# Available
# As Is

# *Available As Is*

## A Midlife Widow's
## Search For Love

### *Debbie Weiss*

SHE WRITES PRESS

Published 2022

Printed in the United States of America

Print ISBN: 978-1-64742-237-0
E-ISBN: 978-1-64742-238-7
Library of Congress Control Number: 2022906627

For information, address:
She Writes Press
1569 Solano Ave #546
Berkeley, CA 94707

She Writes Press is a division of SparkPoint Studio, LLC.

For my father

In loving memory of George Hansen
(July 29, 1959–April 10, 2013)

# I. Marital Status: Widowed

It's four in the morning, and I'm putting together my profile for JDate, the self-proclaimed "largest Jewish dating community worldwide." My husband, George, died fourteen months ago. George was my high school sweetheart, the strong man I curled up next to each night for thirty-two years.

Now that George is gone, I don't know who I am anymore. I've lost the me that I was when I was married, but I've got to come up with something to tell strange men.

This is what I put on my dating profile:

*I'm a former attorney currently writing a book and gardening when I get writer's block. I am fun, witty and outgoing but occasionally shy, irreverent but kind, poised but occasionally awkward, with a wry sense of humor. I can talk about almost anything and am (not so secretly anymore) an eighties freak.*

I'm always hearing about online scams. So best to put right up front that I'm a lawyer, never mind that I haven't practiced in eleven years. Saying I'm a lawyer will probably turn off some people because lawyers are widely regarded as jerks.

I know I was a jerk when I was a practicing lawyer. Now that I don't work anymore, my days are pretty mellow: walking a nearby trail, taking a yoga class, writing in my journal, and planting a few nandina shrubs in my garden.

I still talk to George. During this morning's walk on the tree-lined trail that runs through town, I was overcome by the different shades of green, shimmering and verdant, pierced with red bottlebrush and orange poppies. Afterward, in my garden, the arcing sprigs of my new plants with their neat oval leaves seemed so fragile.

*George, I'm sending them love, hoping they'll take to their new home, hoping that somehow my love will reach you as well. Maybe things look more intensely beautiful, because even in a world without you, I still want to live.*

Of course, I don't put any of that in my profile. I don't want potential dates to know I still chat with my late husband. At least I no longer expect him to answer back. And that's progress. I know I'm alone and it terrifies me, but I'd better leave that out too.

I worry I'll sound terribly retro as I search for a man in an age when so many women have chosen to be single. And having spent over ten years working with male lawyers, I can see why.

The profile questionnaire looms.

I try to imagine the prospect of having sex with a new man. Failing that, I try to visualize going out with him for a nice dinner. Failing that, I go to the kitchen to get a dark chocolate truffle.

**Me:** *50 years old* (a terrible age to be newly single), *5'9, athletic build, green eyes, red hair* (originally brunette, but I have a great colorist, and deeply insecure).

**Location:** *Danville, CA.*

Danville is an overpriced suburb forty minutes southeast of San Francisco. But in 1970 when I first met George at his parents' pool party, it was all walnut trees and rolling hills dotted with ranch houses, just like Walnut Creek, where George lived ten minutes away.

My dad and his mom worked together as nuclear physicists at Lawrence Livermore National Laboratory. Our moms cooked and decorated their homes out of *Sunset*, a lifestyle magazine offering "the best of the West," which seemed to involve miniature cactus gardens and dips made with mayonnaise and those tiny precooked shrimp. George's first words to me were "Do you want to see my model train set?"

He was the cutest boy I'd ever seen, slender with olive skin, a pile of black curls, and huge brown eyes. But he was an older boy, eleven to my seven. Worse, my mom had just cut my bangs too short, and I felt like a fat-faced elf in my navy bikini with the dorky white piping. Tongue-tied, I followed George into the den, aware that he too was wearing only black nylon trunks. I could smell the chlorine on his skin as we stood next to each other, embarrassed when our hands touched as he showed me how the engine car worked.

I thought about him long after I'd gone home.

**My past relationships:** *My relationship was my life.*

I might as well say I wish I'd died along with him. Delete and try again. I roll over and plop my iPad on the untouched pillow next to mine.

*My relationship, singular, was great while it lasted.*

George was a software developer, the technical lead on Quicken, Intuit's personal finance program. An engineer's engineer, he wanted to be only with me and his computer. I wanted to be only with him and my books. Both of us were introverted only children who never grew up.

We lived in our own little world of two, watching the same noir films over and over—*The Maltese Falcon*, *The Big Sleep*—seeing new camera angles each time. We tracked down rare record albums—a Talking Heads EP on red vinyl, a foreign pressing of Joy Division on blue.

At least every other Saturday, George drove us to San

Francisco to find obscure records and DVDs to add to his collection. We made complicated recipes that needed weird ingredients, like monkfish liver or five different kinds of chili peppers, eating whatever he wanted in our two-person universe.

When he wasn't working or cooking, he was doing projects like the home theater system that dominated our living room and that, since he was a perfectionist, he never finished. When people asked why we didn't have kids, we always said, "We're having too much fun being kids." That, and our living room was an unsafe mass of wires.

I don't believe that everything happens for a reason (one of the worst things to say to a widow, by the way, as if my husband's death were necessary to forestall a plague of frogs). There was no reason for George to die of cancer at the age of fifty-three. He was a truly great guy, loved by his colleagues.

When he died, they wrote me letters about the many engineers he'd mentored, his uncanny ·bug-fixing abilities, and his adherence to his motto, "If you can dream it, I can build it." But mostly they told me how happy and upbeat he was to be around, even after his diagnosis, always ready to do anything from dreaming up new features to helping move office furniture.

Continuing on is the hardest thing I've ever done in my life. I didn't think anything would be harder than when my mom died, leaving me alone at ten to be raised by my dad. See "nuclear physicist," above.

I thought my memories would be enough to sustain me, but they're not. They're like looking at pictures of food when you're ravenous. Perhaps looking at photographs of men on JDate will be more satisfying. I might even find someone to ask me about my day.

**My ambitions:** To sleep through the night. That way, I might not follow through on dumb ideas like this one, typing my dating profile in the dark like some kind of stealth operative.

I want to be sleeping next to someone I love, not hunched over an iPad at four thirty in the morning, trying to market myself to strangers.

In the movies, the middle-aged widow played by Diane Lane mourns with spunk, as if she's just lost an argument instead of a husband. Surrounded by dear friends at a seaside restaurant with a golden sunset as her backdrop, the wisest character, usually played by Morgan Freeman, tells her life is still worth living.

An attractive guy keeps staring at her because she still looks stunning; there are no bags under *her* eyes (basically, she's just wearing less eye makeup). We know she'll see him again because he's played by a big star like Richard Gere.

Within a year, she opens a cute new dog-grooming business, fulfilling one of her dreams, and in walks Richard with a dirty labradoodle, fulfilling another. They move to a renovated cottage in the Hamptons after her grieving is compressed into a short montage. Her late husband is transmogrified into the shooting star that flies by offering its blessings. #secondchances.

I watch movies about widowed people and throw cocktail olives at the screen.

I'll be like that guy in *Sideways* who winds up by himself in a crummy restaurant chugging the wine he's been saving for a special occasion because he has no one to share it with.

*My ambition is to find someone I can fold myself into so I'm not alone anymore.*

Delete—that sounds mega-needy.

So, my ambition is: *to find someone who gets my sense of the absurd and to master the crow pose in yoga.* What goals would anyone list on a dating site other than that they're trying to find someone special? That's why I picked JDate. It looked pretty clean, so I hopefully don't have to hear if someone else's wish list includes Roman orgies and ketchup.

***Things I could never live without:*** *My late husband.*

Duh. But that's not going to attract any men. When I googled the most popular words used in dating profiles, "friends and family" kept popping up. I never bothered to make friends when I was married, so when George died, there were no concerned calls or bereavement casseroles or people I could lean on other than my dad and stepmom.

George used to say he spent so much of his time working that he wanted his free time to be for the two of us. At the time, it seemed like enough.

I limited my world to just one person, and despite the fact that my mom died young, I'd forgotten that people are mortal. Trying to sound lighthearted and carefree, I write that I could never live without *Neil Young on vinyl, irony, chocolate frozen yogurt, and vinyasa yoga.*

***My favorite books, movies, TV shows, and music:*** *Movies by Wes Anderson and Fellini. Also* Blade Runner *and* Donnie Darko. *For music, the eighties. (*I Wanna Be Sedated!*) TV show:* Mad Men. *Favorite writer: Haruki Murakami.*

My answers will inform my prospects that I'm an intellectual snob and a bit of a geek. But my list doesn't include the things I really love. That would be too personal. It shows who I want to be—someone detached and artistic, who doesn't seem too suburban despite being a lifelong suburbanite. I want to be someone who seems unquestionably cool, even if I am curating a cliché.

I've read Murakami, but really I live for rereading Laurie Colwin and M. F. K. Fisher, delighting in descriptions of eating eggplant alone or nervously ordering a meal in French. But I don't want to explain to my dates that I return to Fisher because my dad introduced me to her writing, and I read Colwin because she found comfort everywhere.

In college, George and I used to see Fellini films at art house cinemas, but my favorite part was sharing a marzipan chocolate bar. On my own I watch romcoms, laughing at, but loving, the silly endings where everybody finds love. But I don't want my prospects to scoff at me for watching chick flicks.

I feel a twinge at being opaque while trying to find someone who'll love me for the rest of my life. Then again, based on my movie choices, maybe romance is all about curation. I'm not going to mention my blog, *The Hungover Widow*, the name I gave myself based on my excessive Manhattan consumption during my first year without George.

When my mom died, my dad and I acted as if she were on vacation; we didn't talk about her disappearance. It worked, except I couldn't concentrate on my homework and I was overwhelmed by all the new chores and I hated having meatloaf for dinner every night and she was never coming back and my heart hurt.

This time I need to talk about my loss, even if only to a blog, but if my dates knew about it, they might think I'm too geeky. Then again, putting in my profile that I read articles about SEO might make me seem younger.

My fantasy is that if a guy really wants to impress me, he will suggest we both reread *Hard Boiled Wonderland and the End of the World* so we can discuss its noir influences on our first date over decaf (we're over fifty, after all) cappuccinos and apricot scones. I think reading a book to get to know someone is utterly romantic.

George didn't enjoy reading or wasting time sitting in cafés, so this time I'm going to indulge myself. The Ramones reference is sly, but I want to appear fun and maybe weed out anyone who doesn't get it. Although at the moment, sleep-deprived and missing George beyond belief, I probably appear more scary than fun.

**I'm looking for:** *A time machine to take me back to when George was alive.*

Another loser answer. So, here goes: *I'm looking for someone who doesn't take himself too seriously but is not flakey, who is smart with a sense of humor and a little edge.* I have to accept that no one will be George.

**My ideal relationship:** *I'll know it when I see it.*

Like pornography. At least, I hope I will. But after getting up to eat another truffle, I find that the evil dating site has obliterated the soothing powers of raspberry-infused dark chocolate.

**On Saturday nights I'm typically:** I read lots of other profiles before answering this one. Evidently, most people are barbecuing home-cured salmon with their many close friends on teakwood decks they've refinished themselves, drinking a rare unoaked single-vineyard Chardonnay—even though my hunch is that they're alone watching Netflix, eating a desiccated tuna fish sandwich left over from yesterday's lunch.

Why lie? We're all looking for someone to be with or we wouldn't be on this site. Let's be honest.

*On a typical Saturday night I'm surfing the internet just like everybody else.*

**My perfect first date:** *Has me really looking forward to the second one.*

Obvious, right?

**Online name:** Let's try song titles. "Sweet Little Ramona." Too coy. "Cherry Bomb." Too sexual. "Suite Judy Blue Eyes." Doesn't apply to a person. "My Sharona." Pronoun issues. Being my own Sharona doesn't make sense, and being *your* Sharona sounds too forward. I'll be "Lady Writer." It's fitting, and online dating feels like throwing myself into dire straits.

**Marital status:** *Widowed.*

Posted.
Now what?

## 🍓 II. The Man from The Ex Files

"You're the first Jewish girl I've ever been interested in, so my mom's okay with the fact that you aren't into cooking."

Ben, my first prospect from JDate, emailed me that message before we met in person. "She even asked me, 'What would you rather have, a star in the bedroom or in the kitchen?'"

I thought I'd scored a date with a grown-up prom king. A mortgage broker with an MBA, he was a six-foot-tall Alec Baldwin lookalike with a scruffy beard and broad shoulders who clearly worked out a lot. I've always had a crush on Alec Baldwin.

"Being a Jewish American princess, I can be uninterested in both," I emailed back.

"Now I know you're really Jewish," he answered.

Fourteen months after George died and three four-hour lunch dates later, Ben and I were venturing into new territory: our first dinner date. He'd be picking me up, and it made me nervous to think about, staying over on my sofa, since he lived over two hours away.

Originally from New York, he told me he had a Francis Sinatra complex and he saw us having a very cool, Art Deco kind of romance. But even before we'd met I should have noticed that despite his clever messages, he never asked me anything about myself. He had cast me in the unnamed role of "the girl."

I'm sorry, George, if this were one of those Vaseline-lensed, backlit cancer movies, you'd have given me your blessing from your hospital bed to go forth and again find love, with a few white petals floating by your window as a hackneyed symbol of mortality. But in real life, you shooed me out of your hospital room, saying I should go home and eat dinner, you'd be fine, you'd see me tomorrow. Except that you died that afternoon.

But please don't think my deciding to date is any reflection on you. Since you're dead, you won't even know what I'm doing. Yet for some reason I sense that you do.

Since I was raised by an eccentric nuclear physicist, my social skills have never been that great. Since I was with George starting at the age of seventeen, they never had a chance to get much better. When I talk to people, I'm always worried I've said the wrong thing. Although people who don't worry about what they say are far worse.

I'd been preparing to date, asking for more ab work in yoga, having my hair freshly reddened, throwing away all my alcohol only to restock it six weeks later after deciding I'd been way too rash. Give or take a push-up bra, I was ready to enroll in Remedial Middle-Aged Dating.

Checklist:

1. Do not talk about George on dates.
2. Read *The Five Love Languages*, recommended by girlfriend Nancy.
3. Visualize my ideal man as recommended by girlfriend Laura.
4. Eat more salad and less carrot cake as recommended by skinny jeans.
5. Really, do not talk about George.
6. Rein in expectations (which will be hard after George).
7. Chardonnay is not a food group.

○ ○ ○ ○ ○

I pulled on dark jeans, not wanting them to come off, but in a few hours, I might be kissing a new man. I tried on a few different shirts, finally settling on a navy V-neck T-shirt, and hoping the neckline wasn't too low, with a matching cardigan. Over the past year I'd remodeled my kitchen and master bath, trying to kill the stigma of loss that lived in the deferred maintenance of chipped tile countertops and delaminating cabinets, needing to banish that weird girl from junior high who was bullied for wearing the wrong kind of jeans.

I drowned out George's voice saying he didn't like the cardigan and I should return it, as if he were still reviewing my clothes. I applied macaron pink lip gloss and blotted. Glancing in the mirror, I concluded I did not look widowed.

It felt surreal to be getting ready to go out with someone besides George. My man was dead, yet here I was attempting to have fun with a new one.

When George got really sick, my caregiving had been flawed, riddled with impatience and sadness. I didn't deserve to be happy. Yet here I was trying to be. And my attempt was so adolescent, pink lipstick and skinny jeans, ankle boots and fantasy kisses. Having only known a life with George, I couldn't imagine a grown-up future with anyone else.

Were George's and my places reversed, I couldn't picture him going on a date, tucking a bright new button-down into his jeans, getting his car washed, and making small talk over dinner. I could only see him sitting at his computer, coding into the evening, then saying, "Well, kitten, got a lot done today," telling me about his workday as if I were still there, then going to the kitchen to eat a solitary dinner, perhaps his favorite salmon salad with Gruyere on wheat. Only one sandwich to make now.

I ignored the shadowy presence next to me in the mirror,

my guilt reminding me I didn't deserve a new life no matter how many self-help articles I read about love after loss.

My last and practically only first date was with my husband.

"I can't believe these are your records," George said, thumbing through my collection of mostly FM staples—Journey, Steve Miller, Kansas, with a few Elton John LPs thrown in. We were standing next to the record player in the little stereo room of the house my dad and I shared, alone in the middle of a holiday party.

It was 1981; I was seventeen and he was twenty-one. I wanted to reach out and touch the black musical notes marching across the narrow white tie he was wearing with his red shirt.

He looked pretty much as he had when we first met, only taller and even better looking, like one of those skinny, dark-eyed, curly-haired guys in New Wave bands like the Romantics or the Records. We were exactly the same height, so I could look right into his eyes.

He claimed to be majoring in pinball but was in fact studying engineering at UC Berkeley, a National Merit Scholar with almost perfect SAT scores. He thought of himself as a rebel, but one who still lived at home and had scored an internship at Hewlett Packard.

"Don't you know about punk rock? Haven't you heard of the Ramones? 'Rocket to Russia'? 'Road to Ruin'?" he asked.

"What are you talking about?" I said. Almost involuntarily, I tossed my hair over my shoulder. He might have been speaking a different language, but there was a current of electricity running beneath his words.

"I'll stop by and bring you some tapes after school." The current had sparked.

I was a nerd with no experience with boys, but I wanted to go to my senior prom. So my dad threw a party and invited George and his parents, hoping I could procure him as my prom date since George was one of the few boys I actually knew.

I had subterranean status in my high school's pecking order, a result of my being really shy and having been raised by my dad, who understood quantum physics, Jungian archetypes, and Japanese battle strategy during World War II but knew nothing about teenage girls.

Anything feminine I'd had to figure out for myself by reading Judy Blume novels and the instruction booklets that came inside boxes of tampons. My dad covered his ears only half- jokingly and yelled, "Stop, stop, I'm Jewish!" if I uttered the word "period" or "cramps." "Maxi-pad" threw him into a tizzy. In his world, high school girls wore plaid skirts, used no makeup, and never menstruated.

George started riding his bike by my house on Tuesday and Thursday afternoons, the days that he trained for a two-hundred-mile bike tour. Suddenly, all the other days of the week receded.

As promised, he brought me tapes of his favorite music: one day the Talking Heads' *More Songs About Buildings and Food*, the next day, Blondie's *Plastic Letters*. The following week it was The Clash's *London Calling*. Each tape was labeled in turquoise ink with the typing perfectly centered on a purple-edged sticker. You could tell already that he was going to be an engineer.

"Check out 'Lover's Rock'—the lyrics are really funny, even though they're dirty," he said, blushing a little and handing me the Clash tape. "And if you're in a really bad mood, listen to 'Clampdown.'"

After he gave me the day's tape, I'd watch him ride away on his bike, clipping his feet into the pedals, so cute in his white Colnago cycling outfit. I always wished he could stay longer, but I didn't know how to ask. I'd think about the way he smiled at me as if he were sharing something really private, and I'd wonder what would happen if he ever got off his bike and came into the house.

The music George gave me explained everything I hated about my suburban high school—a place where sports were revered, conformity was required, and no one in the administration had ever once asked me about my future plans. But I already had an early admission to Mills College, a small women-only liberal arts college in Oakland just forty minutes from home. Not surprisingly, my dad had picked it out for me.

I had no idea where I wanted to go to college, only that I needed to stay close to home to keep an eye on him. You never knew when a parent might vanish.

One day George came by in his regular clothes—black jeans and a tight black-and-red striped T-shirt that was exotic by my standards—and driving his old blue Toyota instead of riding his bike because it was raining. I asked him in, trying to stop that fluttery feeling in my stomach.

We sat close together on the long white leather sofa in the living room, my knees up, rain pelting the glass doors, the room dim in the gray light. George put his head on my shoulder, surprising me. I stiffened, then softened against him, everything heightened, the feel of his damp shirt against my arm, the water droplets in his curls, the smells of fresh rain and hair conditioner and hope.

"I'm afraid of thunder," he said. "Aren't you?"

"No." Did he think I was a wimp?

"Then how am I going to kiss you?"

I decided I was afraid of thunder. I'd never made out before, but a little later I was no longer afraid of kissing, at least with George, a pink warmth rising deep in my stomach, the ocean landscape above the sofa soft and blurry, the air still yet charged.

"I love you," George murmured into my long brown hair.

"That's impossible. You don't even know me," I said, catching my breath, trying to sound casual, taking my arms from around his neck. I decided this must be some kind of older boy college game.

"Yes, I do. I've known you for years." He laughed a little, but his voice was solemn, like he was trying to tell me something important. I realize now he was letting me know he'd chosen me way before this kiss, and he expected us to be together for a long time.

"Do you want to go to my senior prom with me?" I said tentatively, too immature to think past the summer before college started.

"Sure," he said. Mission accomplished.

We had been together ever since.

Oh, yeah—remember to rein in expectations.

"You have fashion sense," Ben said when he picked me up. I liked the way he looked in his polo shirt but said nothing, not wanting to appear too forward. We had dinner at the venerable John's Grill in the city; romantically dim and retro, the restaurant is the setting of Dashiell Hammett's *The Maltese Falcon*.

Ben ordered us shrimp salad, medium-rare steak, and red wine, like Frank Sinatra—or George—would have done, but in my nervousness it all tasted like nothing. I picked at my food, trying to make sure I didn't drop anything in my lap, anticipation crackling between us.

After dinner, Ben took selfies of us under the "John's Grill" sign, both of us grinning. He looked over at me, a bit bashful, as if he couldn't believe his good fortune. I was lit from within, my hair glowing even redder in the neon, surprised to be feeling happy again after such a long time. We walked through Union Square holding hands.

"I canceled my JDate membership a few days ago," he said. "So many people just want to date for the sake of dating. They see one person a few times, then move on to someone else. I want real emotional intimacy instead of just infatuation."

"Well, I had love, and I want to find it again, but I'm not in any rush," I said, trying to sound ready to be with a new person, yet not overly eager. With every word, I attempted to radiate emotional health, or at least a decent approximation, but I should have been asking what he meant by intimacy, and why he needed to emphasize the word "real."

"I'm so lucky I found you before I went offline," he said, squeezing my hand.

"Awww . . ." Almost involuntarily, I flipped my hair over my shoulder.

"I'm thinking of going home to upstate New York to visit my mom soon," he said. "I'd love to show you where I grew up." In my fantasies, I was practically a member of the family, his mother teaching me, the first Jewish girl he'd ever brought home, how to make her famous latkes (not that I actually knew whether she made latkes) while Ben looked on proudly.

Back at my house I settled Ben on the sofa, pouring red wine into long-stemmed glasses, taking off my boots, and tucking my feet up. The wine tasted of blackberries and promise as I giddily looked forward to our first real kiss.

"I need you to know something," he said, taking a sip of wine, then putting his glass down and looking deep into my eyes. "For a long time, I've been really unhappy."

"Oh?"

"After my divorce, I fell in love with someone."

I pulled my V-neck T-shirt up a little higher. He then launched into the story of "The Blonde Who Ruined His Life." An ex-live-in girlfriend, she wrecked his finances, was mean to his kids, talked him into buying a house he couldn't afford, then cheated on him with a guy she met at the gym.

"After her, I sort of lost hope." He concluded what seemed like hours after launching into his tale of woe. I surmised that we would not be kissing passionately, dazed by our good fortune at having found each other.

I looked down at my empty wine glass. His was empty too,

but I didn't want to offer any more in case it prolonged the conversation. So much for promise.

I couldn't believe this was the same guy who'd written me a hilarious story about Jews inventing jazz music so all the lyrics were about fiscal prudence. His virtual foreplay may have been irresistible, but in person he was serving warmed-over blonde.

By the end of the evening, I felt like I too had lived with this breast-enhanced hottie. Why did he feel compelled to tell me about her boobs? Could this really be modern dating—Ben confessing his romantic failures at my house so I couldn't even leave?

"Well, it's getting late," I said, taking our wine glasses to the kitchen, pausing at the counter and wishing I didn't have to go back to the living room.

Maybe he rambled on when he was nervous. We said goodnight after getting ready for bed, he in the sweatpants and a T-shirt he'd brought in his overnight bag. I was in a modest sleep shirt and boy-short undies.

I asked, "Do you want to lie down on my bed for a few minutes just to see what it feels like?" I wasn't ready to have sex yet, but I at least expected to be wanted.

"I want to communicate about my past in real depth before anything physical happens between us," he said primly, declining to enter my bedroom.

I thought I might die of boredom before that happened.

My adolescent diet of Judy Blume and the copy of *Fear of Flying* I'd found in my dad's den hadn't prepared me for this. We parted for the night, and I closed the bedroom door behind me. I was unable to sleep, picturing him on my sofa dreaming of his ex-blonde, unconsciously willing her back into his life. Why else would he have talked about her so much?

The next morning, I took him to brunch at one of Danville's nicest restaurants—after all, he'd come so far to see me—but the blonde was only an appetizer. Over eggs Benedict and mimosas on the outdoor patio and late into the afternoon back at my house, he told me about yet another breast-enhanced blonde who'd wounded him, an ex-wife he was still sad about, and a brunette he'd loved deeply but who hadn't loved him in return, shattering what was left of his already fragmented heart.

Now I knew. *Real* emotional intimacy to Ben meant listening to him wax ad nauseam about his exes, precluding any intimacy, real or otherwise, with his current date.

We would not be one of those laughing couples reliving their sexy Saturday over Sunday brunch. George hadn't much liked going out for brunch—he thought it took too much time away from his projects—but Ben was far worse. He was Robert Hays in *Airplane*, recounting his epic story of lost love to the passengers on the plane. I had a bit part as one of his listeners.

"I know you understand pain," he said, finally wrapping it up. I wanted to throw my mimosa glass at his head. I hadn't realized that was my main selling point. Was he even attracted to me? Or had he just thought a widow would be less demanding and more willing to spend the rest of our lives sitting shiva for our losses, tacitly agreeing to live in the past because the present could never measure up?

*But my partner died*, I wanted to scream. *I had no choice but to be alone. You just had really poor judgment. Repeatedly.*

I thought about how George never complained, not when he was getting his chest zapped with radiation, not during all-day chemo, not even when he was dying and couldn't breathe because his lungs were filled with fluid. I had a George-o-me-ter in my head, a dial that measured every man by how George would have acted, whether I wanted it to or not. Now it was saying, *Back away. This guy is a total pussy.*

Ben finally left midafternoon, having turned my sofa into a therapist's couch. I'd gone from a sparkly red object of desire to a dull brown urn in which to deposit his pain.

The sharing of agony was not one of the five love languages. Acts of service were, but I'd done all the serving, listening, and offering up comfort while he filled up my poor empty urn with his tears, leaving them to mingle with George's ashes. Remembering my guilt the night before, I realized I'd gotten the date I deserved after all.

If this was my first foray into dating, I had to be cursed, despite remodeling my kitchen and wearing the right kind of jeans. Karma was apparently stronger than designer denim.

After Ben left, I went for a long walk on the trail that ran through Danville and into the next towns, stepping quickly past the sounds of music and splashing coming from the homes, smelling the barbecue smoke, passing the placid dog walkers and the mothers with their strollers, unable to return their smiles.

I was pretty damn sure I looked widowed.

I could have told Ben what real pain looked like, about George's last days, the ones I kept going over, measuring them out like spools of black ribbon.

George was fifty, his stomach extending a little farther each year as his cookbook collection continued to grow, topping out at two hundred pounds on his five-foot-nine frame, his hairline receding, his curls thinner and shot with gray. But his smile and his brown eyes were the same as the day we met. I always saw the eleven-year-old boy from the pool party peeking out at me.

One spring morning in 2009 he said, as if he were running out to buy more cream cheese, "I'm going to Kaiser." He mentioned a sore on his chest that hadn't healed, and wanted to have it checked now that he'd finished coding Quicken for the year.

That was George: his schedule and Quicken's were one. Almost every weekend, he volunteered to be on call for bug fixes despite my pleas for a reprieve. Even his business card said "Mr. Quicken." He returned early that evening, saying only that the doctors were running some tests. But he'd been gone more than six hours. I knew it had to be bad.

The following Tuesday he announced, "The bad news is I have metastatic male breast cancer." He smiled widely to defuse his words, as if they'd be less frightening under a veneer of optimism. "The good news is they say it can be treated with everything—pills, radiation, chemo, even surgery."

*So it needs everything,* I thought.

Later, I googled. "Metastatic" meant "stage four." The survival rate for people with stage four breast cancer was low, though exactly how low I was afraid to find out. Obviously, the odds of survival were much higher when the cancer was discovered before it spread. George's records revealed that his had spread to his bones, liver, and brain. I stopped researching after that, but everything I found told me we were living on borrowed time.

We had four good years after his diagnosis, but by the winter of 2013, the cancer had finally claimed him. Down to one hundred fifteen pounds, his face all shaggy with purple hollows, his body harlequined with bruises, he looked like a starveling Rasputin.

The face on the pillow next to mine wizened, and the terra cotta bedding I'd once found so cheerful became as funereal as dried blood. He'd caught pneumonia that January and never really recovered, spiraling swiftly downward, the death sentence from his diagnosis finally coming to pass.

Every morning I pushed him into our home office, trying not to let the wheels of his chair get tangled up with the cables from his oxygen tanks, and stationed him behind his desk. He was still working, attending all his meetings remotely, his colleagues unaware how terrible he looked. He spent his days coding a product for people to budget their long-term goals when he himself had become short-term.

"Hey, kitten, in an hour could you bring me a cup of green tea and four Triscuits covered with Underwood Chicken Spread?" he asked every morning, turning on the computer he'd built himself that was so much faster than the ones at work.

That would be his breakfast—all he'd eat until dinnertime, when he would have a similar plate plus a few token bites of whatever I was having. Even though he could no longer cook—he could barely eat—he still chose what we had for dinner, although the steak he requested stuck in my throat, and he'd throw up his few bites later that evening, thinking I didn't know. Outside, the February sky was pearly gray; the sun had disappeared.

"We're going to have to deal with this," I said day after day.

"Deal with what?" he asked impatiently.

"With how sick you are," I said, putting my hand over his on the keyboard to stop him from typing.

Again I would hand him the photo on my phone of the gaping holes cancer the merciless sculptor had carved into his lower back. I'd moved from using medium to large-size bandages, worrying about infection, scared I might be making him worse.

"I have to get to work," he muttered, waving me away, even though the pictures showed inches of bone poking through the tears in his skin.

To say George was in denial is an understatement. I'll never understand how he turned his brilliant mind back on itself to deny reality, how he could look in the mirror every morning and think he was beating cancer. He could still write code in C++ and HTML, but he was speaking to me in the language of avoidance. No matter how many times I tried to wrench him into reality, my words were incomprehensible to him.

I could have learned his language, white blood cell count, radiation, oncology department down the hall, but it was as if I had only a textbook—George wouldn't teach me conversational cancer. So my sentences were like my high school French class when we kept going over what's in a bowl of fruit or *une salade*, but the words were meaningless because they had no context.

I wanted to ask him what it felt like during chemo and if he was afraid of dying. Was there anything he wanted to do before he passed, and could I please do it with him? I was like a toddler clamoring for attention, waving my arms and shifting from foot to foot, exclaiming, "We don't have much time left!" while he drowned me out.

Then there were the things I was afraid to ask, like what it felt like to be in a body that was disintegrating and how much pain he was in. And the things I wanted him to ask me, like how it felt to be losing him, and what I was going to do without him— but we no longer understood each other.

We usually compromised whenever we argued, but if we couldn't, he'd win by sheer tenacity. As his health declined, that tenacity had become a survival mechanism. I watched him from the doorway and wondered who he had become.

I will always regret that he went through what must have been the most frightening experience of his life by himself. But I genuinely believe that he genuinely believed he was going to defy death.

He died in the hospital on April 10, 2013, still convinced he was going to get better and come home. He was fifty-three years old, and I was just four months shy of my fiftieth birthday. George had always taken care of me, and I couldn't stop thinking that the one time he really needed me to take care of him, I'd let him down.

But I wasn't about to share any of that with Ben.

Ben called a few days after our "sleepover," announcing, "I'm done talking about my past. I said what I had to. Now I'm ready to focus on *us*." I'd liked him so much before he started nattering about his exes and their boobs, and he was so great looking that I agreed to another date. Maybe we could finally move on to my love language of touch.

But when he arrived at my house, he greeted me with "I

canceled my JDate membership, but you, Debbie, you remain active. I can see how much time you're spending online."

I'd replaced most of my candid profile photographs with professional shots, telling myself the pictures were for my future career, whatever that might be. But actually, I'd listened to a TED Talk by a woman who found her ideal man online. She explained that because men are visual, she'd put up more flattering, professionally taken profile photos of herself. A year later, she and her perfectly matched husband were celebrating the birth of their first child.

I too was getting more responses with professional pictures. I put prints of them on my office shelves, blocking the remote-controlled car George had been working on when he died, willing myself to be the carefree, smiling redhead in the photos. That woman looked open to anything, a far cry from the real me, a widow of fifteen months crying alone at her kitchen table, wondering how to go on living without her *bashert*.

"I've only just started dating after being with one person for thirty-two years. I'm not ready to be exclusive," I said, my anger flaring. "Besides, you didn't seem that into me. Or if you were, you talked about your exes so much I couldn't tell."

*Why* had I agreed to a second date? He couldn't kiss me, yet he could track my time on JDate like a passive-aggressive hall monitor.

"I'm trying to figure out where love goes," he said. "I want real love this time. For the first time in a long while, I was actually excited about someone. You. I was even thinking of asking you to come to New York with me to meet my mom. But you just want to date other people."

Despite my inexperience, even I understood new love didn't flourish while being strangled by the ghosts of girlfriends past. Perhaps his ex-blondes hadn't been so bad—he'd just driven them away by going on about his ex-wife so much they couldn't take it anymore.

Ben was clearly causing his own misery, telling each new woman about her predecessors in excruciating detail. Unless he only did that with me, which made it even worse.

Maybe he expected me to heal him with my widow super powers. And when I failed, as of course I would, I'd become the latest in a long line of women who could never succeed because his injuries were just so damn profound, at least to him. Oddly enough, the mother he described as a disciplinarian evidently never taught her son that he needed to let the other children take turns talking too.

We spent the evening strolling through San Francisco's North Beach, getting drinks at a bar where the Beats used to hang out, looking into the church where Joe DiMaggio and Marilyn Monroe got married, stopping at shadowy little Italian restaurants, getting Caprese salad at one and arancini at another. He said our pasts made us who we were. I said I'd had enough death in my life.

Our only photo from that night was the one I took of the quotation by John Steinbeck embedded in the sidewalk outside City Lights bookstore: *The free exploring mind of the individual human is the most valuable thing in the world.*

Ben was certainly doing a poor job of exploring me. At one point, he did lean over to give me a long kiss on the neck, but ruined it by saying, "You liked that, didn't you?" His voice sounded oddly malicious, as if he were giving me a tiny taste of creamy cannoli, then taunting me for wanting more.

Back at my house, clad in his sweatpants and T-shirt, he asked to lie down on the bed next to me. But after stretching out over the covers, he smirked and said, "So, can you tell which girl really destroyed my faith in love?"

"Um, I guess it's the blonde," I stammered. I hadn't realized there was going to be a test on this.

"No," he practically snapped. "It was Kathy."

Ah, the sweet but emotionally damaged brunette. He'd climbed onto my bed only to invite his exes in too. Now I knew. He used his great looks as bait to reel in unsuspecting listeners.

"Time for you to go back to the couch," I said, channeling my blogging persona, the Hungover Widow finally vanquishing Ex-Girlfriend Regurgitation Man.

"It will soon be time for us to become physical," Ben said solemnly the next morning, as if things had gone swimmingly the night before. "I'm not small." Suddenly, he moved my hand to his semi-erect crotch.

I pulled my hand away faster than a grossed-out twelve-year-old. Touching his penis was supposed to come after the wildly passionate kisses, like the fade in a Nicholas Sparks movie. Having sex with Ben would be like trying to mate with a depressed albatross. That dick belonged to Kathy in perpetuity.

"We aren't going to work out," I said. His weird kiss on the neck, then backing away; his jumping on my bed, then testing me; and now this awkward, unprovoked offer of genitalia suggested something was really off with him. Perhaps he was uncomfortable with female sexuality, offering yet another reason for all those exes.

To my shock, he started crying, repeating to himself, "It's okay, poor unloved middle child who never got what he wanted. It's going to be okay."

He'd seemed almost hostile with his "guess the exes" game; I hadn't realized his problems ran far deeper. Through all his talking, I'd just wanted him to cheer up and take his shirt off. I hadn't seen how injured he was, that his heart wasn't just battered but had likely been broken in childhood.

That would explain the weird baiting, then backing off. Suddenly, he'd turned from a controlling egotist into a little boy who needed comforting, and I didn't know what to do. None of this made me like him any more than I had before.

"Are you going to be okay? Is there someone you can call?" I asked, desperately casting about for ways to avoid spending another day as his anointed healer.

"My therapist is out of town," he said. "I'll call her when she gets back."

We hugged awkwardly after he gathered up his things to go, no longer the prom king from central casting but a zombie from *The Walking Dead*. Ben was an ambulatory cautionary tale, a man who spread his pain like grass seed, lessening it for himself by strewing it among others, never thinking they too might be fragile. He could have had any number of futures, but he was so immersed in the past he precluded all of them, as if happiness were a sin and he needed to take everyone down with him.

He should have just been honest in his profile: *Looking for a woman to share my pain. Degree in abnormal psychology a plus. Must enjoy long walks watching me cry, romantic dinners listening to me talk about other women, and sex where I cry out their names instead of yours.*

Listening to Ben's language of self-imposed misery reminded me not to feel too sorry for myself. Unlike many other widows and divorcees, I got to keep my home, which George had paid off when he was diagnosed, and I didn't have to work because I'd received his life insurance benefit and had a dad who would help out if necessary. I could continue on just as I had before.

If my life felt empty now, it was because I allowed it to become so hollow when I was married. It just hadn't seemed that way at the time.

Many people didn't get to have anywhere near the thirty-two years I had with George. But night after night alone, I still couldn't convince myself how lucky I was. Dove-gray tile aside, a bathroom remodel can only go so far.

I thought a new man was the answer, but in reality, I was living with so much guilt it was almost all I could think about, no matter how hard I tried to bury it under new sweaters and kitchen sinks. The obvious lesson I learned from Ben was I needed to look forward. But I hadn't yet figured out that the *real* lesson was my need to reconcile with the past.

I went on another long walk, thinking that if I fell and sprained my ankle, I had no one to call to pick me up. When I got home, my plants were the only living things there to greet me. And when I died alone, I'd better do it really close to the front door so one of those irritating real estate agents who was always stopping by would catch the stench and call the police.

I crossed the streets gingerly, as if I was ten years old and my mom just died and my dad was reminding me to look both ways.

# III. Running Away to Home

IN THE SUMMER OF 1973, I was nine. My world was suffused with color, the sunlight intensely yellow, the sky immeasurably blue, the pool turquoise, and the lawn a deep green. But my mom, Thalia, statuesque and curvy with auburn hair and green eyes, started spending all her time closed up in the bedroom, abandoning her bridge games and gardening projects. My dad, Mort, tall, freckled, and scholarly, told me her back hurt.

There was no one to bring me Pepperidge Farm Goldfish while I read, or to teach me the crawl in the swimming pool, or to make a new recipe from *Sunset* for dinner, explaining each of the steps while I stared off into space, daydreaming I was friends with the girls in my Betsy-Tacy books. Dad started coming home early from work every day, like he was afraid to leave Mom alone for too long. He told me not to bother her while he was gone.

I wondered what was going on behind that closed bedroom door, and I stood in front of it for hours, as if being closer could help me to see inside. But I was afraid to go in, worried I'd wake her and make everything even worse.

A few weeks in, my dad said calmly, "Deborah, we are going to the hospital."

He drove my mother and me to Kaiser Hospital in Walnut Creek in his big, blue Plymouth Fury. Mom was still wearing her pink-and-green I. Magnin hostess outfit, a checkered blouse that tied at the neck and a quilted, flowered maxi skirt. She'd gotten out of bed to make dinner that night, hunched over the countertop as she grasped it with one hand while I scampered around trying to help. I didn't understand how sick she was, only that she seemed so tired, her eyes ringed with dark circles so big they stained her cheekbones.

Dad and I waited in the hospital emergency room for hours before she finally emerged lying down on a gurney, smiling and waving cheerfully as she was wheeled back into the dark bowels of the hospital. He took me home, but he went to the hospital the next day and every day afterward, arranging for the neighbor's teenage daughter to babysit me. He never took me to the hospital again.

"When's Mom coming home?" I'd ask every day when he got back from seeing her.

"We don't know yet. We'll see."

"When will we know?"

"We don't know that either."

"What's wrong with her? Is her back that bad?"

"We're not sure yet."

"When will we know what's wrong with her?"

"Enough, Deborah."

My dad looked exhausted. If Mom were getting better, he wouldn't have looked like that, and he would have been able to answer my questions. I pictured my mother sitting alone in her hospital bed wearing the cream-colored bed jacket with little blue flowers my dad had brought her from home as the doctors shuffled in and out of her room. She seemed to have moved into the hospital. I started letting the cat sleep in my bed even though I wasn't supposed to.

After she'd been in the hospital for about two weeks, Dad came home and said, "She's getting worse."

*How much worse?* I thought, but was too terrified to ask.

Home had become so quiet—no more Wagner blaring from the stereo because my parents were going to see *Das Rheingold* in the city on Saturday night, no Mom chopping tarragon in the kitchen, no Dad talking to her about some work problem I didn't understand, no Dad letting me make his nightly gin and tonic and laughing when I accidentally poured too much gin.

"She's caught pneumonia," he said three weeks after she was hospitalized.

*When is she going to get better?*

I longed to ask, but I didn't want to make him mad. He was always on the edge of yelling, his patience stretched wafer thin as he shuttled to and from the hospital. I was afraid to ask him to take me with him in case it made him even madder. I spent that summer alone, reading or watching cartoons, the cat sitting on my lap, looking at me with pale blue eyes.

Two days later, Dad came home from the hospital and said, "She's in a coma."

On TV shows, people got better after being sick, but they rarely woke up from comas. Dad couldn't shield me anymore— my mother was going to die. I pictured her lying in bed in her hospital gown, looking like she was asleep, but really, she was already gone.

Had she forgotten about us when she fell into the coma? Had any part of her fought to stay alive, to remind her how much she loved us, even as she drifted away?

Three weeks after she'd been admitted, my dad took me for a drive around town in the Fury. Danville was pretty empty back then—a few stores, not much landscaping. He pulled over into an empty parking lot, the wide expanse of dusty blue seat between us, and said, his voice breaking, "Your mommy's probably going to die."

I'd never heard his voice shake before. And he'd always

referred to her as "your mother" or by her first name, "Thalia," not "Mommy." He usually talked to me like I was a small grown-up. Trying to talk to me the way he thought people talked to children was the tip-off. He felt sorry for me.

"She's already dead," I said.

He flinched, his face suddenly crumbling before he put it back into place. "You're right. She died three days ago."

She'd died on August 9, four days before my tenth birthday. I remembered her waving goodbye to me from her gurney as they'd wheeled her away, still looking perfectly fine. The hospital had eaten my mother.

My dad and I drove home in silence, not knowing what to say to each other.

When he brought her stuff home from the hospital, I started wearing her bed jacket to sleep, trying to find some shard of the warmth I used to snuggle with. I ate the black licorice she loved even though it tasted like fennel, a vegetable I truly detested.

I still saw her in my bathroom mirror, trying out different hairstyles before going to a dinner party with my dad. She was nervous about how she looked, which was silly because she was so beautiful no matter what she did with her hair.

I searched through his desk drawers looking for answers and found nothing except a pre-printed form from the Neptune Society, with her name misspelled as "Thallia," saying my mother's ashes had been scattered at sea. In Greek mythology, Thalia was the muse of comedy. At ten, I had discovered irony.

Next to the announcement was her gold wedding ring. It had been cut in half.

I had been stronger at ten than I was at fifty. At ten, I could heal myself by sitting on my closet floor reading Laura Ingalls Wilder and holding a stuffed tiger, probably because I wasn't thinking about the future. Alone at fifty, drinking Manhattans and listening to The Rolling Stones' "Sway" over and over on

George's turntable proved far less comforting, probably because the future was all I could think about.

No one ever told me the details of my mother's death. I remember I heard the words "anemia" and "pneumonia," but not much else. There was no funeral or memorial service, no counseling or follow-up.

Thalia's death at forty-two seemed a biological embarrassment never to be discussed. Dad didn't talk about it, and I didn't want to upset him by asking. My mother had gotten sick and vanished. Exactly how it had happened didn't matter.

The actions inside our house were small and muted—meals were cooked, laundry was done, beds were changed. I got a house key, a daily list of chores written out by my dad, and a stranger in my house: an afternoon babysitter, a disaffected blonde high school senior who started showing up after school and occasionally made out with her boyfriend on our couch until I tattled on her to my dad.

Every night for dinner Dad and I had meatloaf, super lean meat drying out in the oven as it melded with hunks of carrots and celery. The sides bubbled up in the pan, and the top was covered in an atomic glop of tomato paste that promised nothing good underneath. It emerged a pallid brown flecked with pink, the crests charred to black bleeding to nuclear red underneath. A murder of ingredients. I didn't know where this recipe came from, only that it was the only thing my dad knew how to cook.

"Not meatloaf again!" I wanted to scream, but I knew I couldn't. My dad was doing the best he could.

Before Mom died, his time alone with me was limited to Saturday afternoons at the museum or the planetarium, so he didn't know what to do. Kids were supposed to eat nutritious meals, and he was providing one. I wondered what he would have chosen to eat if he were by himself.

What would a man want to eat after his wife just died? Probably nothing. He would have come home from work and had a gin and tonic plus a few crackers or nuts. That meatloaf was for me.

When Dad cut into the loaf, the steam rose up, the brown smell of defeat, of too little fat embarrassed by its own presence. He augmented it with broccoli and an anemic salad of iceberg lettuce with a few pallid tomatoes.

The house had turned gray, a fuzziness overlaying the bright blue kitchen cabinets and counters chosen by my mother, her awful white vinyl recliners with the chrome trim, and her fake fur white pillows that felt like fiberglass, all of it the height of 1970s suburbia pretending it lived in New York.

I wondered why we couldn't get a live-in housekeeper like the families with dead mothers got on *Family Affair* or *The Courtship of Eddie's Father*. She could have done my chores and made us dinner so we didn't have to eat meatloaf every night. She could have asked about my day when I got home from school and brought me milk and homemade chocolate chip cookies.

Everyone knew a sad kid was supposed to be taken care of, not greeted with a list of chores. Dad should at least have told me how great I was doing, but I was pretty sure he thought only in equations.

We did have a cleaning lady who came every other week. Dad gave her some of Mom's old clothes, and one day she arrived wearing my mom's pantsuit—polyester salmon-colored slacks with a matching Pucci-print tunic. I'd last seen my mother wear that outfit to host a bridge game, when I'd helped her put out little pastel-covered mints that tasted as lackluster as they looked.

I wanted to tell the cleaning lady that those clothes were too nice to wear for cleaning the house. Mom only wore them when company came over, even if they were ugly. But Mom had taught me I needed to be super polite to the cleaning lady so she didn't think I was treating her like a servant. So I hid in my bedroom, not wanting to see my mom's clothes stretched out on a different body.

Didn't the cleaning lady understand that she was wearing clothes that belonged to someone else? Someone who was alive just a few weeks ago? Someone who was my mother?

My dad always yelled at me because I did dumb things; I didn't finish my math homework and forgot my house key at school. I was mad at myself for that stuff too. One time, he told me to stop letting the back door slam shut, and when I let it happen again by mistake a few minutes later, the look in his eyes was pure fury. I knew he loved me, but he didn't seem to like me very much.

I was mad at Mom for wearing ugly salmon slacks and spending all that time worrying about her hair and not trying hard enough to stay alive. She always had to nag me to clean up my room, to do the few chores I did have. Maybe I made her more tired by being so unhelpful. So tired that she got sick and died.

I wanted endless sick days watching old movies with cups of hot chocolate and the cat on my lap. I wished I could have told Dad, and my fifth-grade teacher and the mean school principal who yelled at me for running in the hallway, that my mom had just died and it was a big deal and everyone needed to be nicer to me.

But I never spoke up. I had learned from my dad we did not appear weak. We handled everything on our own, from mealy brown meatloaf to blood-red sorrow.

By my teenage years, things had gotten a lot better. My dad had grown a beard, started wearing a tiger's eye necklace, gotten into transcendental meditation, and learned how to deal with me. He picked one or two things he wanted me to do, like remember to clean out the pool filter every day and to change the cat litter once a week, and he let everything else slide.

In response to my questions—at fifteen I started to wonder if the cause of my mom's death was genetic—my dad told me her internal chemistry had gone off-kilter, starting with the anemia, which caused her body to fail all at once. She caught pneumonia in the hospital and had a heart attack soon after being admitted, and had gone into the coma from which she'd never awoken.

Dad had never taken me to visit her because he hadn't wanted me to see her lying there unconscious. He assured me her death wasn't anything that could be passed down to me.

By then, the white vinyl armchairs had been clawed by the cat and stained with blueberries, the carpets too had been clawed, the cabinets were chipped and had never been refinished, but we didn't care. We lived like two graduate students in someone else's house. That someone else was my mom, whom we nicknamed the Saint, acknowledging that people often idealized the dead. But we were just really pissed off at her for leaving us.

My dad had expanded his repertoire beyond meatloaf and broccoli to become an accomplished, if messy, cook. It was thanks in part to our watching PBS cooking shows together.

"We have a visiting physicist coming from France to have dinner with us on Saturday," Dad would say on a typical Wednesday night, thumbing through one of his cookbooks. "I'll make Jacques Pépin's rack of lamb with mushrooms and sautéed spinach with pearl onions."

I'd wash the colander full of mushrooms, and he'd slice the ends off the onions because that made my eyes hurt. "We'll double the garlic, though," he'd add with a wink.

I looked forward to hosting our dinner parties—though not to cleaning up the mess he made from cooking his mushroom duxelles. I preferred his friends to kids my own age. His friends acted like they were still kids, but they'd read more books and didn't shun me if I acted smart, the way the kids in my school did.

"Just no curry," I'd say. He'd learned to cook by making the same dish over and over, varying the ratios of ingredients. Since he liked things spicy, his curry phase often wrought havoc on my stomach.

"I'm guessing you'll want to make dessert?" he would always ask, grinning.

When I was thirteen, he came home from work one day to discover I had made my mother's—actually, Julia Child's—chocolate mousse. I had missed the velvety taste so much that I'd figured it out myself, and was comforted by the sound of a wooden spoon scraping the sides of a double boiler and the smell of dark chocolate filling the kitchen as it melted.

The mousse tasted just right, but I had misread the recipe and used ground coffee beans instead of liquid coffee. The result was both a dessert and a diuretic.

Still, from that day on, I think my dad saw me differently, as someone who could join him in his endeavors instead of just following orders, as someone who might be interesting enough to become his friend.

After that I baked lots of desserts. It was the only way I could get my health-conscious dad to let me have sweets. I loved contributing something to our dinner parties, having secretly eaten my first attempt, the failed chocolate fondant that never thickened, hours earlier. I would plunk down a St. Honoré Cake or a genoise with coffee buttercream frosting, radiating false modesty and practicing my junior high school French with our visitors.

If my dad ever felt sorry for himself, or thought I was a burden to him, he never let on. Despite my mother's death, I was well-loved, and my childhood was full of books and museums and too much opera.

One evening, as Dad was driving us in the Plymouth (now three years older and filthy with no Mom to complain about it) to see *La Cenerentola*, an opera based on the story of Cinderella, he said, "There are so many stories about girls whose mothers die and their fathers marry wicked stepmothers. You know I'd never do anything like that, don't you?" Steering the hulking beast through traffic, he feigned nonchalance, but I could tell he'd been thinking about this for a long time.

"Yes, Dad," I answered quickly. "I know you're not stupid."

My mom's death taught me the rule of impending disaster: get a high LSAT score, hope the cat doesn't die. I'd gotten a very high LSAT score. Soon after, the cat died prematurely.

At twenty-five, after I graduated from law school and passed the California bar, I started working as an insurance defense lawyer and accepted a job near home, since I never knew what might happen if I ventured too far. A few months later, George and I moved into our first apartment together.

When I was thirty, we bought our first house, a little off-white stucco bungalow in a tract just ten minutes from my dad's. George chose it, ruling out my choice of an older non-tract home he said would have taken too much time to fix up. Soon afterward we got married. And when I got stressed out practicing law, George urged me to quit.

I was a retiree at forty and was relieved to stay home with an empty answering machine, a copy of *War and Peace* by the fire, and numerous pots of green tea. George took care of everything, from paying all the bills from his computer to providing me with a life almost without anxiety—and as someone who suffered from anxiety, that was perfect. Eventfulness was for other people.

I kept telling myself I'd get another job, but I hadn't much liked venturing out into the world. I've read that people sometimes stay the same age they were when they suffered a great loss. In that case, I never grew up beyond the ten-year-old who wanted to stay home after her mom died. When I quit work, I finally had all those sick days I wanted, only now I called them yoga and gardening and being high maintenance.

I felt like a failed feminist—I'd tried to be a competent professional, but competence meant spending all day with other lawyers being mean to me, which reminded me of being bullied in junior high, and it meant having to get my algebra homework done on time . . . I mean, having to meet my litigation deadlines. I had so many choices, it was exhausting. Best to ignore all of them.

A piece of my brain became scrambled when my mother died, and it got stuck trying to understand mortality. In *Motherless Daughters*, Hope Edelman says, "When a daughter loses a mother […] her longing never disappears. It always hovers at the edge of her awareness, ready to surface at any time." She also says the hardest age to lose a mom is between seven and eleven, because by then you're mature enough to understand death, and you know it's pretty scary.

After I quit work, my biggest demand of the day was standing taller in the tree pose in yoga class. But I think that's when George started to see me as fragile. When he was diagnosed, he told me, "The doctors are such gloom-and-doom types; if I listened to them, I'd already be dead. So I'm not going to listen to them. I will always tell you the truth, but you'll hear it only from me, not from them."

"What does that mean?" I asked. He sounded as if he were delivering a proclamation.

"You'll talk to me, not the doctors."

I knew he was thinking of my mother dying at the same hospital where he was going to be treated. I had been thinking about it too, but I still wanted to be with him. Later, he wouldn't let me go to his chemo or doctor's appointments with him.

He was trying to protect me, as he always had, even though it left me the child to his grown-up. But my voice had fallen into disuse after years of not being needed—I thought I was so close to being happy that I never challenged him. Now I didn't know how. Despite being a lawyer, I hated confrontation.

In the beginning, he drove himself to the hospital and reported to me after his medical appointments.

"The oncologist can't believe how well I'm doing. He said my white blood cell count was almost normal. The nurses can't believe I still work full time."

Later, when he was in a wheelchair, he took a medical transport to the hospital—he refused to let me drive or come with him, and still assured me he was going to recover. But I never heard the medical staff say those things. Or anything else, for that matter. He waved me off when I asked how he planned to live when he wouldn't even let me take him anywhere. Like my father, he did not appear weak.

Had I asked, he would have said he was protecting me. He was William Wallace, riding into battle, defeating cancer single-handedly and returning home to his princess, locked safely away in his castle. Or perhaps he was just George Hansen, an engineer of self-described "almost infinite bandwidth," taking on one more task.

The week of our final Thanksgiving together, over George's protests, I grabbed the phone as he was ending a call with his oncologist. I asked if the hospital could get George into a program for the newly wheelchair-bound to help them work with their chairs. "That program is limited to patients who are expected to recover," the oncologist said brusquely, as if I should have already known.

That's how I learned George was expected to die.

Yet still I didn't confront George—I just ordered us a turkey dinner from Whole Foods since he couldn't stand up to cook anymore. I was afraid that piercing his relentless optimism might drive him to his death. That oncologist had made my husband sound like expired yogurt; I had to let George believe whatever he needed to in order to survive.

But really, I was wrapped up in my own denial like a child hiding under her blanket after a nightmare. If my seemingly healthy mother could die in the hospital, maybe my terminally ill husband could have a miracle cure, even as I watched him disintegrate.

I needed to believe he was going to stay with me. I was unable to picture a life without him—I couldn't push the blanket aside and accept this nightmare was really happening, still the child who couldn't believe the person she loved best in the world was going to die.

So we didn't talk about how to care for him or how he wanted the end to be. We didn't laugh over our memories—like the time we circumnavigated the island of Hawaii in a rented Toyota Tercel—or say how much we loved each other.

Our mutual denial became a second disease, preying on our weaknesses, his need to be infallible, my inability to confront him, and it deprived him of what should have been abundant care followed by a well-planned death.

But unlike when my mom died, I was a *de facto* adult, one who, in fact, had spent a large part of her professional life doing research. When George's reports failed to match reality, I could have contacted the oncology department and demanded a meeting. Had they refused to talk to me, I could have argued my rights with the same tenacity I'd used in my legal practice. But I succumbed to my own denial, and in doing so, I failed both of us.

Once he was gone, I kept reliving the worst of it, cursing my nonexistent voice and wondering if our lives might have been different if only I'd intervened.

"He doesn't know where he is. He's not breathing right. Please come!" I cried into the phone after dialing 911, even as George begged me to hang up, shouting, "I won't go!"

But that Sunday morning in April, for the first time ever, he'd been addled, uncertain where he was, gasping for breath, struggling to stand although he'd been in a wheelchair for months.

The room smelled of death even as the sun came pouring through the blinds.

"You have to go," I told him, my insides crumbling. "I can't fix this." His bandages had come loose, and he was bleeding on the sheets, but he was too agitated for me to get close enough to retape them.

"I'll never forgive you for this," he rasped, thrashing around on the bed, his body so skeletal he looked more dead than alive, his eyes wild and mouth twisted.

He was someone I'd never seen before, fighting an imagined enemy or perhaps just the wife who didn't understand him. I could only hope in his confused state, he'd forget I was the one who'd admitted him to the hospital, and that the George I knew would return to me.

The paramedics probably knew the way to our house. They had to come a half-dozen times over the past few months to lift George back up after he'd fallen from his wheelchair, each time reassuring me, "You were right to call us. You can't lift him."

But I still felt responsible, waiting by the door in my bleach-stained sweat suit for the ambulance. I prayed for it to arrive faster, digging my fingernails into my palms as George lay twisted on the floor, pretending he wasn't in pain, telling me not to worry.

They'd taken him two months ago in January when he couldn't catch his breath. That time he'd been in the hospital for two weeks with pneumonia. He could never breathe right after that.

This time they measured his respiratory numbers, and the paramedic who looked like Sam Elliott circa *Tombstone*, his voice deep and resonant just like the real Sam, said, "We're taking him."

George calmed down, cooperating with the paramedics and assuring them he was fine, but he was lying in a pool of his own waste, and I had no idea how to move him to clean it up. I left George alone with the paramedics, telling myself it was because

I'd upset him, but really it was because I couldn't bear to see what was left of him.

Maybe the cancer had finally eaten into his brain. Just a few minutes ago, he'd been acting like a crazed animal.

"I don't know what to do anymore," I sobbed, perched on our dining room table, my bare feet digging into one of the sand-colored leather chairs.

By now, he should have been getting a lot more care than the two mornings a week my dad's home health care guy Gene came by to help out. But George wouldn't let me hire anyone else.

"You have to be strong for him," Sam the paramedic mumbled, his eyes averted like he'd rather be talking to the floor, as they wheeled George by me on their way to the ambulance.

My biggest sin as they wheeled him away was that I felt only relief. He was no longer on my watch. The paramedics even bagged the soiled sheets for me to throw away. But what I needed was absolution.

Every Sunday night after George died, I kept reliving his final Sunday morning at home. The scurrying little rodent that lived inside my rib cage started scratching to get out. My temples thrummed and the room swirled, signaling the start of my weekly anxiety attack.

I'd been reading *On Grief and Grieving* by Elisabeth Kübler-Ross and David Kessler, which says, "It feels as if it were somehow your fault. You were there. In your perfect hindsight so many things stand out that could have been done differently." But Kübler-Ross doesn't say how to stop the terrible movie playing on repeat in my head.

*It's not your fault,* I would tell myself. *He died of cancer. You couldn't have changed anything.* But the rodent kept on burrowing as I walked through the house. *Here's your fridge, your fireplace, your television, your book, your bottle of red wine. Relax with them.*

*Live in this reality. If you can learn to live with your memories, you will replace chaos with power.*

But it never worked. The anxiety beast kept chewing on my nerves like they were electrical wires. Looking out my window into the darkness, I knew the same backyard was out there, yet I wouldn't have been surprised had it vanished, redwood trees, patio furniture, and all.

*How much more of this life do you want?*

With my breath coming in gasps, I would leave to go over to my dad's. He still lived only ten minutes away.

"Good evening, Deborah," my dad intoned in his rich baritone from his royal-blue armchair. "Care to join us for some red wine? I believe there's still some pork tenderloin left with some broccolini, perhaps?" I turned down the pork but accepted a glass of wine with a square of dark chocolate.

My dad and stepmom, Jane, eighty-three and seventy respectively, were both recovering from different ailments. He'd had a flare-up of his blood disorder, and she'd had a hip replacement. They were pretty much housebound, both relying on home health care during the day.

With his long gray beard, penetrating sky-blue eyes, and crown of white hair, my dad looked like a wizard, old but still powerful. Jane, a retired pediatrician—she was one of seven women in her medical school class at Stanford University—had sandy gray hair and eyes that beamed empathy. Whatever your problem was, she would listen and care about it.

They always ate a late dinner watching several prerecorded news hours on the BBC followed by old episodes of *Masterpiece Theatre* blaring away at high volume. I had never understood why they'd wanted to hear the news three times, the same disasters repeated in triplicate in plummy British accents.

My dad reached out a hand from his wheelchair. Jane pushed herself up painfully from her chair to give me a hug.

I was home. At least this house hadn't turned on me.

The place was virtually unchanged since I'd left for college. He and Jane never renovated the kitchen, and it had disintegrated as the years passed. The paint on the white-and-blue cabinets was worn away, the white floor tiles were cracked, and the dark blue Formica countertops were buckled and burned.

But it brimmed with purchases Jane had instructed the home health care aide to buy from the farmer's market. There were crimson carnations and pink-tipped white lilies in vases cluttering the glass-topped kitchen table. The counters were covered with blue stoneware bowls filled with rosy tomatoes and amber persimmons. The antique rug, with its weaving of animals and trees, glowed a light red.

My own house was sterile. My fruit bowl was empty.

"Sorry, I'm falling apart again," I said.

"You're not falling apart," my dad said. "You're going through an understandably difficult time. It was different for me when your mother died because I had you to raise. I had to keep it together." He paused for a moment.

"Or maybe I just wasn't very emotionally aware," he added.

I think he secretly believed smart people should recover more quickly than other bereaved folks, as if their superior neurons could see them through. But grief didn't work that way. After my mom died, I had struggled to hide my inability to concentrate, and spent hours poring over my math book, trying to will myself back into being the "mentally gifted" minor my elementary school IQ test said I was.

"You were better at this than I am." He'd managed to stay a grown-up. I'd devolved into a toddler.

"You will get through it," Dad said with certainty, "And I predict you'll be happy again someday. I was in time, and you're a lot like me. Look what happened. I found this." He flipped his thumb toward Jane, who lifted her shoulders in an exaggerated shrug and beamed back at him.

They'd met at the Commonwealth Club in San Francisco. He thought she was too young for him—she was thirteen years his junior—so he wasn't interested until she mentioned that she was a doctor. Then he invited her out for sushi. She'd been divorced from her first husband for years by then, with no children, and my dad had had enough child rearing with raising me on his own. They'd been together for thirty-five years.

"I don't know how to get through this," I said.

"Look, I remember when you were twelve," he said, "and you were having trouble with some girls at school. You started telling me about it and I interrupted you with a plan of action. You explained that what you needed me to do was to listen and hug you. I can do that now, but I don't have any solutions."

He waited for my response.

"So," he said, when none came, "do you want to talk about general relativity, or should we watch TV?"

I settled in with them to watch old *I Claudius* episodes. My breathing slowed, my heart stopped pounding, and the rodent went back to sleep. My little family was still there. Death hadn't swooped in to take them, at least not yet.

I tried not to stare at Dad to make sure he looked okay. He'd gotten awfully thin. I knew premature widowhood was a random event, yet I couldn't help wondering if it was genetic.

I wanted to move back home, to lie on the lawn next to the aqua-colored oval swimming pool like when I was a teenager, my mind filled with nothing but self-absorption. Being a grown-up was overrated. Then again, unlike my dad, I'd never really been a grown-up. Neither had George.

I imagined that I would be the mom who checked on her kid fifty times a night to make sure he was still breathing, probably forever destroying his sleep patterns. Anyone could die at any moment, and since I couldn't even drive to a new place without getting lost, I probably wouldn't do too well at keeping a helpless little human alive.

When I was thirty-eight and nearing the end of my child-bearing years, I asked George yet again if he wanted kids.

"Not unless you do," he replied. "I have you to take care of. I don't feel like I'm missing anything."

"I love that you feel that way," I said. "I'm happy just the two of us."

We would stay our little family of two. As children raised like miniature adults, a home without kids seemed normal.

After he died, I wondered what we lost by staying essentially the same people we were in college—in love with each other, but never maturing enough to want to share that love or to make the sacrifices that came with parenthood. George had allergies, so we'd never even gotten a pet. We were always two kids alone together, living out our childhoods for the second time.

But he had been the one in charge.

Jane kept an air mattress on the living room floor so I could sleep over on nights like this one. "If only you knew now that your life will get better in the future . . . ," she said as she brought me the sheets and blankets to make it up. I flopped down, the light and sound from the TV flooding in from the family room, grateful to be sleeping anywhere but at my house with its two resident ghosts.

One of those ghosts was George, torn and helpless, as he took me to task for failing him. He didn't even talk. He just looked at me sadly, with a few tears escaping down his sunken cheeks.

The second ghost never existed in real life, but she was the person I would have been had my mother lived. My mother Thalia died before I saw her as more than "Mom," but she was a psychiatric social worker. She stopped working after she had me, but my dad had told me she was planning to go back. The copies of *The Female Eunuch* and *Sexual Politics* on our bookshelves were hers.

She and my dad had spent the first year after they got married living in Europe. Before that, she had been the only woman on the chess team at Rutgers University, where she'd earned her master's degree in social work. Clearly, she had been extraordinary.

My ghost came to life after George died and I started thinking about alternate universes. My ghost lived in Seattle, grilling salmon for her two adult sons, while her husband was on his way home from work. Unlike me, she had grown up knowing what motherhood looked like and wasn't obsessed that the people she loved would suddenly die. Or she lived in Malibu writing Zen koans, was unafraid of being alone, danced in divey clubs, and spoke her mind without hesitation. My ghost was who I would have been if I wasn't afraid of everything.

During my freshman year of college, I tried to break up with George. I'd been thrilled to go to fraternity parties and discover that, unlike high school, the boys actually wanted to talk to me. George said I'd soon discover the parties weren't all that, and he waited for me at my dorm on Saturday nights until I came home.

Once, when I was very late, he even tracked me down at a party and carried me out to applause, just like Richard Gere in *An Officer and a Gentleman*. At the time, it had seemed so romantic—the girls in my dorm certainly thought so—but I think that's when I relinquished other paths. By junior year, I was set on stability, straight As, law school, and George, the boy with whom I had a future.

Had my mother survived, we might have traveled together—she had cousins in Scotland she visited every few years—or she might have encouraged me to spend a college semester abroad, and I might have discovered I liked the world. Based on her reading choices, she might have advised me not to settle down with my high school sweetheart until I'd learned how to spread my wings. Perhaps she would have tried to convince me not to give up the law because women of her generation had to fight for their careers.

As it was, I blamed her for leaving me with the rule of impending disaster.

"When Mom died, you kept me in the dark," I said to my dad one morning after a night spent on the living room floor. Actually it was early afternoon, because he's practically nocturnal. He was sipping the green tea his home health care aide had brought us. "And when George died, he didn't tell me anything either. Is that why I'm so messed up?"

*Is that why I can't bear to be alone, thinking I'm always in the dark?*

"You had thirty-two years of living in a fairy tale," my dad replied, accepting his protein drink from the aide, then grimacing at the taste. "And you expected it to last forever. Having it end was a shock. You've gone through a lot of loss for someone your age, but you aren't messed up."

"But no one ever tells me anything," I said, sounding like a petulant thirteen-year-old who was too young to be told anything.

I thought of the hours I spent waiting for my dad to come home from the hospital to tell me about Mom, and the hours I spent waiting for George to come home from the hospital to tell me what his doctor said. I had cried secretly on my way to school so my dad wouldn't notice that I was sad, and I had cried on the living room sofa while George was at chemo as I imagined the liquid going into his arm drop by drop. He didn't even know I was afraid. We did not appear weak.

"When your mother died, the clinical model was to keep kids in their normal routine if they seemed to be functioning well," said Jane, in full pediatrician mode as she came to sit with us. She lowered herself carefully into the armchair, still in pain. "Giving them counseling or talking about the death was thought to disturb them."

"Deb-or-ah," my dad said, drawing my name out as he always did when he wanted me to listen, "I wasn't trying to deceive you. I did the best I could at the time. I never signed up for dead wife duty."

Suddenly he looked defeated, no doubt remembering those early days when we were both stressed beyond imagining—when he had to put dinner on the table every night and make sure the cat was fed and the house didn't fall down, which might very well have happened, considering the way Mom disappeared. It had been a constant effort to impose order on what we knew to be chaos, where anything might happen, even your worst nightmare.

"I know. You were the best omni-parent ever," I said, trying to bring the light back into his eyes with the name I'd given him for being both mother and father to me.

I remembered the Saturday afternoons that he picked me up from Mills and took me to the Good Earth Café in Berkeley, where he spent hours helping me with my calculus assignments and proudly wore the Mills College sweatshirt I'd given him for Christmas. We ordered coffee for him and hot chocolate for me as we went over derivatives and integrals, time and space, velocity and acceleration; and got more and more refills. We were two veterans who'd defeated a hostile universe together and come out pretty damn well for it.

Until the universe struck a second time. Being the ten-year-old with the dead mom should have been enough.

Google backed me up on this: The American Cancer Society predicted the lifetime risk for breast cancer in males was around one in a thousand, which meant that just one-tenth of one percent of all breast cancers occurred in men. So why had fate chosen to gift my husband with it? And why had his usually uber-rational mind fallen into denial, leaving me with another ghost of myself, that strung-out caregiver who passed by me in the hallway as she whimpered because she couldn't help her beloved.

I grabbed a handful of dried apricots and left to go home, driving slowly by the couples out for their evening walks. They had flesh. I had a living room full of George's stereo equipment I'd never liked in the first place and still didn't know how to use.

Grief was a silent house.

# IV. The Man with the Diamond Chip on His Shoulder

"I CAN'T BELIEVE I'M CONTEMPLATING dating someone who lives in Danville," Lowell said fifteen minutes into our first date, which was a casual brunch at a restaurant exactly equidistant between our two houses.

Another JDate find, Lowell was a multitalented artist, writer, and director; sixty-seven years old; five feet ten; and a bit plump with a handsome, pixyish face, a roguish mustache and goatee, and dark gray hair brushed back from a high forehead.

He wore a pale green suede jacket over a matching green plaid shirt, the collars carefully placed to overlap. I had on white pedal pushers, a flowy striped cardigan, and oversized sunglasses perched on top of my head, trying out for the role of bourgeois hippie chick.

Once we sat down, I recognized him as the guy in the brown Mercedes station wagon who'd repeatedly cut me off while I was driving over as he kept switching lanes, oblivious to the other drivers. I just hoped he didn't recognize me as the one who'd honked and sped by him, cursing after he cut me off for the third time.

We'd emailed during the month that he was in Paris. He sent me photographs of his historic mansion in the Berkeley Hills and the brochure for the Stinson beach house he was selling.

No doubt he was pleased when I wrote back oohing and aahing over its beauty and asked how he could bear to part with it. I'd written him about Colette, Julia Child, and M. F. K. Fisher, trying to sound smart and Francophile-y. I kept playing Joni Mitchell's *Court and Spark* over and over on George's turntable, lingering over "Free Man in Paris," waiting for him to return.

I was awed by Lowell's Bohemian affluence, old money dressed in a "careless paisley scarf and antique kimono" kind of way. Lowell's dating profile said he wanted to share his bounty. Perhaps he was a man of substance.

After Ben, I needed someone whose cup was overflowing with promise instead of sorrow. Lowell was entrenched in so many projects I saw myself as both his muse *and* his attorney, meshing my solitary life with his social one, and finding my calling so I could escape my ghost. Of course, that was assuming we actually liked each other.

Oh yeah, remember to rein in expectations.

"You look just like your photos, which is rare," he said by way of greeting. "When I first saw your profile, I honestly didn't think you were that attractive, but when you put up those professional shots, I thought, *There's going to be a lot of competition for her.*"

"Could be," I said coyly, flipping my hair. Score one for the TED Talk, but ignore the fact that Lowell was the sort of man who wanted to compete for a human trophy.

"When did your husband die?" he continued.

"April 2013."

"That's pretty recent. Are you sure you're ready to be in another relationship?" he said, his voice nasal and high-pitched.

"Um, yes." If I hadn't thought so, I wouldn't have gone on JDate. We both ordered lattes and poached eggs. He specified several times to the server that he wanted his *very* lightly poached.

"I host parties and concerts for my foundation. I need a partner who can act as hostess at my events," he went on.

"That sounds great. I love talking to people." Actually, I had no idea whether or not I could act as a hostess. I might not even make it through breakfast.

"I travel a lot and spend one day a week at my foundation in the city," he said. "My partner needs to be flexible, available to travel on short notice or stay at my place if I need someone at home."

"Okay." I was looking for love; he was interviewing for an administrative assistant.

"I want to adopt a dog with my next partner."

"Mmmm." I wouldn't be acquiring anything anytime soon that would predecease me.

Then he made the Danville comment. In his emails from Paris he'd said several times, "You don't seem very Danville," apparently intending it as a compliment. But Danville is lovely, framed by rolling hills, its streets lined by old shade trees, home to an impressive, modern library and a well-curated independent bookstore.

Moreover, bashing the suburbs isn't terribly original. I'd answered that Berkeley had an undercurrent of anger, as if some great socialist revolution had failed, but everybody still got a Volvo.

In the restroom, I dabbed at my mascara. My eyes tear up when I get angry, a terrible trait in a lawyer.

Lowell wasn't just oblivious; he was arrogant. But he was also interesting, unlike anybody I'd met before, with his own music foundation and an Emmy for documentary filmmaking.

His profile said he wanted to be part of a couple who was "lively, fun, social, and spirited," and he described his ideal woman as "very attractive, youthful, and petite or slender," specifying an age range ending far below his own. Concerned about the slender requirement, I'd lost a few pounds in preparation for our date.

When we first started emailing, Lowell had answered my question that yes, several women on JDate had messaged him objecting to his profile's physical requirements and pointing out how badly he himself failed to meet them. But I so wanted to be partnered that I ignored his desires being limited to appearances. Nor did I question why I was changing to meet them.

I was so used to having men take the lead—my father assumed I'd go to graduate school, George made our decisions, the partners at work dictated how to handle our cases—I put my faith in patriarchy, and a particularly archaic member of it at that.

Lowell wanted a girlfriend to plug into his world, no adjustments necessary. I had nowhere else to be, so I went back to the table and started fitting in, hoping to become his leading lady.

Six weeks after George died, the Saturday evening of Memorial Day weekend, I had gone to a beginner's swing dancing class at The Two Left Feet, a local dance studio. My hair colorist told me when she was single, swing dancing had saved her life—apparently, she'd found Western Swing and the Lindy Hop to be particularly vivifying. I figured it wouldn't hurt to try; I just wished I had someone to go with me.

I used to joke with George that I had to pay for my friends. I saw my personal trainer twice a week and my colorist, massage therapist, aesthetician, and nail technician once a month. I knew several women at the gym, and I kept in touch with a few former colleagues and classmates, but I had no one to call on the proverbial day when you're losing what's left of your mind. That Saturday of a three-day weekend, I might have been the only person in Northern California with nowhere to go and no one to be with.

My isolation was epic. At least once a day, I pulled out the drawer where I stashed the last T-shirt George had worn. When I held it up to my face, it still smelled a teeny bit like him, the clean, earthy smell of the old George mingled with the metallic, medicinal odor of the dying one. I'd also saved the beat-up leather gloves he'd used for maneuvering his wheelchair, the leather soft against my face as if I could still feel George's touch.

*Okay, put them away and close the drawer—now.* But I couldn't. *Okay, do it now.*

I was sorting through George's stuff, throwing out thirty-two years of accumulated geek paraphernalia. Look, George, there go your boxed sets of *Mission Impossible* and *Dr. Who: The Tom Baker Years*, joining your *Avengers* collection, every single goddamned episode since 1961. They were so boring, yet you insisted we watch them with dinner.

I'm taking your record albums out of their plastic sleeves, getting fingerprints all over them on purpose to summon your ghost. There go Ferrante and Teicher. Bye-bye mint-condition Jethro Tull. *Please, George, come back to me just this once, and I'll never ask you for anything ever again.*

That black leather jacket you wore to your first Ramones concert? Into the charity pile. Hey, you abandoned me.

Each night before making my first Manhattan, I'd write out my to-do list for the next day:

1. Call George's stock options broker again. Threaten to sue if no one will talk to me.
2. Call car loan bank again. Ask to speak to a manager.
3. Call Intuit benefits again. Try to figure out COBRA coverage.
4. Do not threaten to kill employees at bank, brokerage, and benefits companies.
6. Collect life insurance.
7. Do not blow it all on one grand futile gesture. George wouldn't have wanted an eighties tribute concert

in his name, and besides, most of the Ramones are already dead.

8. Buy more bourbon.
9. You're doing great even though it doesn't feel like it.

Sometimes, I'd hear a sob that sounded like an animal in the wilderness, only to realize it was the sound of my own voice. The raven of loneliness had settled on my shoulder, and I thought I might die. It had even begun to whisper that death might be a good idea.

After many days and nights alone, the idea of trying a swing dance class didn't seem any dumber than anything else. I was a single person. Time to start doing single person stuff, even if it was only going to a dance studio. By myself. To hang out with strangers. Six weeks after my husband died. It sucked, but in my isolation, it seemed like an attempt at resilience instead of an exercise in masochism.

Pulling on a black sweatshirt and dark jeans, I stepped into a soft spring night only to discover I was surrounded by couples, some laughing and holding hands or otherwise in pairs where both of them were still alive. Some of the women were wearing gauzy flowered dresses or spaghetti-strapped camisoles covered by lacy shrugs.

I was a specter in my dark clothing, emerging from my lair like Nosferatu to peer at the living, uncertain of how to interact with them. I wished I could skip the class and ask a few of the friendlier-looking people to join me for a drink. *I want to tell you about my husband, George,* I would have said to them.

Country music blasted from the dance studio. The front room was filled with women in prairie outfits and men wearing Western shirts discussing where to buy the best dance shoes. I was a Morrissey fan who'd stumbled onto the set of *Hee Haw*.

"Is it okay to come here without a partner?" I asked the smiling lady manning the entry table. She looked to be in her early sixties, trim in her Levis and checkered blouse, her hair springing up in silver curls.

"Sure," she said, "People come in alone all the time. They come here to be social."

"Okay," I said, then blurted out involuntarily, "I . . . I've never been here before. I'm a recent widow."

I was hoping she'd say, "Go home. You don't have to do this." But instead she directed me toward a studio in the back and said, "I'm a widow too. I'm sorry for your loss, honey. C'mon in. This is a great place to meet people."

I wondered whether I'd ever be healed enough to do what she was doing—sitting alone, cheerfully manning a counter where couples passed by her all night long.

A few pairs of dancers were twirling around the back studio, focusing intently on each other. There was only one unpartnered dancer, a grinning fellow, far shorter than I, with feathered blond hair and a mustache, wearing a brightly flowered Hawaiian shirt, a thick gold chain gleaming around his neck. His head came up to my boobs. My high-necked sweatshirt had been an inspired choice.

"Face each other and clasp hands loosely," said our teacher, a tall bearded man wearing a wedding ring, an accessory I'd just started to notice. Too late to leave. I hadn't realized how peeled I'd feel in a room full of strangers.

My partner helpfully told me each move he was going to make in advance, but it made no difference. I stepped into him and swung under his arm, which in my case meant having to duck . . . and then I was lost.

I was the kid in PE who never served the volleyball over the net because I thought everyone was watching me, guaranteeing I'd fail. But I had widow's brain, where my head was flooded with molasses, cutting off many of its synapses.

I was imprisoned in a bobbing box of two, my hand on my partner's shoulder, his on my waist, our other hands clasped out to the side. I saw myself in the mirror reeling about like an off-kilter Goth. My hand in his started to sweat. I didn't want to be touched. I was living out the scene in *Sixteen Candles* where the short guy slow-dances with the really tall girl at the high school dance.

I thought I'd be free at the end of an hour, but my $10 admission included not just one hour of misery but two, a bonus class in ballroom dancing. Between sessions, there was a break for cookies and soda in the studio kitchen. I was trapped in the never-ending youth fellowship meeting from hell.

"My husband died six weeks ago," I said to my partner in an attempt to explain my leaden demeanor.

"Please accept my condolences," he said. "You'll always have your memories to see you through."

Shit, he was nice. Now I couldn't just leave. As we began our second class, he took my hand and said, "Things will get better in the future."

I fled at exactly the two-hour mark when one of the husbands was asking his third question about quarter turns. Making my way back to my car in the dark, I realized it was the first time in years I'd been out alone at night.

A cold fog enveloped me, setting me apart. I was a widow.

Compared to more evenings like that, Lowell looked like heaven. "My new partner and I just adopted a borzoi together," I practiced saying aloud in my empty living room. "He's even going to make a film about it."

A few weeks after that first brunch, I was lying by the pool under the palm trees at the Claremont Resort in Berkeley, wearing my new black, 1940s-looking bikini, waiting for Lowell to emerge from his workout at the hotel gym. Trying out my new persona of sophisticated girlfriend, I pictured myself in a technicolor romance, swept off my feet by a dashing swain, but I was assiduously ignoring how badly I'd miscast Lowell.

I'd been seeing him for extended weekends, packing the new black leather overnight bag I bought for my first grown-up sleepovers and meeting him in Berkeley on Friday afternoons. I was buying my own clothes now, but I was still choosing them for a man.

On our second date, a lecture at a restaurant by a cookbook author that Lowell knew, I chatted with his friends, mentioning locavores, sustainable seafood, and sous vide, trying to sound like a foodie.

"I'm glad you spoke up," Lowell said afterward. "My last girlfriend usually clammed up at events like this one." I hated that kind of comparison that implicitly pitted one woman against another, but I kept silent. I watched him wave and make silly faces to attract the attention of a toddler who had wandered over from a nearby table, but he also looked around to see if anyone else had noticed his performance.

Back at his house, he changed the background music from classical to eighties as he prepared a dinner for us of lamb and cannellini beans and said, "I'm trying to have more fun in my life." We danced around his French-Gothic-style kitchen in a desperate simulation of fun.

"I like the way you move and I like the way you look in my house. Why don't we try spending weekends together and see how it goes? You might enjoy a couple days a week away from Danville," he said as I leaned against the balcony where I'd gone to cool off. "You could stay in the apartment in my basement so we don't have to, uh, rush into anything."

So I became his latest object, sleeping in his bougainvillea-covered apartment while he stayed in his bedroom on the third floor. We made out sometimes—he seemed especially into it in public by the Claremont pool—but he didn't seem terribly eager to go further. In my inexperience, I failed to see how wrong all of this was.

"I'm concerned you're not ready for a real partnership," Lowell said over dinner at the Claremont a few weekends later. "Your loss is fairly recent by recovery standards." He shot a piercing stare at me over his scallops in beurre blanc as if trying to figure out where I was in the Kübler-Ross stages of grieving.

"If I hadn't recovered enough, I wouldn't be dating," I told him yet again, taking a sip from my almost empty glass of Chardonnay and wishing he would ask if I wanted a second one, but afraid to order one for myself in case he would think I drank too much.

"You were in a long marriage, so you probably know how to get along with a man," he said, as if weighing his options.

I kept silent, not wanting to say, "But you're not the man that George was." I silenced the George-o-meter when it warned me that talking about getting along with a man probably meant the man in question was very hard to get along with.

Clearly, Lowell had never considered whether he should get along with a woman. He just assumed she would transform herself to please him like one of those shape-shifting aliens in a science fiction movie.

"You're loopy," he said suddenly, his scrutiny dissolving into a grin. "Like Diane Keaton in a Woody Allen movie."

In fact, I was anything but. I was calculating what my new relationship was worth to me. Back home after my weekends at Lowell's, I'd pull into the garage after evening yoga, linger in the car, put my feet up on the dashboard, and sing along to Counting Crows' "Goodnight Elizabeth" one more time, missing George waiting for me, and trying to prolong the moment before I had to go inside.

Sometimes it felt like I was living in five-minute increments, drawing out my dinner, watching Netflix, and drinking red wine until I couldn't keep my eyes open any longer, prolonging the chill when I climbed into my empty bed.

I might have to do this for the rest of my life, which would be about 3.1 million times, assuming twelve five-minute increments per hour, multiplied by twenty-four hours a day, three hundred and sixty-five days a year for thirty more years. Assuming I survived to be eighty, which seemed like quite enough of this lifetime.

How much was my new relationship worth to me? Too much.

"Hold your legs up. They're so long I don't know what to do with them," Lowell said back at his place after dinner. We were finally having sex, but his foreplay was perfunctory, as if he already knew he wasn't going to enjoy himself.

It reminded me of the way he sent his sausages back without even tasting them when we went out for breakfast, explaining they were always undercooked the first time. Intercourse didn't seem to excite him much either, which was odd because he was hard before we even started.

I should have known Lowell wasn't going to be happy. He carried around a seemingly endless compendium of slights:

"I've come to this bar for years, but they've never appreciated my patronage."

"That restaurant owner picks my brain whenever I come in, but still charges me full price for my meal."

"The guests of my foundation are trying to get me to pay for too many hotel rooms."

I thought if I tried hard enough, I could soothe him, like removing the thorn from the lion's paw. Then I'd become invaluable to him. Like mine, however, his sorrows came from within, and only he could fix them.

"Goodnight," Lowell said. It was my signal to return to my room, having fulfilled my purpose as accessory with benefits.

He'd told me that he was too restless to sleep with another person in his bed, but he'd also let slip that his last girlfriend had. I wanted to ask him why he let her and not me, but he'd probably just consider it for a moment, then give me a negative performance review.

"Did you use Viagra?" I asked as I tied the sash on my new black silk bathrobe. I was puzzled by the disconnect between the erection and the ennui.

"I, um, take something," he said huffily, then added with a little chuckle, "I'm old."

That puzzled me even more. Shouldn't age make a person aware of his mortality, more delighted at the chance to make a life with a new love instead of spending night after night alone in his mansion? But I voiced none of my thoughts and quietly made my way back to the basement.

Lowell seemed to want me in theory, springing for lavish spa treatments on my birthday, taking me to dinner at the latest "it" restaurant, giving me books about Berkeley architecture (one of which even featured his own house). He even took me for a weekend at his Stinson beach house.

Over tea and ginger cookies at a little bakery in Point Reyes, he told me, looking deep into my eyes, "I love it here, but I haven't wanted to come by myself."

George hadn't liked going away for weekends. He found it a waste of time. The last time we'd gone to Carmel, I brought an overnight bag, but George had begged me to come home that afternoon. He bought me a watch to make up for it, but it didn't really.

With Lowell, I saw long leisurely weekends at the coast, even if he complained about the wait at the café at Stinson Beach and took the one empty barstool when we went out for drinks, leaving me to stand by his side. Dashing swain, indeed.

One night, Lowell peered over at me sitting on his white jacquard sofa and said, "I can see you with a big diamond ring on your finger." I'm embarrassed to admit I imagined the vintage black lace dress I would wear for the ceremony.

When George and I got married, we just went to the courthouse one morning and stood before a makeshift altar composed of a chipped wooden desk topped with dusty plastic flowers. I wore jeans. George wore the same outfit he wore every day—a fair-trade Peruvian cotton T-shirt, mountaineering shorts, and high-topped Nikes. He was one of those people who wore shorts every day even if it was freezing outside.

We laughed at the gift box the county provided, with its sample package of diapers apparently for couples who got married in haste. But we had true love. In its absence, Lowell and I would need a lot of embellishments.

I pictured Lowell and myself taking an afternoon class together on Proust, curling up by his enormous stone fireplace on cold winter nights, he with his leather-bound notebook and I with my iPad, reading the lines we'd written aloud to each other, inhaling the scent of woodsmoke, drinking one of the red wines he'd shown me in his cellar but never offered me.

I fantasized about not being alone anymore and, even more shamefully, never again having to worry about money. He was thinking about my finances too, proposing I rent my house out for income and move into his basement apartment. He'd keep the beach house and put it on Airbnb so I could handle the listings and share in the profits.

He said, "It would strengthen my position to have a lawyer on my team." In the movie version of my life, I'd gone from playing the widow to playing the labradoodle.

I walked down the three flights of stairs to my room, turning off the lights as I went, wishing I merited a good morning cuddle and one of the three empty bedrooms next to his on the top floor. I wanted to shout at him that as the third man I'd ever had sex with, he should be trying a lot harder.

Kübler-Ross says, "whether it's four years or four months, having sex again is complicated. The 'right time' depends on the person, the relationship, and what feels okay inside."

He was the one that made sex complicated, and I didn't feel okay inside. I worried I wasn't to his taste, like a sausage that needed more time on the grill.

I knew I could still have great sex. During my first few months of widowhood, I spent my evlenings drinking Manhattans and watching *Weeds*. After a few drinks, I could pretend that the main character, Nancy Botwin, also a suburban widow, was a real person and we were going to hang out together the next day.

While Nancy dealt pot to college students onscreen, I'd look up my old high school classmates on Facebook. I'd discovered the girl who bullied me in junior high was married, had three children, and had become a family therapist. Her husband was still alive. I fantasized about killing her, since fate apparently wasn't into justice.

The sole bright spot in my life was my new friend, Gene, the home health care aide to George and my dad. George had met him through my dad and liked him, and had asked him to come by to earn some extra money by taking care of him after I pleaded for more help.

Gene stuck out in Danville like a sore, but very hip, thumb. He was forty-two, six feet tall, and weighed 240 pounds. He was half Mexican and half American Indian with tawny skin, great muscles, a mohawk, and round, childlike brown eyes.

He was covered in dark blue tattoos—he called them "prison style" even though he'd never been to jail—of everything from Yosemite Sam to the scales of justice to a portrait of his ex-wife.

After George died, Gene often texted me, "How's your day going, beautiful?" A self-described cinephile, Gene's hobbies included being a movie extra, attending film festivals, updating his IMDB page, and having his photo taken with celebrities.

When I answered that I was on my way to see my trainer or home watching *Grey's Anatomy* (extra points for getting through the cancer episodes), he'd answer, "Pump some iron for me," or he would text me a selfie he'd taken at a screening with one of the actors. Aside from my dad and stepmom, Gene was the only person I talked to almost every day. He was keeping the raven of loneliness at bay.

One night, thoroughly pissed at having been reduced to imaginary friends, I threw my martini glass at the living room fireplace and watched it shatter on the hearth, spewing shards of glass over the living room floor. As I stepped around the broken glass to make another drink, I pretended there was somebody watching me, noticing how cool and nihilistic I was.

My phone buzzed with a new text from Gene.

"Whatcha up to?"

I called him. "I'm sorry, I'm sort of falling apart," I said. "I broke a glass. It seemed like fun at the time." Gene told me later I slurred my words when I was drunk. I'd always thought I sounded fine. Oops.

"Are you okay? Don't step on the broken glass," he warned.

"What does it matter? Everything's so awful."

"I'll be over in thirty-five minutes."

By then he'd taken me to several movie screenings, all very casual, just a couple of friends hanging out, sometimes grabbing a bite to eat afterward. I'd last seen him a couple of days ago, when he'd stopped by to pick up some of George's power tools as part of my project to clean out the garage. There were so many that he'd taken to stopping by a couple times a week.

"I'm just here to avoid rush hour," he always said with a wink.

The garage was almost unbearably hot as I'd shown him what to take away. His muscles had strained under his Slightly Stoopid T-shirt as he'd lugged everything out to his truck. The evening breeze had just started to penetrate the heat, and the sky had turned indigo. When he had hugged me goodbye, I'd felt an electric shock followed by an all-body tingle—a jolt to somewhere I'd never been before.

Knowing he was on his way, I'd snapped into cleanup mode, leaving the broken glass but tidying up the kitchen. I tossed the takeout containers into the trash. I showered and changed into a clean tank top. There! Pathetic, but not sloppy.

Not being alone was worth the loss of my self-respect. I didn't cut my feet on the broken glass, a scenario I'd been perversely looking forward to. Once I fell apart, I got to be in pieces. I could stop making all those phone calls and going to banks and mailing out death certificates when nothing was going to make any difference anyway.

Gene got to my house just as I had finished tidying the kitchen. I fell into his big hug.

"Be careful, beautiful," he said as he went to get the vacuum cleaner. I gave him a paper bag for the larger pieces of glass, then retreated to the living room sofa with my arms wrapped around my knees and wondered what was going to happen after he cleaned up.

When he was done, he sat beside me, holding me as I slumped against him.

"I'm sorry," I said yet again, enveloped in Gene's arms, softened and electrified at the same time. "I just couldn't stand to be alone anymore."

"I know, sweetheart. I said you could call me whenever you want," he said, rubbing my back. The tension in my shoulders started to liquify. "Do you want to lie down for a bit? Did you sleep much last night?"

"About four hours, on and off."

Gene and I lay down on the couch, his arms still around me, his skin velvety and warm, as if steam was running underneath. His muscles felt smooth as I ran my hands down his arms. He smelled like honey and laundry soap. Or maybe just like something I really wanted.

"You must hate me," I said, although I knew he didn't. This wasn't my first depressed, after-hours phone call.

"Yes, I hate you, you crazy, beautiful thing," he said, laughing softly.

Then he kissed me, hesitantly at first, as if he were afraid that I'd push him away, then with more force, like he'd been waiting a long time for this. He pressed closer to me on the couch, taking his shirt off. Hesitantly, he lifted up my tank top, moving it over my head slowly, waiting to see whether I'd stop him. But I was transfixed, cold and warm at the same time.

Then he drew me into him. His skin was like food. I'd been starving, I just hadn't known it.

"God, you're hot," he moaned, running his hands over my hip bones and pulling down my shorts. I was frozen, embarrassed to be so exposed, yet excited to be wanted after so long. He kissed me deeply, moving his mouth from my neck to my breasts.

I felt an avalanche of little sparks, gasping as they became more intense. This was my last chance to tell him to stop, but I couldn't. I was engulfed in a spreading heat that was convulsing in a huge release.

Then he plunged into me. It had been so long since I'd had sex I felt like I was losing my virginity for the second time. It was the first time I'd been with anyone other than George. I was filled with a warm throbbing, made powerful by Gene's desire. It was the first time I'd ever felt that way.

George and I had fallen together like puppies. After so many years together, even before he got sick, we were more best friends than lovers—sex had pretty much dwindled off—but I had been content that way and thought my desire had receded with age, never considering whether I wanted it back. George and I hadn't really talked about it.

But this was different. It was incendiary yet almost choreographed, an infusion of life into what I thought was long dead.

I hadn't had sex for nearly two years. At fifty, I figured I was done with it. Sex was for other people.

Kübler-Ross has this to say: "We would suggest, however, that seeking counseling or a bereavement group is usually better than seeking sex right away in order to sort out your feelings." But none of the grief books tell you that good sex is far more cheering than joining a book club or tackling that pesky junk drawer. And aside from suggesting you get massages, the books don't say what to do when you're desperate for human contact, whether you know it or not.

In one night, I doubled my numbers. I reawakened my sex drive. That had to be imprudent—what if I couldn't put it back to sleep? What if the fates punished me by making my dad relapse?

Being with Lowell, however, was going to mean putting many parts of myself to sleep.

A few weeks after that first attempt at intimacy, I was photographing Lowell in his backyard as he stood beside a whole roast pig oozing porcine goo. He was hosting a catered picnic for thirty. It had been an auction item for the annual Berkeley Public Library fundraiser. The pale sunlight set off his terraced backyard with its huge boulders, old oak trees, and artfully placed outdoor antiques.

I'd directed the caterers when Lowell had been overcome with a sudden last-minute fatigue, then I mingled with the guests, discussing all things Berkeley and noticing how pleased he was when we scored a few dinner invitations. One Berkeley notable even commented on how well I fit in.

Lowell was too exhausted to summon me to his bedroom that night, so I stayed in the basement, nursing a pounding headache I hadn't yet realized came from holding my tongue for far too long.

Especially after he told me what my spot at the picnic would have cost if I hadn't been his guest.

He almost hadn't invited me at all. We'd had our first argument the week before, when his Mercedes had been sideswiped.

I called him as soon as I got his message, but he was out to dinner. When I finally reached him later that night, he said he was fine, if a bit shaken up. But the next afternoon he emailed saying, "A car accident isn't a birthday, but I still need attention without having to remind you about it, especially when I'm ill. I shouldn't always have to initiate contact when you're in Danville mode."

Never mind that he wasn't ill enough to cancel his dinner out. Now my hometown had become the bastion of all things inconsiderate. I called him and explained that I hadn't been in touch because my doctor's appointment ran late. I'd wanted to keep my minor ailment private; otherwise he probably would have complained that I'd failed to disclose I was defective.

"We just spent three days together this past weekend," he said, his voice becoming a screech. "We even called each other 'boyfriend' and 'girlfriend.' My girlfriend should care enough to contact me the morning after I'm in a car crash. I was in a car crash, Debbie, a car *crash*. My girlfriend didn't call me this morning, but all my friends managed to, even Peter." Peter was a crotchety, retired book publisher.

I refrained from saying I hope he'd enjoy sleeping with Peter.

"Our relationship lacks the requisite intimacy," he continued. "I feel you haven't been listening to what I say."

I thought that was all I'd been doing. Ben too had said he wanted real intimacy, which seemed to be shorthand for a woman who functioned as an indefatigable sounding board.

"Lowell is a traditional sort of guy. If you want him, you're going to have to bend to accommodate him," my dad said when I asked him for advice. "He's not going to change." This was ironic, coming from a man who'd changed enormously after my mom died, including learning how to control his own considerable temper.

When I'd previously told Dad about the age difference between Lowell and me, he said only, "I hope he manages to stay healthy." But when I asked my dad if he'd ever criticized his dates the way Lowell did with me, he went blank, then shook his head in disbelief and suggested I return to the drawing board. My mother probably would have told me I was setting back the cause by dating Lowell in the first place.

George was considerate to everyone, even the peevish design team on Quicken who refused to change their drawings after he'd explained multiple times they were almost impossible to code. He'd just smile and do his best. The George-o-meter was set to "Run," but I couldn't bring myself to end it, worried that I'd die alone because Lowell was my last chance at companionship. It seemed the final insult in a life marked by death.

Remembering how he made me breakfast and had my latte waiting for me at cafés, I decided his love languages were quality time and acts of service. So I held back my own complaints and told Lowell I wanted to make up. He said he'd see me the next day at the Claremont, but arrived far later than he said he would, then went to work out at the hotel gym as if I wasn't even there.

As the sun began to set, I sat shivering by the pool and pulled my clothes on over my swimsuit. I finally understood. His true language was resentment. Dissatisfaction was his version of foreplay. Now he was exacting punitive damages, which probably excited him more than our lackluster times in bed. Yet I still wanted to succeed. I still thought I could change him.

"Companionship" is such a dull word until it's taken away from you.

o o o o o

Gene provided companionship for a while. It was a balm after what I'd been through. I'd woken up one morning to find two heavy stainless-steel watches on my nightstand—the one Gene had forgotten from the night before and George's, which was there because I'd taken it out to remind me. To remind me of what I wasn't sure, perhaps as a touchstone for memories of better times or a censure for being with someone else. But for the first time in a very long while, life felt yummy.

"Want to go for burgers, Del?" Gene asked after we'd seen a movie at the Castro Theatre in San Francisco. Del was short for "Delicious."

He called me his hot girlfriend, far from the ragged cancer wife I used to be. We walked over to Orphan Andy's, swinging our clasped hands, ordering our favorite meal, burgers topped with blue cheese and sautéed onions. "Bloody as hell," Gene told our server with his trademark wink.

"How should we describe the movie to our friends?" he asked. He took pictures of us at all his premieres, then posted them on Facebook to show his five thousand virtual friends what he and his Del were up to.

"Overly indie and earnest. Too many scenes of lovelorn twenty-somethings staring off into space at diners," I said, well aware that we too were sitting at a diner, looking like middle-aged teenagers who'd just discovered love.

Through Gene's connections, we went to several screenings a week, a pair of cinephiles living through the movies. I'd forgotten what it was like to go to the city—or anyplace else, for that matter. Suddenly, there were so many sights to see, people to watch, and pizzas to try.

A film at the Kabuki Theater meant a trip to Japantown with

its stores selling manga, action figures, and custard with fruit. An afternoon premier at the Castro meant taking in its famed crème brûlée truck, its much-hyped naked men, and its bakery selling anatomically shaped cookies.

I floated down the street, with my chocolate-frosted, penis-shaped cookie in hand. I was embarrassed every time I took a bite.

"My burger has a melty center, just like someone else I know," Gene said. He took a bite, widening his big brown eyes in mock innocence.

"It has better buns," I said. I was a size six, down from the size ten I'd been when I was married. Since George's death, I pretty much gave up eating anything other than bourbon and carrot cake. Only alcohol and sugar tasted like anything.

The cream cheese frosting dissolved on my tongue in a pleasure I didn't deserve. I had the flat stomach I'd always wanted but, despite the four moisturizers I layered on twice a day, it came with sunken eyes and dull skin thanks to a lack of sleep and my liquid dinners.

"We just need to get some more meat back on yours," Gene said with a shake of his head.

On the Sunday the paramedics took George away, the ingredients for Coquilles St. Jacques were in our refrigerator. George had suggested I make it for dinner, to try to recreate the festive evenings we used to have.

That Monday night, I made the dish in his absence. I sautéed the scallops, thickened the cream, and added the Pernod for flavor. I ate it with the Montrachet he'd instructed me to buy and sat at the dining room table instead of the kitchen counter, as if by having the special meal he'd planned, he'd know from his hospital bed that I loved and waited for him. He died two days later.

I'd avoided the kitchen after that. Apparently, it could kill from afar.

With Gene, I could have eaten two burgers. They tasted like ecstasy. The juice ran down my fingers; the outside was lightly charred and the inside pink and meaty. The sharpness of the blue cheese cut through the unctuousness, and the caramelized onions added that final layer that sent it into the realm of orgasmic.

I was starting my recovery with food and sex, giving both a second chance, even though sex was a memory and food had failed me in the past.

Once diagnosed, George started cooking like a fiend, and what used to be a hobby had become an obsession. On weekends, we'd hit Tokyo Fish in Berkeley, hoping for scallops still in the shell, laughing at the phallic looking *mirugai* clams, getting a flat of my favorite *uni* as he read off the list of ingredients from his cookbook by Chef Morimoto.

Sometimes we went to Bryan's in the city to buy the ingredients for *Larousse's Lobster à L'américaine* or Steak Diane, special occasion dishes he made to show me that nothing had changed. I pretended to believe him, but as we wrestled lobsters into pots of boiling water, all I could see was George sitting in his chemo chair.

On the ride home from the city, Gene kissed me at stoplights. I kept my eyes open, watching for them to change, looking forward to making love once we got home, my new pale green sheets tangled around us like benevolent sea creatures.

The morning after the picnic, we went out for breakfast, and I waited for Lowell to sing my praises. But all he said was "Can't you offer to pay for once?"

"Not after all I did yesterday," I said, attempting a joke, but he just looked down at the floor, apparently dismayed, as he adjusted the drape of his long gray scarf.

He usually paid for meals, but I got the check this time, including the doughnut hole he plucked from its glass case and ate at the counter, exclaiming peevishly, "I'm hungry," offering me a bite only after I glared at him.

Everything crystallized for me in that moment—I knew there would never be love. He'd always be calculating how much he was giving to this relationship, how much I was, how much rent he could be collecting on the basement apartment if I wasn't there. He was not a man of substance, after all.

I missed Gene's and my Sunday morning breakfasts, when we'd roll out of bed and sit at the counter at The Alley Café, ordering the best French toast I've ever tasted, light and eggy almost like a soufflé, with maple syrup mingling with a dusting of powdered sugar.

This was breakfast as a continuation of sex, drowning in irresistible sweetness. I was a different person with Gene, someone younger and carefree who didn't layer on four different kinds of moisturizer, who wore his old flannel pajamas that were so big they practically fell off and were softer than anything I owned.

Lowell gathered up one of the two newspapers on the counter to read at our table. I'd previously explained that he should take only one section of the paper at a time so the other diners could read it too, but we differed on newspaper etiquette.

"Thank you for breakfast, but next time, it would be nicer if I didn't have to ask you to pay for it," he said as he sat down again, the master gently thumping his misbehaving labradoodle on the nose.

My headache returned. I had failed at being my half of that aspirational, but probably insufferable, couple described in his dating profile.

"Next time, it would be better if I didn't have to ask you—" he repeated, after I failed to whimper my remorse. He unwound his scarf as gently as if it were alive, placing it on the back of his chair.

"I. Get. It," I said, cutting him off, my house-smoked salmon tasting only of recrimination.

I stood up to return a section of newspaper to the counter and came back with another piece because I didn't want to share his. The young woman sitting next to us stared at me from behind her chic black-rimmed glasses, probably telegraphing me to just leave already.

"You never bring food. You refuse to bring meals. Every other woman I've been with has at least offered to bring food, to pay for things, to think about *my* pleasure," Lowell suddenly bleated.

"I *have* bought dinner, and besides, you have tons more money than I do. I drive forty-five minutes each way to come see you. I edit your writing. Did any of your other girlfriends ever do that?" I said, pathetic in my insecurity, dreading another round of who did what for whom. "If you're this unhappy with me, you should handle it in private."

He'd previously told me about his glamorous, but emotionally withholding, mother, saying I reminded him of her. I'd assumed he meant physically, but as he ranted on, I felt his vitriol toward her come pouring out on me, seeking revenge against all the women who'd wronged him. He'd also told me about his last two ex-girlfriends, who, of course, were young and beautiful, and who, of course, hadn't done enough for him.

"I needed to tell you now. My shrink doesn't want me to feel resentful," he said, his words bathed in triumph. I pictured his scarf strangling him like a fat cashmere snake.

"Now I feel resentful," I said calmly. "I'm leaving."

I thought life with Lowell would be all of a piece, unlike my relationship with Gene, my family on one side and the boyfriend they could never accept on the other. A few weeks after Gene and I became lovers—we were practically living together in my state of advanced neediness—I saw George's parents for the first time since he died.

His mother, Isabella, was a petite Chilean woman in her

mid-eighties with a bob of black hair and red lipstick. She was usually dressed in a silk blouse with a pussycat bow, her necklace tucked neatly under the loops. George told me that in her youth, she resembled the actress Dorothy Lamour. His father, Bob, was an amiable, bald, retired chemist from Wisconsin who loved sharing his wealth of knowledge on topics ranging from history to photography.

I shooed Gene out of bed early that morning so that he'd be gone by the time my in-laws came to pick me up. If they found out I had a boyfriend only four months after George had died, they might think I hadn't loved him enough.

"Del, it's good that you've finally grown a pair. You can't be afraid of them forever," Gene said on his way out.

He was right. I was terrified of them. I should have just said no when Isabella emailed asking if I'd like to join them for Sunday brunch.

*No, I would not like to join you. It's nothing personal.* But of course, it was everything personal.

Isabella and Bob met in the 1950s when he came to Chile as a graduate student. She went back to the United States with him and eventually earned a doctorate in physics at UC Berkeley. But despite having spent much of her life in California, she still seemed to live in the matriarchies of her youth and expected the children, which now included me as well as George, to be available on command.

Half the population of Chile seemed to visit Isabella, and she had expected George to have dinner with all of them. I tried going to some of her events when George and I first started dating, but there was always another one she demanded we attend.

"Boundaries," I'd intone loudly whenever he got off the phone with her. During my junior year of college, I convinced George to rent an apartment so we could have our own place, but over my protests, he still went back to his parents' house on weekends. After six months, he gave up the lease. In my twenty-one-year-old view, Isabella and I were rivals for his attention. And she had won.

When I started law school at UC Davis, she asked me to help her talk George into getting a graduate degree, justifying it by saying we would both be in school at the same time. With her doctorate in physics, she expected George to get a master's at least, but I refused to be her intermediary.

She complained to him he was fat; she hated the way he always dressed in mountaineering shorts and tennis shoes. Couldn't he wear slacks and maybe a nice blazer like her other friends' sons?

I came to dread seeing her red lipstick and pussycat bow, the plates of empanadas she directed George to pass around at parties as if he were still eleven years old. She'd complain to George that he never attended the symphony with them, and in return, he'd play her a snippet of the Dead Kennedys' "Holiday in Cambodia."

But George and Isabella had met in the middle, both loving the *bossa nova* of Antonio Jobim. At family dinners, I saw him looking over at her with love.

I zipped my feet into uncomfortable little ankle boots because Isabella hated sneakers, and grabbed a long cardigan in case I had to hide inside of it. For George's sake, I too would meet in the middle.

That Sunday morning, the three of us were seated on the outdoor patio at Bridges, one of Danville's nicest restaurants, surrounded by red-leafed Japanese maples and limpid ferns. Sunshine dappled through the foliage, and a stone fountain gurgled nearby.

"Did I ever tell you about the crazy fireworks I used to detonate back when I was a boy in Wisconsin?" Bob asked, but really he was saying, "It's good to see you."

Isabella chatted about their book club, visits with mutual acquaintances, trips to the Rep and the symphony, but really she was saying, "We're continuing on with our lives. You need to too."

I couldn't tell how they really were beneath their veneer, doing more in an effort to remember less, but I didn't want to pry. Isabella still drove forty-five minutes to work each day at Lawrence Livermore and still did research and wrote physics papers. Any crack in her routine could have hurt her.

Like me, they must have woken up each morning with their first thought of the day being that George was gone. Perhaps they smiled at each other weakly, tacitly agreeing to complete their schedules and act like nothing was different, yet the order of the world had ruptured, the child dying before the parent, and, like me, they must have always been thinking of him.

I wondered about my in-laws' conversations when they were alone. If they reassured each other their Georgie was finally at peace, or whether they asked each other in hushed voices, *If Debbie had contacted us sooner, do you think he might still be alive?*

"Watch out for guys who are after your money," Bob said, tucking into his BLT, then pulling out all the bacon with a frown. "Especially if they find out you own your own home."

In all our years of eating out together, I had rarely seen him happy with his food. He used to download lots of free software, then call George in a panic, demanding immediate help when the downloads wreaked havoc with his computer. Not such a terrible sin in retrospect, but at the time, it was just more reason to stay away.

Isabella once told George she would quit work to babysit for us when we had children so that I could keep practicing law. Responding to her repeated questions about when that might be, he finally told her that asking another woman about her reproductive choices was the height of bad feminism. But she loved her work, and giving it up would have been a great sacrifice to her. Add in my perpetual absence, and she must have thought she couldn't do anything right by us.

Watching my in-laws gently tease each other, each claiming the other had chosen a disastrous tour of China, Isabella liking the restaurant they'd tried the night before while Bob protested his lamb was all gristle, I realized I'd missed them. Seeing them again was like finding something I'd lost long ago and finally realizing how precious it was. A silk ribbon encircled the three of us, binding us together.

"I'm sure Debbie won't fall under the spell of any gigolos. She's too smart for that," Isabella said, turning to me and giving my arm a little squeeze. "But you are a young person. You should start dating again. It's bad to be alone all the time."

I thought about Gene and wanted to jump into my ramekin of crème brûlée. I couldn't tell Isabella about him. Although he certainly wasn't a gigolo, with his high school education and patter about the celebrities he'd met, he was the wrong sort of boyfriend to introduce to my highly educated in-laws. I tried not to squirm in my seat, still feeling his touch from when we made love that morning.

Isabella might have initially liked Lowell with his cosmopolitan style, but I could hear her saying after a couple of evenings listening to him talk about himself: "He is too old for you and he is absurd!" Bob would have seen right through his pretensions from the start.

A few days after our argument in the restaurant, Lowell emailed saying I should come over for leftovers and that I'd done well at the party, my job as hostess apparently having changed from freeloading to an act of service. He put "love" above his signature for the very first time, offering me a tiny crumb.

He was so entitled by money and maleness, expecting slender ingenues wearing designer lingerie and proffering homemade gougeres to line up to meet him. Had he been a woman, his expectations would have been shattered like a faux Meissen plate.

I'd approached him like the bar exam, thinking if I could win over a man so discerning, I might be worthy of love. But I should have seen that underneath his disparaging other people was an overflowing font of self-loathing. I threw out my copy of *Court and Spark*, which I'd played obsessively before I met him, unable to stop hearing his nasal voice superimposed over the lyrics.

"Dear Lowell," I typed, "You have unleashed your second uncontrolled litany of complaints at me in two weeks. Clearly, I am not the person for you." I kept retyping and deleting the line, "And a narcissistic dickwad is not the person for me." In the end I omitted it. *Be a grown-up.*

I breathed deeply and hit send, wishing I'd left in the dick-wad line, but the Hungover Widow was done with the pig and the ham. My spine tingled from regrowing my backbone.

Lowell should have been honest in his profile: *Sycophant wanted. JD with a specialty in self-abnegation a plus. Must enjoy canoodling in public but sleeping alone, pandering to my unresolved Oedipus complex, and listening to me complain about lowering the asking price for my beach house. Know that you will never be enough.*

Lowell was available only as is. I was the idiot who'd chosen to spend six weeks with him, thinking I could improve him, but I'd learned not to overestimate my powers. I couldn't expect to change the men I dated.

They were probably going to be middle-aged if not older and used to their way of life. I was too, actually, even though I thought of myself as malleable, ready to slot into the life of the next man I loved despite needing my daily forty-five minutes on the cross-trainer and my restrictive diet of salad, and everything in its place lest the world start to crumble.

I also learned from Lowell not to shut up for too long. If something felt that terrible, it probably was. But what I failed to learn was that the love I needed was self-love.

This was not a Jane Austen novel where the right landed

gentleman married the Widow Weiss. It was a reverse fairy tale where the princes I kissed turned into frogs, or in my case, dyspeptic Jewish men. I would have to find my own way through the haunted forest. I still haven't replaced my copy of *Court and Spark*.

Things didn't go very well with Isabella either. Two weeks after that first brunch, she invited me to lunch at Bridges, this time just the two of us. We sat outside again, everything just as pretty as it was the first time, the fountain burbling along with her as she told me about my in-laws' upcoming weekend in Carmel. She ordered a Bellini and the wild prawn salad; I asked for a Bloody Mary and the burger.

Then she adjusted her sunglasses, handed me her phone, and said, "This is a picture of Georgie at rest. I find it comforting to look at since he was in so much pain at the end."

I looked down to see a photograph of George laid out in his casket. I turned to ash and almost dropped the phone in the butter dish. The ribbon that bound us together stretched way too tight.

*That was on her phone?*

It wasn't the sort of thing you showed your book club, thumbing through your photos saying, "Here's how the kitchen remodel is going, and here's a photo of my son taking a really long nap." That thing looked like a wax work with a sunken yellowish face and closed eyes, like something that had never even taken a breath. I didn't see how it could be a comfort to her, but didn't want to ask. We'd never really had any deep conversations before. I put my sunglasses back on.

"Debbie, when Georgie got sick, how come you never told me?" she asked a few minutes later, pouncing while I was still reeling from her show-and-tell.

Our drinks arrived, hers in a delicate champagne flute, mine in a chunky tumbler, the sides dripping with condensation. So we were having our first deep conversation after all. Sweat broke out along my hairline. I took a long drag of my Bloody Mary. She took a piece of bread, then moved the basket toward me to share.

"It was George's decision not to tell you about his illness," I told her, and pushed the basket away. "I couldn't go against his wishes even though I disagreed with him. That's why I couldn't call you until he was admitted to the hospital."

I wanted to tell her how I had begged George to tell his parents he had cancer, arguing with him they deserved the chance to spend time with him in case anything happened—too afraid to use the word "die"—but he always refused, claiming he had too much work to do.

He never considered whether Isabella might blame me for his absence or whether she'd be in even more pain when he died, wondering why he'd excluded her. But it was too late to tell her now that I couldn't change anything.

Our food arrived, and I let my burger grow cold on the plate. Its meaty smell was nauseating, its thick red patty just more dead flesh. I imagined her wild prawns trying to squiggle away like little pink commas.

I thought she'd be angry and protest that I should have changed George's mind or gone behind his back, but she surprised me, taking off her sunglasses for the first time and saying, "I have an answer to my question. We will not talk about it anymore. We will just be friends."

That night, I rolled myself into Gene's warm bulk, trying to forget that hideous photograph, but it was weeks before I stopped waking in the middle of the night seeing George when he was no longer George.

A few weeks later, Isabella held a memorial service on July 29, George's birthday. She invited some of his colleagues and old friends, including an ex-friend of his who'd tried to attack me in my twenties and whom I hadn't seen since.

She hadn't known about the attack, but it was vintage Isabella, scheduling something in George's honor without consulting me, then demanding my presence on short notice. I spent the day walking on Ocean Beach with Gene and thinking how people never really changed after all.

After the memorial, Bob called my dad and told him he and Isabella never meant to upset me. With George's death, Bob's voice had become strained, as if it was hard for him to talk in a world that could be so unfair. Imagining him making excuses to my dad in that tired voice forced me to see the hurt he was trying to disguise. In some ways, I was all they had left.

They invited me to another lunch, this time at their favorite bistro in the Napa Valley. The bright sunlight slid down the green hills, through the grape vines, and onto our marble-topped table.

"When Georgie was ten, we went on a trip to France," Bob said. "At every restaurant, he'd order the Crepes Suzette for dessert. Even though he was just a little boy, he'd look up at the waiter and say imperiously, 'Crepes Suzette.' He must've eaten his weight in crepes."

Bob's face was no longer as gray as it was right after George died, but it would always remain a few shades paler than before.

"Let's order the crêpes suzette for dessert," he said after we finished our entrees of buttery cassoulet, which for once, he seemed to enjoy very much.

We each got our own plate of crepes, even though the three of us could have easily shared one portion. Raising our forks, we each took a bite, powdered sugar on our lips, the crepes spongy and tart with the flavor of orange liqueur.

Bob lifted his cup of decaf espresso and toasted, "To George."

"To George," Isabella and I echoed, raising our cups to his. Now I knew, they had forgiven me.

On the drive home Isabella surprised me by inviting me to go with them on a three-week cruise of the Baltics. "It is time you saw more of the world," she said.

The trip was lavish, but it was too soon after losing George, and I was still living underwater. I have only scattered memories of the cruise, standing for hours at a museum in Bruges looking at a Chagall of a young couple holding each other as if they'd just discovered love—they looked a little like George and I used to. At an abandoned Estonian prison, I took a photo of fuchsias shot through with razor wire, seeing them as a metaphor for life, beauty entangled with pain, each bringing the other into sharp relief.

But I got people's names wrong at dinner even though I'd sat with them just the night before. Skulking through the Hermitage and the Catherine Palace, all I wanted to do was curl up next to Gene's toasty warm skin. After the day's excursions, I spent my nights drunk in my cabin, texting with him.

"I MiSS U. I luv you. I CAN't wait to C U."

He always answered immediately, and I knew he was waiting for my messages as he followed our ship's path on the cruise line website as we made our way through the Baltic Sea. When he picked me up at the airport, I flung myself into his arms, believing I was in love, but perhaps just relieved to be saved from my emptiness.

I didn't know Isabella had seen Gene and I together at the airport, but at our next lunch together, she casually commented, "That young man with all the tattoos must be your boyfriend. It is good that you are not alone."

I just nodded sheepishly, awaiting her words of judgment, but they never came. Not all people were incapable of change—I could only hope I was one of them.

# V. The Widow's Diet

A SHOPPING LIST FROM MY FIRST YEAR OF WIDOWHOOD:

1. Precooked chicken.
2. Premade spinach salad.
3. Premade Caesar salad.
4. Do not cry if anyone at the store asks where George is.
5. Nonfat yogurt (the boring kind).
6. You may not buy any more carrot cake.
7. Nor any more chocolate fro-yo.
8. Do not cry if no one lets you out of the parking lot.
9. Manhattans are not a food group.
10. Hang in there. It ~~will~~ might get better.

# VI. Dating Like a Man

"I REALIZED I WAS SO EXCITED TO SEE YOU again because you haven't been divorced so you're not broken like the rest of us," said Denis, another JDater.

We were on our second date, walking through the rose garden in Golden Gate Park in the late September heat, surrounded by wilting petals in pink and yellow. I'd never thought of widowhood as an attractive trait, and I couldn't see why he thought a widow wouldn't be broken, but I didn't quibble. I didn't want to appear tarnished.

He passed me the thermos he'd brought, filled with a homemade ginger-and-mint infused vodka concoction. I took a sip, feeling quite daring. All we'd done on our first date was sip iced tea over a quick lunch.

Denis was my age, half white and half African American, with close-cropped graying hair and matching beard, wire-framed glasses, and a stocky, barrel-chested build. A politician with a PhD in environmental studies, he was raising three teenagers and running his own company to combat climate change. Not surprisingly, he had very little free time.

But he was fun and hip and frequented cool places like small music clubs, pop-up diners, and cap-and-trade emissions conferences. Despite his impressive résumé, he gave off a shy graduate student vibe, as if he was aware that he was a bit of a geek. Best of all, he had a magnetic smile. It was as if he enjoyed wherever he happened to be. It was a pleasing change after Lowell.

"What are you looking for?" I said.

"I need to take advantage of the time I have when the kids are with their mom. When I do have time to spend with someone, it tends to be pretty intense," he said. "I'm searching for real emotional intimacy."

That damn word again.

"What does that mean?"

"It means we can tell each other anything. And we can feel close to each other without having to be together all the time."

That was my clue this relationship was going to fail. I should have already known from Ben and Lowell: Woman as sounding board, check. Limited availability (with the other men emotionally, this time physically), check. Misplaced expectation of closeness, check. But back then I didn't know how to decode.

Denis told me about the classes he was taking on the art of preaching, about his recent trip to Kenya with his kids, and about the book he was writing about global warming.

As we walked through the de Young Museum, he said, "It's a little embarrassing, but I usually cry when I'm moved by art."

It seemed like a line, especially since we were looking at some hyperphallic neon Keith Harings, but I thought I saw a tear fall from his eye as we stood before a solemn painting of parallel columns entitled *Justice*.

"Can I kiss you?" he asked at the fly-casting pools, taking my hand as we sat close together on a bench and watched the anglers cast their lines. I agreed, thinking he wasn't as shy as I'd thought. After the park we walked over to Ocean Beach and strolled along the waves. The beach was crowded and warm. Our date ended seven hours after it started, with a long hug goodbye at the train station.

To be committed, I needed far more time than Denis had to give, but I pushed that thought away as too early to worry about. Perhaps I could be satisfied with temporary scraps of happiness, like ordering one glass of champagne instead of the entire bottle. My relationship with Gene had flamed out spectacularly. Maybe taking it slow was a good idea.

"This is to keep away the other guys," Gene said, setting a big bowl of my favorite chunky guacamole in front of me on the kitchen table.

He'd half mashed the avocados, diced the onions and tomatoes, and added lots of garlic. He'd even fried the tortilla chips himself. He got himself a glass of water, frowning at the bottle of red wine I'd set on the table. The other guys comment was a joke. I didn't know any other guys.

"You've never really had even one drink?" I asked yet again, trying to reconcile his abstemious habits with his wild past.

"I told you I've never drunk alcohol or taken drugs. I always want to be in control. Especially because I used to hang with gangsters. That's why I had my name tattooed on my back—in case something happened to me and the police had to identify my body," he said.

His delivery was so unaffected that I believed him, and a little shiver ran through my body over my bad boy's checkered past. His gangster days had ended long before he'd become a home health care aide.

"I'm afraid I'm using you," I said, taking a gulp of wine and making the confession that had plagued me for weeks.

Gene had the mind of a child, all immediacy and emotion, seeing everything in black and white with nothing in between. Before George died, I could think in the abstract. Should my widow brain ever choose to reknit itself, I might need a boyfriend who could too.

But Gene just said, "Use away. I'm organic, free range, and locally grown."

I had the feeling he'd deployed that line before. He told me he'd slept with ninety-two women, and while, in my renascent adolescence, I felt flattered to be chosen by someone so experienced, I also knew grown-ups didn't usually share this kind of information.

"I don't have the willpower to give you up anyway," I said.

"Other than dealing with casinos, candy shops, and jewelry stores, willpower is overrated," Gene said, employing another no doubt favorite phrase. It was as if he'd seen too many Humphrey Bogart movies. I suppressed Jane's analysis of children and their use of repetitive language.

But a few weeks later, as he drove me to yoga, Gene said, "Your pants are too tight. I can see everything right through them."

"No they're not," I said, wounded. "They're just Spandex. Everyone wears them."

I went on high alert. We'd been together a few months now, and recently he'd become moody. He said my clothes were too sexy, even though they were the same skinny jeans and T-shirts I'd always worn. A few times, when I couldn't go to a screening with him, he claimed I'd already agreed to go, even though I knew I hadn't.

One morning at the yoga studio, he gave me a long kiss goodbye, then stationed himself on the bench outside the door to wait for me until class was over. "You don't have to waste your time waiting for me," I said.

"You're ashamed of me," he said, glaring at me through narrowed eyes. Suddenly, the sunshine was too bright, my yoga clothes felt uncomfortably warm, and the women entering the gym were giving us odd looks. Heavily inked men with mohawks were rare in Danville, but it was Gene's petulant scowl that embarrassed me, nothing else.

When I emerged from the studio, Gene was still sitting on the bench. He kissed me as if we'd been apart for weeks. He made me uncomfortable with such a public display. I wondered what I'd done to make him so insecure, but I couldn't come up with anything. It couldn't really be my clothes.

I thought of how gentle he'd been taking care of George, carrying him to the shower, then bandaging his wounds, all the while joking with him like it was just a social visit. But this Gene was a different person.

His morning goodbyes were becoming longer every day. "I love you," he'd say, having already dressed for work, his white smock covering his shorts and T-shirt. It was incongruous with his flip-flops; maybe he wasn't so cool after all. His huge body stretched over mine in the bed; his weight bore down on me.

"I love you too," I'd answer automatically.

"You better," he'd say, lingering before he got up to go.

It all went downhill from there.

The Saturday after our trip to the park, Denis and I went to an arthouse movie, followed by a late Italian dinner in the city where we ate prosciutto and melon at the bar and compared glasses of Brunello and Amarone. We sat with our thighs pressed close together as he told me about growing up with his ultra-liberal parents in New York, and how he'd spent his senior year of high school working with horses on a ranch, and how he'd been a sexual late bloomer.

I drank my wine a little too quickly and tried to forget the older, silver-haired couple who'd sat next to us at the movies, holding hands and exchanging private smiles. The woman had looked so content she'd glowed from within. They had a future George and I never would.

Back at his place, Denis said, "You can't leave until you've had some of this." He popped open the special champagne he'd shown me before we'd left for the movie. We kissed on the sofa. His hands wrapped around my waist, then ran over my thighs.

"I was hoping you'd stay over," he said softly.

"Okay," I said, shocking myself by agreeing so soon. I'd wanted some cheerful sex after breaking up with Lowell, but this was only our second real date.

He took me to the bedroom, took off my clothes, and then pulled his own off so quickly it made me giggle. We changed positions several times—it was if he had to get through them all to earn another graduate degree. It was oddly cerebral, yet also exciting. Perhaps I wasn't as shy as I thought I was.

That night I learned that I didn't need an emotional commitment to have sex. After thirty-two years with one man, it was a revelation. My dad had brought me up to think all boys were after one thing, and a good girl's job was to say no. Otherwise, a boy might think the girl wasn't so good after all. He might even tell all the other boys that she wasn't. When I was growing up, my dad used to joke that I only had to stay celibate until I was forty, but considering he winced upon even hearing the word "vagina," he didn't want to know if I wasn't.

With Denis's three teenagers and his complicated professional life, we would never be that couple at the movies. We'd probably never even achieve the emotional intimacy he wanted, which, judging from past experience, seemed to mean unconditional acceptance regardless of merit.

But I could say yes to sex just because I wanted to, without considering whether we'd ever combine households or meet each other's families or even whether we'd spend another night together. Sex and ephemerality could coexist. I might yet become a modern woman. But was Denis ever going to come out of the bathroom?

"I was on the phone," he said, finally getting back into bed, looking sheepish. "I needed to make sure the kids wouldn't be coming home too early in the morning." He put an arm around me and turned off the light, as if we'd done this many times before. To my surprise, I slept well.

In the cold, clear light of morning, I looked over at him sleeping next to me. A good girl didn't sleep with a man without loving him, and having known Denis only two weeks, I did not love him.

I was widow thin and my hair was dyed bright red to hide my roots, and, for once in my life, I was trying new things. But my sleepover now felt like a manic attempt to seek relief from my memories of my husband as a cute college senior and, far worse, of my husband as a dying man racked with cancer, each image superimposed on the other.

Denis rolled over and gave me a sleepy "Hi." He was staring at me with something that looked like love, but it was only because he thought he'd captured me. I didn't care that I was naked because he couldn't see what I was thinking. How was I going to get through another Sunday? Would we go to breakfast and act like a couple? Would it just feel worse because we weren't and never would be?

I wanted to become a different animal, no longer a beloved wife or devastated widow, but something harder. I wanted my heart to be a vestigial organ, and have my needs revert to Maslow's basics—food, sex, shelter. No moving up the emotional hierarchy. That could hurt.

I hurried into my clothes to go home, turning down Denis's offer of breakfast. Dating had become a survival mechanism.

"You treat me like a moped, fun to cruise around the driveway, but you won't take me into the street," Gene said over dinner one night at Giovanni's, a ramshackle restaurant in Berkeley with perfect homemade gnocchi and faded murals of Italy covering the walls. His face screwed up like an oversized child's. "The way you hugged me at the airport after that cruise, I knew you loved me, but now you're just looking around for another guy."

It was a warm fall evening, the streetlights turning on just as the sun set and bathing everything in a yellow glow. I'd been feeling happy, just a girl out on a date with her boyfriend.

I told him I wasn't looking, but it wasn't true. Lately, I'd been daydreaming about a new boyfriend I could introduce to my family, someone calm and professional, who made sense to them so they wouldn't worry about me. I stared down at my menu, my appetite gone.

Gene's hours at the home health care agency had been cut back. I worried that he wouldn't be able to afford his place anymore. His apartment was just a few small rooms in a neglected wooden building on an asphalt lot devoid of landscaping. His living room was overflowing with free movie paraphernalia, DVDs spilled from the shelves, signed promotional posters covered the walls, and autographed T-shirts and programs cluttered every surface. The only things he'd paid for were his Manchester United soccer jerseys and programs. Although he never lived outside the Bay Area, Gene fancied himself a Brit.

I could picture him driving over to my house late one night, with the back of his truck loaded with soccer jerseys and DVDs, saying he'd been evicted and had nowhere else to go. Then he'd park his truck in front of my house, permanently blocking the view from my living room, and I'd never be free.

Without asking, he'd designated us "in a relationship" on Facebook, leading to congratulations from his many virtual friends. Mature adults didn't do this. But I was a mammalian widow and craved warmth like a newborn animal. I was too weak to go back to being cold again night after night.

"Who're you flirting with?" he suddenly demanded. "You've been flirting with someone ever since we got here." I'd smiled back when the restaurant bartender smiled at me. He recognized me from our prior visits.

"Nobody," I answered.

"Yes you are. I saw you making eyes at someone across the

room. You got all smiley. You always get all smiley with people," he said, glaring down at the table. I explained about the bartender, but Gene seethed in silence.

"Why are you mad at me? I didn't do anything wrong," I said after a few minutes. I hated the pleading tone in my voice. My stomach was in knots as I picked at my veal marsala, but he just looked away. I wished I'd ordered a glass of wine instead of abstaining to please him. Earlier that week, I'd gotten some new yoga pants in the mail and Gene suggested I try them on for him. I'd refused, feeling a crimp in my spine, thinking back to the days when George used to review my clothes.

Anyone looking over at us would have seen a big guy with a mohawk in black nylon shorts and a thin red-haired woman with droopy eyes in a loose denim miniskirt. They would have seen him quickly inhaling his meal, looking angry, and seen her staring down at her plate, looking sad, while neither of them talked to each other during the entire time.

That woman looked defeated.

*You cannot continue to live like this.*

Gene put his arm around my shoulders as we were leaving the restaurant, pulling me close. "It's all right, sweetheart," he said. I pulled away from him. That night, for the first time, he dragged out making love as if he were trying to imprint me.

The next day, I ended it. I finally realized he was becoming dangerous.

A few weeks after our first night together, Denis asked me to meet him on a Saturday morning at his place, but kept pushing back the time. Finally, he said to come over in the early afternoon, then left me sitting outside fuming in a late summer heat wave, reading yet another of his texts saying he'd be right out. He was still waiting for his kids to leave for their mom's. I watched his neighbors slowly drag a dilapidated sofa out to the curb.

Lately, he'd been changing the times for our dates at the last minute, then saying, "You should take public transportation if you're going to be so upset," when I arrived flustered from rushing to meet him on short notice. A couple times he chose expensive restaurants, like the tapas place he took me to after an environmental rally—"Come at four. No, wait, come at two"—where he ordered enough Jamón Serrano for four and a pricey Rioja, and only asked afterward if we were splitting the check.

"This isn't working. I waited around all morning for you. I'm a lawyer, a decent enough professional person to meet your kids. I hate sitting outside like the other woman," I said when I finally saw him. I was listing my credentials to reassure myself, more than him, of my propriety.

"I kept pushing the time back so the kids would be gone so we could make love," he said. "You could've come in."

"You never invited me in," I said.

We tried to salvage the day by going for lunch at a romantic inn on the Bay. We sat on an artfully distressed brown leather sofa in a bar with pale green walls and honey-colored hardwood floors and ordered truffled popcorn and pink champagne, but the day felt sullied after that morning.

I wondered if he hadn't let me in the house with his children because he thought they could tell we were sleeping together, but I didn't ask. We knew each other well enough to have sex, but not enough to talk about anything sensitive.

But isn't this what I'd done to Gene? I had kept him away from my family because I thought they wouldn't approve of him, even though he'd overcome so much to become a home health care aide, including his prior gangster lifestyle and a terrible car accident in his twenties. His body looked like an enormous comic book. I didn't want Daddy to know I was sleeping with the help.

Gene had done so much to bring me back to life, and in return I'd quarantined him from my family. Now I knew how it felt.

"I don't want to pay for that," I said when Denis ordered a charcuterie plate. I was sick of funding his addiction to luxury pork products.

"This probably isn't the right time to talk about this," he said, after we'd each had a glass of champagne and a few handfuls of popcorn, "but I think we should get tested."

"Why? Do you think I have something?"

"No, it means we really like each other. You haven't dated a lot, but getting tested means we want to take it to the next level where we stop seeing other people," he said, scooping a heaping tablespoon of duck rillettes onto a piece of baguette and maneuvering it into his mouth.

"I don't think I can even afford to eat out with you," I said, trying a bite of pork pâté before realizing I wasn't hungry.

After our first night together, he'd sent me an exquisite arrangement of tropical flowers. But my stock had decreased and my wallet had been opened once I'd been caught, yet another "rule" I would have known about had I dated more when I was younger. For someone so loquacious, Denis didn't seem to speak any of the five love languages.

The George-o-meter moved to "not for you," but I ignored it, thinking I was just being old-fashioned. Maybe testing meant something in the modern world, but to me it just sounded sterile, like wrapping your heart in Saran Wrap instead of falling in love.

Fixing my front gate or coming to Danville instead of asking me to meet him yet again at his place would have been romantic. My first love language was touch, but after handling everything by myself since George died, I'd discovered my second was acts of service.

So many things around the house had stopped working. I called it "Widow's Entropy," where the house knows its master has died and goes into mourning, breaking down in pieces. To me, love looked like Gene cleaning out my fireplace and fixing my broken fountain. It looked like Gene buying soup and cheese when we went grocery shopping, and sneaking a package of his favorite Oreos into the cart, and explaining that smoked salmon and pretzels did not make a meal while he shook his head in disapproval and ran a finger over my protruding collarbones. Love looked like him staying with me all night and being there in the morning.

"Wow, no one I've dated has ever spoken up to me like that," Denis said. "I'm actually a great cook. I could make us dinner sometimes." So modern daters could talk about exposure to disease, but not what they could afford to pay for a meal.

"Plus, I'm always coming to Berkeley because you say you don't have time to come to me," I said.

"If I didn't do what I do, I wouldn't be the person that I am," he said with a self-congratulatory smile. "Besides, you've only really known Danville. I want to see the world and I don't know that you'd be up for it."

He'd made comments about my "Danvillity" before, usually accompanied with a little smirk as if to tip off some invisible observer about how uncool I was. I guess spending my life with George in one place and caring for him until his death didn't count for much, even if it did mean I wasn't "broken like the rest of us." I was beginning to see what Denis meant.

"It depends," I said to stall for time, falling back on the stock answer we used to equivocate in law school.

I guess this was what he meant by being intense—splitting the bill for way too much overpriced ham, getting tested so we couldn't see anyone else, then traveling together if I wasn't too "Danville." When you were young you got declarations of love; when you were older you got statements of intractability and requests for medical exams.

Besides, I was the only one of us with enough time to see other people. Manipulative Man was trying to take away the Hungover Widow's freedom in return for only a few scattered hours. That wasn't enough to keep the raven of loneliness at bay. I doubted there'd be any more flowers.

I watched Denis polish off what was left of the charcuterie plate, smiling as if he'd made me a pretty good offer. We'd only slept together a few times, yet he was attempting to annex me like a wayward territory.

As a former lawyer, I could tell when someone was trying to out alpha me. It had just never happened before under the guise of romance.

Lowell and Denis appeared different; one was so archaic while the other professed to be modern, yet both offered their exclusivity like a prize, never thinking about what I wanted. Both of them just expected me to conform to their lives like plastic wrap clinging to stale leftovers. Even Ben had wanted me to stop seeing other people despite offering only a running monologue on his exes. Were all men this solipsistic?

"Let's hold off on the whole testing thing for now," I finally said. Denis was demanding too high a price to be my Saturday night savior; I would have to look elsewhere. Without asking, he picked up the check.

He too needed to rewrite his dating profile: *Are you seeking someone who's rarely around but expects you to be exclusive? Who trashes your plans on short notice? Who shames you for wanting more? If you've ever wanted to feel like the other woman, then I'm your man.*

We left to go for a walk on the beach. He walked quickly ahead while I lagged behind, taking in the deep green cliffs and the Cypress trees. The sand was so hot it hurt my feet, and I remembered my walks on the beach with George.

When we'd first gotten together, I'd named us "the Fog Chasers" because we loved walking on the beach in the fog. After George's diagnosis, the waves took on an elegiac quality, saying the things neither of us could voice. I was consumed with fear for the future. For the moment, though, we had that time together, gilded by uncertainty, and I savored it. George had refused to speak of his illness, and I had craved the ocean.

When we got back to Denis's place, we stretched out on the bed while he fielded calls from his daughter, who wanted to come home to get her laptop. He finally met her at the door, computer in hand. I had echoes of that morning at the curb, feeling that I was someplace I shouldn't be. Missing George beyond belief, I got up to go home.

"You say you want to leave, but you were snuggling your butt right up next to me," he said smugly.

Given the way I felt, I doubted I was snuggling, but even if I was, so what if my butt had a mind of its own? It didn't mean I had to stay. I'd been right in not wanting to be vulnerable with Denis. I was beginning to wonder if he had different standards, seeing desire as natural in a man but as an admission of weakness in a woman, like it was something to be capitalized on.

"Say the word and we can go to the Claremont for the night, if you want," he said as I headed for the door.

I felt like one of the horses he'd herded during his senior year on the ranch—trying to corral me hadn't worked, so now he was offering a carrot. He thought he could manipulate me, seeing only a sheltered housewife, not someone as intelligent as he was. He was not as blatantly patronizing as Lowell, but he was still patriarchal.

I left quickly. The drive home seemed much longer than the way there, and the sky was so dark. I thought about how badly things had ended with Gene, and wondered why I couldn't get anything right.

Kübler-Ross says: "Since holidays are for being with those we love the most, how on earth can anyone be expected to cope with them when a loved one has died?"

George and I used to research our Thanksgiving recipes weeks in advance. He would be at his computer with me looking over his shoulder, resting my chin on top of his head as he decided between Beef Wellington or Turducken, carrot or asparagus soup, potato casserole or baked yams. I'd take the recipe for Dear Abby's pecan pie out of the binder, the newsprint yellowed and stained. It was our one constant every year.

We'd spend the two weekends before the holiday shopping, pairing the dishes with wines. We'd spend the day itself cooking with an *X-Files* marathon in the background and finish up in bed with homemade pecan pie topped with whipped cream, watching the final episode, the one not suitable for daytime viewing. I used to sleep well back then.

My first year without him, I had no one to spend Thanksgiving with. My dad and Jane didn't really celebrate the holiday. They ate sometime after eight, their meals prepared by their home health care team. My in-laws went out of town every year to spend the holiday with the same old friends. The grocery store put out a display of their famous pecan pies.

The rodent started gnawing and I couldn't quiet it. I started going over to my dad's house late at night again, unable to stop myself even though I knew it exhausted him.

Almost involuntarily, I called Gene. I had no one else. In that moment, my life had dwindled down to a single fact: I needed my own caregiver to stay alive through New Year's Day.

Gene had somehow managed to become a member of the Academy of Motion Picture Arts and Sciences, scoring invitations to private screenings of the movies up for Oscar consideration. Almost all the movies that year seemed to be about alienated people.

It comforted me to watch them drown at sea, or fall in love with operating systems, or trek cross-country for unsuccessful family reunions. It comforted me even more to come home late with Gene, scarf down a frozen pizza, then fall into bed with him, no longer alone like the characters in the movies.

On Thanksgiving Day, Gene and I went to a steakhouse he liked in San Francisco's Union Square. The streets were packed with people admiring the enormous Christmas tree and much smaller obligatory menorah. People ice-skated at the temporary rink and lined up hours ahead of time for sales. The store windows were full of Santas, glitter balls, and real live puppies and kittens up for adoption.

The restaurant was dark and elegant. We ordered rare rib eye steak with pearl onions and mashed potatoes. I pretended to enjoy it, but I really hated the impersonality of it all, the rushed pace, Gene frowning when I ordered my first glass of wine, the waiter failing to ask if I wanted a second.

After dinner, as we walked through the crowds, I stopped to give a dollar to two guys playing old Simon and Garfunkel songs. Suddenly, Gene stalked off ahead, dropping my hand.

"If that gets you off," he said.

Once I caught up to him, I asked him what went wrong. "What do you mean?"

"When you gave that guy the money, he said, 'Nice tits.'"

"No, he didn't. He said thanks."

"I heard him say it, and you just smiled like you liked it, all flirty the way you always are."

"That's not true. And he couldn't have said that. I'm wearing a coat. He couldn't even see my tits."

"I swear that's what I heard," Gene said.

I started walking away from him, dodging the throngs on the crowded sidewalk, my arms crossed in front of me for protection, the sky dark and the air biting. The one person I relied on was completely unreliable. Once again, the switch that controlled his jealousy reflex had flipped for no obvious reason. I'd been a fool to think it wouldn't.

I could have gotten lost in that crowd, and no one would have known what happened to me. I looked for a place to sit down and figure out how to get to the nearest train station, but the cafés all had lines, and there was no room to wait for an Uber.

"Let's go," said Gene, coming up behind me.

"No. That guy didn't say that. And even if he did, it wasn't my fault."

"That's what I heard. Really, I did. But c'mon, sweetheart, let's go home," he said, reaching for my hand.

It was easier just to go with him. The streets were so full I was trapped in a malevolent custard. On the way home, Gene tried to make conversation, talking about the celebrities he'd seen over the years in Union Square, the upcoming screenings we could go to. He said he might even be able to wrangle us an invitation to the fabled Skywalker Ranch in Marin with its fabulous pre-movie buffets.

But I had turned to stone. When we got home, I put my purse down on the kitchen counter. I took off my coat and hung it up neatly in the hall closet. I walked to my bedroom and considered. Did I really want to do this? *Yes.*

"You have to stop being so crazy jealous. I can't fucking take it," I said, punching the wall over the bed, hard for emphasis, but it didn't break the plaster.

Gene watched me, horrified. My hand didn't even hurt; it might have belonged to someone else. I thought I saw tears in his eyes as he reached for me, but I pulled away.

I had warned him: I will hurt myself more than you can. I'd made a Hobson's choice, taking the one horse available rather than walking alone through the holiday season. We went to bed, and Gene, back to being the sweet boy I believed him to be under the misplaced wiring, wrapped himself around me as if to absorb my pain. I felt nothing.

Over the next few weeks, Gene and I went to more and more movies. The bruises on my hand faded from black to purple to yellow. I took photos of him standing over the stove stirring skillets of turkey fajitas, chorizo taco filling, and tomato bruschetta topping. He grinned like one of the celebrity chefs on TV.

I photographed him shirtless, stretched out on my bed like a sunning sea lion, mugging in mock embarrassment, his torso a mural of blue ink. I did not invite him to come with me when I went to see my dad and in-laws for the holiday.

On Christmas Day, we took selfies as we lunched at the Empress of China, the famous gilded restaurant in San Francisco's Chinatown decorated with fairy-tale lanterns and peacock feathers. George and I had gone there for dinner the night of my senior prom. It was scheduled to close in a few months—a fitting end to the life I'd known.

The bruises on my hand had finally disappeared. But by then I understood why a person might need to go into denial in order to survive.

A few days after my disastrous date with Denis, I was watching an episode of *Weeds* where Nancy Botwin has passionately dispassionate sex with a drug dealer on the hood of his car. I had a sudden revelation: I no longer had to be monogamous. I'd just assumed a woman like me would be.

But I no longer had to be a woman like me, which meant being a good girl, which meant dating only one man at a time. The possibility of being in two or more sexual relationships at once had seemed utterly taboo, like ordering two desserts at a restaurant.

But why not? Denis had been my gateway drug between love and ephemera. Why not invite more men into the mix? I could see Denis as well as anyone else I wanted to, like ordering both the crème brûlée and the chocolate mousse if I were craving more sweetness than one man could offer.

Kübler-Ross says, "Grief is also the shattering of many conscious and unconscious beliefs about what our lives are supposed to look like." Since I couldn't make my life look the way I wanted it to—like a princess smothered in love riding a purple unicorn—I'd take another tack. I would stop expecting any sort of commitment. I would not be herded.

I would date like a man, emotionally detached, collecting experiences for their own sake without any sticky hope for more. I'd take the love out of my language. It wasn't that I was cursed; I'd just been setting the wrong parameters.

These would be my college years to experiment. I was just living them for the first time at fifty-one.

"I'm not finding anyone that great," I said to my dad on my next visit. He no longer resembled Richard Harris in his final appearance as Dumbledore. He was fully recovered from the flare-up of his blood disorder the previous year, his face once again filled out, his eyes no longer sunken into his cheekbones. I could finally stop worrying about him, at least as much as I was capable.

"Most middle-aged single people are single for a reason," my dad said, sipping from the green tea Jane brought over to us. She, too, had made a full recovery from her hip-replacement surgery.

"When I was dating," he continued, " I can't tell you the number of women who said I was the only grown-up man they'd met since they were single. I was the Bay Area adult male. Our spouses had the poor taste to die, but other people were divorced several times or they've never been in a long relationship. Statistically, you're going to get a very flawed pool." He offered me a bowl of marinated dried plums he'd ordered on Amazon.

"As I'm discovering," I said, taking a bite of plum. My face pruned up from the tartness. By now, I'd met a bunch of JDate guys, serious fellows, a few of whom were nice but to whom I wasn't attracted, and several more who thought they'd been irreparably damaged by their mothers and spent a lot of time discussing it with their shrinks.

"You may have to decide whether you can love a flawed man, which will be difficult after George," my dad said. "After Thalia died, I found that things had changed a lot since I was married. Once when I went to kiss a woman goodnight, she pulled away, and just as I was about to apologize for being too forward, she said, 'Just a minute, let me put my diaphragm in.'"

"Funny you should say that," I said, once I'd stopped sputtering into my tea, "I'm also thinking of dating just to see what's out there. I want to take permanence out of the equation."

"Actually, dating cheered me up quite a bit after your mother died. And you're a lot like me in some ways. You might as well try having some fun with it." He offered me a wasabi-marinated mushroom, watching me manage one small bite before my mouth exploded from the heat.

My dad used to be friends with a psychoanalyst who delighted in asking people deeply personal questions, as if he was peering into their souls to pluck out their fatal flaws. When I was nineteen, he'd asked me at a dinner party in front of everyone, "What was it like going through your adolescence alone with your dad?"

"It went pretty well considering it was the first time for both of us," I'd answered quickly.

My dad dissolved into laughter, and the psychoanalyst never again asked me any personal questions. But my dad experienced the real adolescence, becoming single in 1973 when self-help and sexual freedom were flourishing. He was the popular one, sporting a navy-blue turtleneck and matching Mao cap (an unorthodox choice for a government scientist), taking UC Berkeley extension classes on Buddhism, and going out with dozens of different women before finally meeting Jane.

I was the teenage dork who had rarely dated. By college, I was grade grubbing and taking LSAT prep courses, and planning a life with George who, despite the punk rock obsession and torn black jeans, was busy turning his internship at HP into a full-time career. We yuppies couldn't wait to be middle-aged.

I told myself I was content to have no sense of adventure, but now I wished I'd developed one. It was like a neglected muscle that had finally atrophied. Other widows might go on safari in Africa or seek spirituality in India, but that just wasn't in my wheelhouse. Denis had struck a nerve when he said I had only known Danville.

"Ahem," Dad added with a little chuckle, apparently finished with pushing the boundaries of fatherly decorum, then laughing loudly when he saw my face after trying the mushroom. "Maybe I should've warned you about those."

"Among other things."

"I get to give you different advice now that you're a fifty-year-old woman instead of a teenager," he said with a disarming smile.

He'd almost died from a car accident in his twenties. Add in losing his wife at forty-two, being a student of history, and working in a weapons lab, I could see how he became my teacher in the rule of impending disaster.

He was still proud of himself for letting me go to a Neil Young concert on a double date when I was fifteen, but he spent the entire week before telling me not to get separated from the others, nor accept any drinks, nor let anyone see my emergency money, nor let the boy pay for anything, nor—worst of all—be alone with him.

When I came home from college on weekends, he left any new articles on my bed about date rape he'd clipped from the newspaper. In college I was too frightened to take a semester abroad—I'd read *The Women's Room*, so I knew how men could be.

Dad and I had one of our rare arguments when he refused to

let me live alone during my final year of law school since he was paying my rent. I finally won, citing the need for a quiet study environment, but he obviously never suggested moving away. And if he thought I should have waited before settling down with George, he never said so, probably realizing I'd just ignore him.

"I'm out of clever things to say, so you might as well be going," Dad said after we'd both been silent for a few moments.

Whenever I called to say I wanted to visit, he'd tell me three times not to bother coming over if it was inconvenient—he was fine, there was no need to check up on him. I'd have to stop him before he got to the fourth round. He worried he was taking up too much of my time, never realizing he was my mentor in premature widowhood, not to mention my best friend.

"Knees together!" he said as I got up to go. He said it every time I left, only now he added with a wink, "Metaphorically, at least."

Gene and I lasted for a while after the holidays, but one gray winter day, over spaghetti with his special tomato sauce, heavy on the onions and garlic "to keep away the other guys," he glowered at me and said, "You're always staring at people. I can't take you anywhere anymore the way you look at them. I'm too embarrassed."

Unlike his other accusations, this one was true. I did stare at people, wondering how they mastered being alone at night. I wondered if the happy-looking people really were happy, and if any of them were widowed and knew something about survival that I'd obviously failed to learn.

I asked Gene to leave but he refused, his 240-pound bulk sprawled defiantly across my sofa. "I have to be at your dad's house early tomorrow morning and it's a hassle to drive back and forth to my place," he said.

For the first time, there was a physical threat behind his words. I couldn't get him out of my house. I said he could stay the night. He went to the kitchen to do the dishes with a terrible scowl on his face. I sat on the living room sofa, trapped. When we went to bed, I kept to my side, hoping he couldn't feel the bed vibrating with tension. He had become my jailer.

I couldn't sleep, and waited for the first rays of light to filter through the shades. I got up to sit on the couch, feeling too jittery to stay in bed. The house was silent, but his presence felt like a storm. Algebra hours later, like watching the clock in fifth grade waiting for math class to be over, or chemo hours later, like waiting for George to come home from the hospital, the room turned from black to gray. I went back to bed.

At five o'clock, Gene's alarm clock went off and he got up to get ready for work. When he leaned over me to say goodbye, I did not push him away even though I wanted to. I told him I loved him even though I didn't. I waited for the sound of the door to close behind him.

In one night, George's wife on the sofa disappeared. So did Gene's Del. In their place was the woman I'd been when I wanted to live.

I texted him that it was over, but when I checked my phone after evening yoga, he'd texted he was on his way to my place. I drove to my dad's house to avoid him, wishing I'd ended it sooner, yet knowing I never would until he'd done something truly frightening. Resilience does not live in a vacuum.

"I'm in your driveway. Please, sweetheart, just come home. I don't know what I did wrong. We just need to talk," he said, his voice all syrupy bewilderment, so different from last night's threats.

"If you're at my house when I get there, I'm calling the police," I said.

"I'm worried about you," he said, his tone as soft as velvet, "You don't eat enough. How about if I just stay for dinner and then go home?"

After several minutes, I convinced him my threat was real. The Danville police had followed his truck around a few times before because he stood out so much with his mohawk and tattoos. A prior girlfriend had once gotten a restraining order against him. He'd explained it away as paranoia, but now I wasn't so sure.

Thankfully, Gene wasn't there when I got home. Reawakening my sex drive had indeed been imprudent, but I'd been unable to help myself.

I've read that people's physical desires sometimes intensify after losing a loved one, but I never thought it could happen to me, a woman who'd willingly relinquished her sex drive years ago and didn't understand people who couldn't control their own. I never knew my animal needs could take over my rational mind. I thought that only happened to men.

Widowhood made me far less judgmental. For the first time, I could see why someone would go to a bar and find a stranger to bed rather than stay home alone. Not that I actually ever did that, but my body had started making demands, whispering it was still alive, it had been neglected, it needed to be touched. Its pleas were all the more urgent for having just seen death, and it grabbed the first sustenance it could find, even after reason said leave him alone, he's not good for you.

I'd also learned that loneliness was more treacherous than any number of Manhattans. The grief books say not to make any major decisions for one year after losing your spouse. Now I knew why. You might be making those decisions with the mind of a sleep-deprived tween. I'd been acting as carelessly as one.

I should have seen I was torturing Gene, knowing about his jealousy yet resurrecting our relationship, never thinking what reentering his life might do to him, but with grief had come an impenetrable self-adsorption. It was like watching myself in a movie and being unable to hit stop. I had devolved into something extremely primitive.

Yet I'd learned I was still capable of love. And I also learned, finally, to appreciate my freedom.

# 🍓 VII. Widowhood 101

"JUST DECIDING TO GET OUT OF BED in the morning is a victory," said Dr. Sue, my grief counselor, during our first session together. A flaxen-haired, pixie-like woman with trailing purple scarves, she appeared to be in her mid-sixties, but she seemed ageless in a former-modern-dancer kind of way.

I signed up for grief counseling after Gene and I imploded. From George's Kitten to Gene's Del, I had to stop folding myself up like an obedient shirt. I couldn't seem to do it on my own. Kübler-Ross had tried to warn me, saying, "Be careful not to take on new relationships with lots of emotions," but as usual I'd ignored her.

"But I still freak out at home," I told Dr. Sue. "Sometimes I wonder if I should check myself into a mental hospital." George had been gone over a year, and I still couldn't calm down at night.

"No," she said, "You don't need to do that. You're functioning. I tell my patients if they can't stand being at home, check into a nice hotel for a night or two." That sounded fine, but I'd still be alone, except for the security people responding to the wailing sounds coming from my room.

"I was an awful caregiver to George."

"It wasn't your fault," she said soothingly, "You did the best you could under the circumstances. George put you in an impossible situation. He cut you off from everybody who could have helped."

Dr. Sue would tell me some version of this over and over again during our months together, but I still couldn't make myself believe it. Maybe it was just too soon, even though it was true.

In his denial, George had turned down all the outpatient services the hospital offered—a wound nurse because he didn't think he was wounded, a social worker because he thought we were fine, home health care referrals because he'd decided we didn't need help despite my pleas of how overwhelmed I was. After he died, I found out that he'd refused palliative care because he didn't think it applied to him.

Dr. Sue said I had post-traumatic stress disorder, which gave a name to my anxiety attacks. "They should fade over time with talking about it," she advised. "It's worse for you because of the way you lost your mother. George's death is bringing up her loss as well." Kübler-Ross agreed, saying, "You may have lost your beloved, but the grief brings into your awareness all the losses that have occurred in your life."

Yet when my mom died, I didn't feel like I too wanted to die. Probably because I had my dad and because ten-year-olds are more resilient than fifty-year-olds. At ten, I'd opened the closet door and put the stuffed tiger aside—time to do something else—instead of thinking *why bother?* and making another Manhattan and imagining my feet sliced on the glass I'd broken with no one to stop the blood.

I knew my attacks were about George, and they'd stopped only because of Gene. Maybe I could hire a babysitter to bring me my nightly tea and carrot cake, then hold my hand until I fell asleep.

"I feel like I cheated on George being with Gene," I said.

"A guy shouldn't hit on a recent widow because she is too vulnerable," Dr. Sue said, bristling. "He should know better." I had thought of Gene's and my first time together as born of my own neediness, but in truth he'd been flirting with me for weeks before it happened.

The hospital ate my husband just like it ate my mother forty years ago. I had the right to seek solace. It's just that my kind of solace was so undignified.

"I'm worried I've become a sex fiend," I practically whispered.

"You're just normal," Dr. Sue said with a laugh, "it's nothing to feel guilty about. But you need to be alone sometimes, to take the time to grieve, to integrate your loss."

Maybe, but losing my mother at ten should have at least given me the Advanced Placement Grieving Credit so I could skip Introduction to Widowhood 101. It seemed like a verb, to widow: to wail at your husband's graveside, to tat lace, and to wear shroud-like black clothing, as if you too were already dead. Widowhood defined you by someone who was no longer there, like being a negative number.

I didn't want to grieve, and worse, I didn't know how to. When my mother died, the point was to grieve as little as possible. When my dad had asked how I was doing soon after George died, I'd answered honestly that I was relieved he was out of his agony, and he too had been relieved by my answer. Cancer had destroyed George, and his death had been a mercy.

But I'd left out the other feelings, the double loss caused by his denial, and my own denial, and the way we never had talked about anything important as his days crept inevitably to an end. My widowhood felt like a well-deserved punishment. Sometimes I drank too much so I could wallow in my sadness, instead of disposing of it the way it I'd calmly bagged George's clothes and dropped them off at Goodwill a few days after he died.

"Just be careful. Don't fall into something serious too soon," she said as our session ended. "Your homework assignment is to tell at least one new person you're widowed."

A few days later at the yoga studio, I put my mat down next to a thin, stern-looking woman, her black-and-gray-streaked hair pulled back into two pigtails. She told me she came to class seven days a week, interspersing her classes with Overeaters Anonymous meetings.

"I come to class because it gets me out of the house," I said, inspired by her openness. "I was widowed last year."

"I'm a widow too, but I'm happy on my own. I'm done living with anyone ever again," she said vehemently, reaching over to grab her toes, as if to tell me we were finished.

I couldn't imagine ever being like her. Even if her marriage had been bad, didn't she want to find someone new so she could finally be loved? She was a mythical beast, a self-contained widow.

In our next session, Dr. Sue said, "You need to reach out more, to be willing to be vulnerable, to tell people that you're a new widow trying to make friends. Try joining some groups."

"Um, I get really nervous around new people." I'd seen a different therapist for a few sessions when George had first been diagnosed and I'd become frustrated with his workaholism because our time together was limited. That therapist had also suggested I look for connections outside my marriage, but I'd just ignored him, rationalizing I wanted more George, not less of him.

"Try."

"I think I have social anxiety. I spent eleven years hanging out with lawyers, after all," I said with a weak laugh and a deep, drawn-out inhale that sounded like Marge from *The Simpsons*, another irrationally nervous person I totally identified with.

"You'll do fine."

"Honestly, I have a terrible sense of direction and I don't drive at night. George did all the driving."

"Try," she'd said. "You need to stretch a little. To stop being so alone."

"What if I have to parallel park? I never learned to do that. I had these driving lessons with my dad and—"

"Find a parking lot," she said firmly. "I'm afraid our time's up for today."

I sensed relief in her tone. How to explain generalized anxiety—the fact that, since everything made me nervous, I'd constructed a life where I was able to avoid almost anything because I had George to protect me. That's why I'd tried to replicate that protection with Gene. Widowhood meant having to leave the house by myself. Even after dark.

I'd been living in a playpen, and now that the bars were down, I had no idea what to do outside. Maybe Amazon Prime could start delivering social opportunities direct to my door. But like an errant puppy, perhaps I could be trained. I resolved to take on another assignment: I would socialize myself.

For my first foray, I decided to join the Porsche Club of America. I wasn't that into cars, but I'd been isolated for so long I didn't know what I liked to do or where to fit in. I did drive a Porsche, but it was George's car, not mine.

We'd bought it after his diagnosis, when he and I had veered into cancer movie cliché and had bought him his dream wheels, at least the dreamiest we could afford. It was a gently used Carrera 4S in steely metallic gray, with a wicked growl and extra-wide tires. He'd been dying, but we'd been speaking in objects. I'd secretly named it "the Consolation."

After George died, I promised the Consolation I'd find it a real driver, one who at least knew how to parallel park. I even contacted the president of the local branch of the Porsche Club about the best way to go about selling it, but I kept seeing my high-tech guy behind the wheel, grinning as he flew down the hills of San Francisco, at one with his rocket ship.

That car became my armor too. I'd disliked Dr. Sue's use of the word "vulnerable" as something to aspire to. Someone driving a car that badass could never look pathetic, even if she did happen to be a widow. Of course, someone using a car as armor probably had a lot more to worry about than appearances.

The president was so friendly over the phone I started going to the club's monthly dinners and Saturday breakfasts. It was a lot like meeting new people at the dinner parties my dad and I used to host, except that the members of the Porsche Club weren't nuclear physicists.

I drove with the club to tour performance auto shops across the Bay and sample Sangiovese at wineries in the hills above Sonoma, carefully typing the events into my online calendar, trying to commute my sentence of isolation with pancake breakfasts, as if grief could be staunched with maple syrup.

I worried people could see I was stained with loneliness, like a fluorescent dye that was visible only in the dark. The people at the club were kind, but sometimes when I told people I was widowed, they shied away, eyes averted, as if widowhood were a contagious disease and I was Typhoid Mary. They said things like, "That's my worst fear" or "I just couldn't live through that." I had to restrain myself from telling them they would live; they just wouldn't like it very much.

A few men looked uncomfortable, excusing themselves quickly after I told them, as if being widowed meant "seeking dick." I caught a few wives appraising me to see whether I was on the prowl for their husbands. I learned to smile brightly, and hopefully chastely, while quickly changing the subject.

Some well-meaning people said I should be grateful for having had such a long marriage or for having so much of my life still ahead of me, like I was supposed to be Polly-fucking-anna while they turned into Pangloss, proclaiming that everything happens for the best in the best of all possible worlds. Meanwhile, their spouses were still alive, eating all those damned pancakes.

I learned that being with other people didn't quell loneliness. I needed to feel seen. I pretended I was wearing a widow monitor, an electronic bracelet around my ankle that would shock me if I said anything too dark.

But I was learning to propel myself out the front door, to be someplace at a set time, and to engage with others. From the outside, it looked so inconsequential, but I put in a lot of effort into starting to take those tiny steps—set the alarm clock and go, approach those couples at the club dinner, take the empty seat at breakfast, *no, you cannot leave*—and I had to believe it would add up to something. Recovering from grief was initially about survival, but later it was about moving toward life, even if it didn't look like much on the surface.

Most people at the club were welcoming and inclusive, which in itself was worth learning. Sometimes I'd hear another story of loss or I'd talk to someone with a wry wit, and I'd feel a thread of connection that I hoped to strengthen.

I even tried a Track Day with the club where we circled around the track at Thunderhill Raceway in Willows. It started out fine, all of us looking at one another's cars and talking about them, with those who'd made the most modifications for racing having the most to say. But then I had to get on the track.

From the start, all the other drivers were going so much faster, zipping around the curves while my car seemed to totter every time I accelerated. My instructor, a laconic fellow in horn-rimmed glasses and a button-down denim shirt, looked like a high school history teacher. His voice was flat like the teacher in *Ferris Bueller's Day Off* saying, "Bueller, Bueller." He said I was doing fine, but I kept catching him sigh.

He told me to steer into the apex of the curve, brake lightly at the cone at the widest part, then accelerate out of it. I tried, but it was as if I'd never driven before. I braked way too hard and was unable to speed up until it was time for another curve and yet another attempt, prompting yet another sigh from the passenger seat.

By my third loop, I was starting to feel carsick, afraid of falling off the elevated turns, and my stomach lurched. The other drivers stacked up behind me, waiting for me to wave them by on the straightaways, which I did, again and again, each time willing myself to peel my sweaty hand off the wheel.

I'd hoped Track Day would improve both my driving and my social skills, but performance driving was nothing like chatting about coupes versus cabriolets over grilled salmon. Better to stick to activities where I talked to people rather than tried to commune with machinery.

The handout promised, "Much of the fun is meeting up with your fellow rookie drivers at the clubhouse to commiserate over your shared mistakes." My fellow rookies were wearing driving shoes and baseball caps emblazoned with the Porsche insignia. Trying to look less like a widow, I'd chosen pink jeans and high-tops with sparkly laces.

They were already trying to beat each other's times. I was the nerd who was flunking out of driver's ed and everybody else in class knew about it.

I walked out of the clubhouse casually like I was taking a bathroom break and headed for home, forgoing my other four track sessions of the day. I stopped on the road for a milkshake—strawberry, to match my pants. Widowhood was turning out to be a second adolescence complete with shyness over meeting new people, worrying whether they liked me, and a blurring of my sense of self like a lens that couldn't focus. "Porsche driver" certainly wasn't going to cut it as an identity.

Depressed people should probably avoid driving around in circles.

I forced myself to join another club, this time picking the Rotary, that venerable organization (founded more than 115 years ago) that, as its motto says, puts "service above self." That sounded lofty; maybe it would have the secret formula for refocusing a widow, or least getting her out of the house.

"We need more people to man our margarita booth at the next Art and Wind fair. Remember, it's for a good cause!" the Rotary president exhorted at our weekly meeting at a local country club. He never strayed from his script, from delivering the pledge of allegiance to telling the weekly, super-clean joke to asking us trivia questions about Rotary to introducing the evening's speaker.

I picked at my chicken tetrazzini as a spokesperson from the water district gave a speech on quality control standards while visions of my empty bed loomed before me. It was like moving back in time to a more earnest era before the invention of irony.

Through Rotary, I got an appointment with the managing partner of a law firm that specialized in insurance defense, the kind of law I used to practice. But eleven years after quitting my job, sitting in another firm's gray and burgundy lobby, I knew I didn't want to go back.

I'd passed the bar exam at twenty-five and spent the next eleven years at the same firm practicing coverage law, the geekiest branch of insurance defense, which involved interpreting insurance policies, which is just as exciting as it sounds. Back then, women lawyers looked like well-upholstered wedges in suits with padded shoulders, short skirts, high heels, and an exhausting veneer of infallibility.

I used to watch a lot of *LA Law*, but soon I was watching *Regarding Henry* over and over again so I could cheer when Harrison Ford says, "I hate being a lawyer."

So did I because:

1. People got to be mean to me all day.
2. I never figured out how to advance among a group of men who bonded over fantasy football.

3. At my first court appearance, the judge yelled at me seemingly for no reason. Another lawyer told me the judge hated new lawyers, but I didn't see him yell at any of the new male lawyers.
4. I'm fundamentally lazy.
5. Having it all was an evil marketing scheme designed by men to turn women into perpetual motion machines wearing short skirts.
6. Stress is not a food group.

"What are you looking for?" asked the managing partner, when he finally emerged from behind the lobby's double doors. He looked like a corporate Terminator, his slick black hair becoming one with his shiny black suit, his smile more like a smirk.

"I want to work part-time," I said. "I'm looking for a balanced life." I stopped myself from saying my widow's brain hadn't yet reconstituted enough for me to do anything too demanding.

"In that case, I'd suggest you look into law firms run by women," he said, the smile becoming all smirk as he effectively banished me from the patriarchy.

Apparently, not much had changed in the thirteen years since I'd quit practicing. As a new associate in 1988, I was confronted by senior lawyers who tried to build a hierarchy like we were all in a wolf pack, attempting to outmaneuver me so I'd work for them as well as my assigned bosses.

The male associates chatted behind closed doors because they were afraid of being sued for saying anything sexist, which left the women associates excluded from the insider information. I was too inexperienced to know how to push back, lean in, or otherwise get all my dicks, er, *ducks*, in a row.

But I had been a good lawyer and I wondered how I would have fared in a less phallocentric environment where everyone, not only the loudest, was encouraged to speak. On the other hand, judging from this visit, little had changed. The managing partner at this new—yet obviously the same—firm quickly handed me off to a nearby paralegal and retreated behind the double doors where his many drones no doubt toiled away ceaselessly. Apparently, balance was only for women. Real men, or at least real lawyers, reveled in being unbalanced.

Going back to a law firm would just be more driving around in circles.

At my local synagogue, I met with the rabbi, a scholarly man with a wry smile and solemn brown eyes under huge bristly brows that resembled my dad's.

The synagogue was very Northern California, a modern, wood-paneled building set among green hills, with its own vegetable garden, and children dashing around the playground of the religious school next door. The rabbi's sunny office was lined with bookshelves so overflowing with books they spilled onto the floor, just like at my dad's house.

"I was widowed last year," I said. "My problem is that I can't seem to handle being alone."

"How about if we meet for grief counseling?" he said.

"I'd like that, but I think you should know I'm an atheist."

I'd been one since my mom died, preferring to think of her death as a random act rather than the conscious choice of a god who needed to take a Danville housewife, no matter how good her chocolate mousse. An agnostic, George used to joke that if he died young, it meant God was looking for somebody to revamp his computer system. George's coding skills were preternaturally great, but it certainly wasn't comforting to think I'd lost him to a better job opportunity.

"If synagogues excluded all Jews who were atheists, we wouldn't have a congregation," the rabbi said with a big grin, his eyes wrinkling at the corners. "Why don't we meet every other week?"

I agreed. If I got double counseling, both spiritual and secular from both the rabbi and Dr. Sue, maybe I'd recover twice as fast.

"The ability to be alone will give you a great power because you won't be dependent on others. Imagine sitting comfortably alone by the fire enjoying a good book," the rabbi said during our first session. I tried to imagine doing that without hyperventilating or checking my email every fifty seconds.

He suggested I look for a few friends with the potential for real connection and added that perhaps I'd like to attend the synagogue's monthly women's red tent gatherings. I went to a few, but the leader started every meeting by going around a circle with each woman saying what she was most grateful for over the past month. As they listed children and husbands and dear old friends, I refrained from saying, "Hendrick's Gin," pretending my imaginary widow monitor would shock me if I did.

I was an alien from Planet Solitary, peering into the windows of the husbanded and familied before crawling into my spaceship to fly home, unable to communicate with the earthlings because my native language was death.

But a few divorced ladies from the group invited me to a movie night, and another one invited me to lunch. At one of the gatherings, one of the women told a story with real emotion, even using the word "fuck" while a few of the others looked on askance. I knew I'd found a potential friend.

After much consternation, I asked her to lunch—*What if she's one of those people who's always busy? She's popular and I'm an outsider*—but she accepted. Just a tiny risk, but at fifty-one, I was finally learning to make friends.

After each counseling session, the rabbi gave me a blessing. "You will find peace," he said the first time.

"Eventually, you will find love," he said at the conclusion of the second.

"My ex-boyfriend was a home health care aide. I had to break up with him when he became jealous and controlling," I said.

"Aim higher," he said.

Any outing or social contact earned me points in the Thriving Not Grieving game. When my personal trainer asked how my weekend was, I could rattle off an admirable list of new things I was trying and people I was meeting. But my groups felt beige, like Dr. Sue's featureless, institutional office. When Gene used to take my clothes off slowly, the bedroom dimmed to a dark glow; life had become a warm soupy magenta.

Kübler-Ross says just showing up for things is an accomplishment. I was beginning to wonder. I tried a networking group even though I had nothing to sell, nor did I want to buy what the group was selling—custom-beaded rhinestone jewelry, menopause coaching, and wine for all my nonexistent special event needs.

I tried a group that channeled the divine feminine, but the women in it seemed to have mistaken disillusioned for divine. They wore oversized jewelry that rattled angrily when they spoke. I saw myself in ten years, over-adorned with an undercurrent of defeat, trying to find destiny in my inexplicable loss.

Maybe I could find a club for misanthropes, except that it probably never met.

Next, I tried a creative writing class offered by an adult education program. "I'm a recent widow. My husband died of cancer and I'm still trying to make sense of it," I said during the introductions on the first day of class. A gentle wave of sympathy wafted up from my classmates, mostly retirees in their seventies. I looked down, trying to avoid catching anyone's eyes, not wanting to see the pity in them.

The education program was housed in the high school that George had attended in the seventies. I might be sitting in the very classroom where he and his friends had deliberately exploded their chemistry experiments.

The following week, when it was my turn to read, I stood up and began, "My piece is called 'What Not to Say to a Widow.' We don't usually tell other grown-ups how to live, but widow-hood brings out people's inner critics. They tell us to sell our homes or join an ashram, but they won't take the time to get a cup of coffee with us. They tell us to 'get out there,' but I have no idea where 'there' is and I'd probably get lost trying to find it."

When I was finished, my classmates looked at one another as if they'd just been hit, trying desperately to catch the eye of another sane person. All of my writing could be summed up in five words: *I am really pissed off.* But it was better than admitting I was a pariah, indelibly stained by loneliness and guilt.

A few weeks later, my classmate Will approached me after class. A tall, red-haired retired public defender in his late sixties, he was writing a memoir about his three tours of duty in Vietnam. Thirty years sober through AA, he viewed each day as a gift, dedicated much of his life to public service, and even followed a vegan diet. Absent his wicked sense of humor, he would have been otherworldly in his goodness.

"You always excoriate people in your writing. Do you think you'll ever have anything good to say about them?" he asked, his kind blue eyes looking into my hungover green ones.

"Hmmm, I'll think about it." *Not bloody likely*, I wanted to say, but I pictured the imaginary widow monitor around my ankle giving me a little shock.

But he still checked in with me each week, asking, "And how is Debbie doing?"

"Fine," I'd mutter, attempting an unsuccessful smile, hoping he didn't see me as a project, yet grateful he cared enough to ask.

Another time, he said, "During difficult times in my own life, I've tried to help others. And it's always helped me more than it did them." It sounded like he was reading from a Sunday school sermon for miscreant children. Will could have been Henry Fonda in *Twelve Angry Men*, wise and perceptive, trying to get me to see beyond my anger, while I'd already judged the universe as guilty.

Yet I loved the classes. We started each session with a writing exercise, then each of us read our work aloud, from the former civil rights activist writing his memoir to the poet describing the local hillsides to the retired engineer spinning a dystopian fantasy. The rest of us offered praise and gentle suggestions as the two and a half hours of class time sped by. On those Thursday afternoons, I was outside myself.

"Find something you like to do, then figure out how to do it with other people," I posted on my blog. I'd just had to keep looking.

As we were leaving class one day, Will said rather formally, "A few of us meet on Friday mornings at Delilah's house to get feedback on our writing. We'd like to invite you to join our group."

I'd taken other writing classes over the years, sometimes reading my pieces aloud to George, but he never thought I was a very good writer. He always looked a little embarrassed whenever I read my work to him. He said I made everything sound like a legal brief because I added in so many caveats that I took away the meaning. I just shrugged it off, having spent years doing little else but writing legal briefs.

But now I wondered why he hadn't found something to say he liked in my stories about a little girl growing up with her single scientist dad. Maybe he'd been afraid I'd embarrass myself, but I'd only shared my work with my writing class. He'd always managed to praise his colleagues, even when their efforts were less than stellar. Maybe he'd held me to a higher standard, but now that he was gone, I wanted to tell him he should have been more encouraging. I could divine no reason why he hadn't been.

Will's invitation was a chance to be someone more than I had been, someone who did something besides eat grilled salmon and drive around in circles, someone who might actually be able to think. The night before the group met, I printed five copies of my best rant, checked my Maps app several times to be sure of the driving time, then doubled it just in case.

Our classmate Delilah was a former model and later a therapist. She was sixty-something with blonde hair curving around cut-glass cheekbones and huge hazel eyes under a high forehead. When I got to her apartment, she directed me to a low armchair upholstered in pink rose-patterned chintz. Her scruffy little dog nosed around my sneakers.

"This will be your place now," she said in her rich Southern accent.

"It's so good to have you with us," said Lee, surprising me with a big hug and a kiss on the cheek. She was a curvy journalist with a sheath of sand-colored hair, a round, expressive face, a knowing smile, and eyes that had seen far too much.

She read a chapter from her novel about misbehaving diplomats who were fueled by elaborate parties, premium gin, and foreign intrigue. Will read from his memoir, then Delilah read from her antebellum romance about a forbidden love affair.

"If you're writing a sex scene, it needs to actually have sex in it," said Lee, critiquing Delilah's depiction of her lovers' time together. "Don't be afraid to say 'dick and balls.' We all know they're involved." They were great writers, and I was in intimidating company. Their critiques were balanced but definitely unvarnished.

"That's our Lee," said Will. "But seriously, if this was supposed to be a passionate encounter, there would've been more, um, activity. They wouldn't just fall together and then nothing happens until one of them lights the proverbial cigarette."

"You might want to think about adding moisture or dampness

to suggest excitement," I said, thinking about Gene and blushing. For once, I wasn't editing everything before I spoke, no longer imagining the shock of the widow monitor.

When it was my turn, I read aloud, "I was leaving a coffee shop yesterday and a man opened the door for his date, then walked through it himself, letting it close right in front of me, my arms full with my iPad, purse, and mocha latte. Widowhood means always having to wedge my foot in the door because I don't have an extra hand."

As my new writing group scribbled in the margins of my essay, I knew I was exactly where I was supposed to be. And where I would be every Friday morning from that day on.

"Tell us more about George," Delilah said as we were winding down a few weeks later. "You must have some great stories about him."

"Yeah, we want to know more about George," Lee said.

The following Friday, I took a sip of mint tea, breathed in deeply, and began to read. "I didn't understand why we had to go to the Hansen's party because we had our own swimming pool at home, but my parents said I had to go. Little did I know that at seven years old, I was about to meet my future husband."

I could still see eleven-year-old George in his swim trunks, preternaturally poised, reaching out a hand for me to shake, the first kid I ever met who shook hands. His mom had to gently place my hand in his to show me what to do. Of course, I blushed.

I could finally be vulnerable. I'd just had to find the right people to be vulnerable with. But the raven still came to visit me at night, so I turned back to online dating, looking for a way to quiet my memories.

# VIII. Dating for Hoarders

"WHEN WE GET TOGETHER, I promise to give you a baby oil massage followed by seven orgasms.🌹🍑," a gorgeous professional rapper texted me at midnight a few weeks later. He'd contacted me on OkCupid, a dating site I'd signed up for that was much larger than JDate, not aimed at Jews, and hopefully a lot more fun.

The rapper and I hadn't chatted much before that, so I wasn't expecting his offer, nor its accompanying advertisement, an unsolicited nude photo of himself, rear view only, perhaps in deference to my age. I felt myself turn red against the sheets. Maybe he was trying to establish a business selling happy endings to underserved Danville housewives.

"Sorry, I don't feel comfortable with that. 😊," I texted back. "I was about to suggest we meet for coffee." I was relieved when I didn't hear from him again.

*Would you want seven orgasms on the first date?* No, it sounds exhausting.

I often answered the site's compatibility questions and checked out men's profiles late into the night, forcing myself to read the newspaper the next morning instead of jumping back on like an online shopping addict. Except I was shopping for men instead of shoes, and returning most of my purchases since I didn't know what I was looking for in the first place. I told myself I was gathering material for my writing class, but really, I was spiraling into an addiction, imagining an alternate self with every man I dated.

I didn't understand how long it takes to grieve even if you don't want it to. Despite all my dating, widowhood was less like a romantic comedy and more like one of those interminable Ingmar Bergman films where the heroine's psyche slowly disintegrates over time. I'd lost George seventeen months ago, but I really hadn't recovered much, no longer escaping to my dad's house at night, but I was still suffering from insomnia and PTSD. I would have fared far better had I pictured myself as a good friend in distress instead of a lost cause to escape.

I wanted to wear a badge that identified me as a widow, decorated with flowers and rhinestones, because widowhood is nothing to be ashamed of. But a badge would let people know to ignore me when I cried in the grocery store, and not glare at me at the register because I didn't notice my carrot cake was missing a price tag.

Widows should be given baskets of chocolate truffles and vibrators to acknowledge that sexual bereavement is real. And big poofy new beds to enjoy them in because we keep seeing our late husbands in the old ones. And somebody to haul those new beds into the house because we're tired of having to do every last little thing for ourselves. And there should be drop-in centers where people who feel unbearably lonely can talk to each other and watch funny movies together, maybe over milkshakes.

*While in the middle of the best lovemaking of your life, if your lover asked you to squeal like a dolphin, would you?*

Do adults really answer this stuff? Am I dating Flipper? *Skip the question.*

I had iced tea with a songwriting cowboy who managed his family's ranch. He peered at me from under the brim of his hat as if

I were a new species of talking dog while I rambled on, trying to fill up the silence. Later that night he texted me, "You're smokin' hot 🔥. Would you like to come see my ranch sometime? 🐎"

"That sounds like fun 😄," I answered. But that was the last I heard from him. Perhaps he just wanted to meet a lot of people as an end in itself since his profile said he had virtually no free time, but he'd answered an awful lot of those compatibility questions.

*Would you date a cowboy?* Yes, he too was smokin' hot, albeit inarticulate save for emoji speak.

OkCupid listed your answers publicly. After I'd answered enough questions, the site classified me as being primarily motivated by sex, which it also made public, causing me to delete my answers to any question remotely related to sex. It then reclassified me as being primarily motivated by science, which I didn't understand but seemed safe enough to share.

Long live my second adolescence, a major time-suck from doing anything too challenging.

I sipped chai latte with a former child music prodigy.

"I've written five symphonies, but none of them was ever produced," he said, then rambled about moving cross-country and starting over, possibly with a like-minded adventuress.

When I mentioned I was a widow, his monologue slowed down a little, but he quickly revved back up to tell me about the seven musicals he'd scored, none of which had ever been produced either. After our coffee date, he emailed, "Next time let's drive to Point Reyes in your Porsche 🚗." I didn't reply.

*How important is it that your date ask you questions about yourself?* Very, otherwise it's like watching a bad TV show you can't turn off.

*Would the world be a better place if people with low IQs were not allowed to reproduce?*

(a) ~~Yes~~ (b) *No.* So now dating sites dabble in eugenics?

# Available As Is

○ ○ ○ ○ ○

Sometimes I averaged two meetups a day, going to the same café for nonfat chai lattes both before and after my Thursday afternoon writing class. A couple of times, the server greeted me on my second date of the day with a raised eyebrow.

I'd meet almost anyone who seemed appealing and was willing to come within ten miles of Danville. I was scampering around like a rabid squirrel, occasionally collapsing in exhaustion with a mushroom pizza and a bottle of red wine. My life had become a sick experiment in performance dating.

Real people lived with someone they loved. Fake people like me trolled the internet talking to strangers, sitting on their bedroom floors with a virtual life and a disintegrating reality. Then again, reality was pretty nebulous when you knew your life could fall apart at any minute.

My dad used to do experiments at a linear accelerator where he sped up particles to make them react with one another. I'd become an accelerated particle, colliding with the men who contacted me online, enjoying the popularity I'd missed out on in high school. I'd gone from being a pariah to one of the popular neutrinos, but really, I was running around in circles trying to outrun my loneliness. That and my guilt.

During his last few months, I had started yelling at George. On what turned out to be his last Christmas, we had his parents over for holiday tea since not seeing them at all would have worried them. George had tried to disguise his condition and had sat in one of the dining room chairs before they'd arrived. He'd made me hide his wheelchair, and he'd pulled his ski cap down firmly to cover his baldness.

Trying not to implode from collaborating in his deception, I'd served tea and passed plates full of raspberries, pink-frosted cookies, and guilt. We'd argued more since he became ill than during our entire marriage.

Suddenly, his mother, Isabella, had started sobbing uncontrollably, her shoulders shaking, her perfectly lined lips twisting.

"I know," she had said between sobs. "My two brothers, your uncles, died of cancer. I know what it looks like, Georgie."

Bob, usually an incessant talker, became silent, slumping into himself, his face turning gray.

"I won't talk about this now," George had said, adding weakly, "It's Christmas."

If Isabella could leave her hometown in Chile to get a doctorate in physics and become a scientist at a government research lab when very few women did such things, I hoped she'd be able to get her son to see reality, but he didn't listen even to her. His parents had left soon afterward. Neither of them had touched their cookies nor drank their tea. With their eyes downcast, they'd grabbed their jackets hurriedly from the hall closet.

Cancer was when people couldn't look you in the eye anymore. And in George's case, it was rejecting the parents who had only ever wanted the best for him.

"Worst Christmas ever. This is fucking killing me," I screamed after they left, pounding my fist against the wall, wishing I'd never agreed to go along with the charade.

George's face crumpled just like his mother's had an hour earlier.

And that wasn't all. "I need to put you in a nursing home," I'd yelled at him a few months later, angrily rubbing yet another spray of carpet cleaner into the pale gray carpet after he'd lost control of his bowels while working in the home office.

"I'm sorry, I'm sorry," he said over and over from his wheelchair, the tears streaming down his mottled cheeks.

"It's okay, it's okay, it'll wash out," I said in return, realizing I'd just threatened to take away his home, knowing I could never wash away the stain of my words.

And still it went on. "What the fuck is going on? You're getting worse!" I'd screamed, trying to pierce through his denial. "We've got to get more help. I can't do this alone," I ranted, sleep-deprived and amped up from the prednisone I was taking far longer than I should have to control my stress-induced hives. And most shamefully, "This is killing me," I'd said as if I, instead of George, had been the one who was dying.

Now that he was gone, it wasn't just that I couldn't live without him. It was that I couldn't live with myself.

*Is it a requirement that you communicate with your significant other daily in some way?*

Yes. I wanted someone who asked about my day and who told me about his, to keep me tethered to a world without George. Barring that, I'd communicate with random men, untethered to a world that made no sense without him.

I drank Cabernet at Bridges with a commercial realtor who'd previously fronted a punk rock band. He was cocaine-wired. He inhaled his first glass of wine, then slowed down only a little for the next three. For some reason, he kept quoting lines from *Pulp Fiction*, mainly the dirty ones.

I agreed to meet him again because he was pre-boxing Mickey Rourke sexy, but afterward I had to keep wiggling away when he tried to grab my butt in the parking lot while announcing loudly, "I'm going in for the butt." Later he emailed me saying we had no chemistry. I was surprised he could even remember.

*Could you date someone with no impulse control?* No, it was like fending off a bot gone rogue.

My worst date was a hot, dry hike with a patent attorney where I slipped and fell trying to navigate down a rocky slope. He waited at the bottom, unconcerned while I righted myself, surprised that I ended the date early as I picked the gravel out of my palms.

*Would you go on a hike for a first date?* Never again, although his lack of compassion might have been related to his profession.

My second-worst date was lunch with a buff mortgage broker who kept drowning his tuna sandwich in squirts of mustard while telling me how many reps he'd completed at the gym that morning, not that I'd asked. He broke stride only to offer me a bite of his tuna sandwich, raising a limp bun topped with spirals of atomic-yellow gloop.

*What's the most important lesson you've learned since going online?* To limit all first encounters to coffee. #datingadvice

Whenever I tried to sit still, my memories threatened to drown me. The Wednesday after the paramedics had taken George away, his treating physician had called and told me, her voice breaking, "George is expected to die very soon, within days, maybe a month. I'm sorry. I should have been able to prepare you sooner, but he had that order in place." It was the first time she and I had ever spoken.

I was finally hearing the truth. He was always going to die. There had never been a chance he'd recover. I was convinced I'd willed his death because I'd so hated those sleepless nights with the nebulizer.

*I just wanted a break, I never wanted him to die,* I explained to the fates. But it had been too late. I was standing at the kitchen counter, yet I felt like I was falling through space.

I had lost him.

But I hadn't understood. "What order are you talking about?" I said.

"When George was first diagnosed, he put an order in place barring the hospital staff from communicating with you. If you'd tried to call us, we wouldn't have been able to talk to you. I can only talk to you now because he's in and out of consciousness and you're his contact person in case he can't make his own decisions."

A gray wave of disbelief rushed over me. He never told me he'd barred my access to his doctors. *Pretty dumb for a genius, George, since now I don't know what's going on.*

The gray wave of sorrow turned to molten red anger. He had deceived me.

"George won't be leaving the hospital," his doctor said. "But I haven't told him. He still believes he's going to recover and go home. I don't want to crush his morale. I'm so very sorry." I couldn't speak as she hung up.

Very slowly, as if my bones might break, I sat down at the kitchen table. George had thought me too fragile to hear the truth. He'd been afraid his doctors might call our home and speak to me about his impending death instead of the miraculous recovery he'd always talked about.

He'd probably thought I would have obsessed over his prognosis and made the rest of our lives miserable. I'd known that he wasn't going to recover, but I'd thought we had a lot more time left. I saw then that my denial was as strong as his.

But he never should have put that order in place. How could he have coded a new feature in Quicken or chopped the shallots for *Lobster à L'américaine*, seemingly unconcerned that if I called the hospital, I'd have been told my husband had exiled me? I couldn't even get mad at him since he was almost gone, his hospital bed soon to be his deathbed.

I'd left for the hospital after putting on a black-and-white striped T-shirt and white jeans, too tired for color, but I'd stroked on mascara, trying to look extra-sane since the hospital staff probably thought George must have had a pretty good reason for signing that order. *Thanks, George, I just found out you're dying and now I have to navigate eye makeup.*

If this were a cheesy made-for-TV movie, I'd have been a screaming banshee in a tattered sweat suit, reaching into his oxygen tent to shake him awake and demanding to know how he could have deceived me. The nurses would have had to drag me away, whispering amongst themselves they could see why he needed that order in the first place. #crazybitch.

But who wants to think about that when you can meet lots of strange men?

My best date was with a tall artist who was David Byrne sexy with sad eyes and beautiful tapered fingers. At our first coffee date he stared at me as if he were hungry, and caught me off-guard as we were leaving with a long, intense, almost feral kiss goodbye.

"I'm sorry I just wanted to," he texted later that day.

"Why be sorry?" I texted back. But I wasn't always in my body back then.

I didn't realize how much stock I put in having my dates' eyes light up when they saw me, and how diminished I felt the few times they appeared visibly disappointed. I'm embarrassed to have sought validation in the male gaze, but I was worried about being single at fifty, well aware that most men wanted younger women

I'd grown up with images of women being pursued, watching old James Bond movies and sherry ads, and I saw such an aggressive gesture as a testament to my desirability instead of a violation of my boundaries. #MeToo.

For our second date, the artist called on a Saturday night and offered to come to my house bearing vegetarian pizza. Tired after spending the day in the city on a date with a widower who'd talked at length about his troubled marriage to an alcoholic, I'd surprised myself by saying yes.

The widower had spoken honestly and without self-pity, yet I was uncomfortable with him. I later realized it was because he hadn't idealized his marriage the way I did mine. I was so used to spinning the story of a fairy tale with a premature ending, without considering whether I'd really been that happy after all.

The artist vanished after two more dates and several more kisses. After that first kiss, I'm lucky he didn't press things.

I told myself I was being a good widow, putting on makeup and going on dates, telling my social groups I was moving on, getting out there, and all the other clichés designed to reassure the non-grieving that talking to a widowed person didn't have to be socially awkward.

Bad widowhood looked like going to the drugstore in a bourbon-stained bathrobe to pick up an oversized bottle of generic gin and a twelve-pack of Butterfingers. I worried about the exceedingly thin line separating the two.

The same day I had gotten the call from George's doctor, Isabella had met me outside his hospital room, admonishing, "We can't let Georgie's morale down." By now, she and Bob had met with his doctors, and they also knew he was expected to die in the hospital. But even so, we'd still gone into his room and talked to him as if he would be coming home.

Isabella told him he should recover at their house—she would hire a nurse and I could stay over as much as I wanted. She was apparently trying to create the alternate reality where he hadn't excluded his parents. Bob was silent, his skin the same gray it had turned at Christmas, his cardigan hanging off him as if it too were lost.

I'll always wonder what those last months would have been like had George let his parents help us. Bob might have driven George crazy with articles about cancer nutrition he found on the internet, and Isabella would have wanted to go through their old photograph albums with him. But it would have been far better than shutting them out.

Despite our differences, the three of us would have cared for him together, most likely at Isabella's house the way she wanted, and the end, though inevitable and devastating, would have been full of love. Instead, throughout his illness, his parents' presence had been their absence.

I wish I'd gone behind his back at the beginning and told them the truth. Then when he'd died, I wouldn't have felt like an accessory to his cruelty, even if it had been unintentional.

After an hour of discussing homecoming arrangements we were never going to need, George had whispered to me from inside his oxygen tent. His mouth had not been working properly, and his face was swollen, but his eyes were clear.

"You need to go," he'd said. "If you don't go, she'll never leave." I guess he was tired of hearing Isabella talk about his coming home. I knew he would have wanted to come back to our house once he recovered, but as of only a few hours ago, I also knew that he never would. Ever compliant, I left.

Back at my house, I'd gone through the unpaid bills, many of them almost due, accessible only through George's bank account set up on his computer. I called George's room. "What's your fucking Wells Fargo password?" I said once the nurse put the phone to his ear.

"Colnago," he had said in that almost-gone whisper.

Colnago was the brand of bicycle he'd ridden in college. He'd long ago stopped training and had sold the bike. Was that his Rosebud? Did he have any regrets? I would never know.

All I could think about was the order I'd found out about only that morning and how he'd lied to me about how long he'd had left. From the time he had been diagnosed, he must have known he had only a few years at most. Now I was trying to figure out how to get into his bank accounts when we should have spent the past months, if not years, preparing for his death. My anger propelled me into action. Pay the bills, figure out what to do with the taxes that were due in five days, don't think about anything else, I'd see him again tomorrow.

Later that afternoon, I had gotten the call from his doctor—George had died. There would be no tomorrow.

She'd gone to his room to tell him that she needed to be able to talk to me. He agreed with her, then fell out of consciousness. She consoled me that he didn't have to undergo the operation they had been considering to remove the fluid from his lungs. He would never have to wake up from surgery and not understand what was happening to him.

In those first few moments, I felt only relief. He was free of his pain. But my second thought was that once he knew I had to be in the loop, he had lost his will to live.

Just the morning before, I'd gotten the doctor's call that he was going to die in the hospital. When I saw him that afternoon, he'd been lucid, even smiling at me from inside his breathing tent. A few hours later, he was gone. I was suspended in ice; it all happened so fast. His denial had deprived us of any goodbyes, but I didn't think I deserved any deathbed "I love yous."

I don't recall what I did that day, but I did not go back to the hospital. I was just too tired. I think I went into a kind of shock. I do recall phoning my dad and Jane to tell them he was gone, and my dad asking if I was okay. I said I was and that I'd come over the next day.

That night I called my few friends to tell them about George—my aesthetician broke down in tears—as if by telling other people I could make it feel real. But it still didn't. I was never going to see him again. He wasn't there anymore. That conversation about his banking password had been our last.

Isabella had stayed at the hospital after I'd left. She'd been there when George had fallen asleep that afternoon and when he never woke up again. Perhaps after being banished for so long, she had taken whatever time she had left. Being his mother, maybe she had sensed that was the end. She'd stayed with the body for hours, just the two of them. That's what love looks like.

The next day Isabella had called early to say, "We have an appointment at eight thirty this morning with the social worker at the hospital. You should meet us there." I let the call go to voicemail.

"It's too late now," I had said aloud to our empty bedroom. There was no more George. There was only a corpse. I felt frozen, but little else.

I called the social worker and asked him to tell my in-laws they could do whatever they wanted with the body. I just couldn't deal with it. I'd told myself there was nothing to do now that George was gone. But really, I couldn't stand living in shame anymore, shame about my husband's signing that order, and my own poor caregiving, and my failure to convince him to include his parents.

Even our solitary lives had become a source of shame, with no close friends to visit him or bring us casseroles. No one to ask, "Am I doing this right?" No one to come with me to the hospital the day after my husband died.

I had figured Isabella and Bob were angry with me for following George's orders not to contact them, and they probably thought I'd mismanaged his care and maybe even hastened his death. I could not face them.

So, to my everlasting regret, I checked out. I succumbed to a kind of insanity where I was certain that I'd get into a terrible accident if I drove to the hospital, so I just couldn't get on the freeway. Besides, I'd had to do everything on my own when George was alive, so now I was wiped out and I couldn't talk to people and act like I was okay, and nothing mattered anymore anyway.

I wasn't trying to be cruel to my in-laws, yet I left them alone to deal with George's death. I never asked how they were or got their consent to take over or explained I was too messed up to be of help.

Then I called the company that had rented George's oxygen tanks and told them to pick them up as soon as possible. No, they could not get the patient's approval, because the patient was dead, so please just come and get them already. I hurled the nebulizer, the ammonia tablets, and all the other medications on George's side of the bed into the trash. From there I moved on to the cabinets of bandages and Wet Ones and other cancer paraphernalia, seeking to change reality by imposing order.

I went over to my dad's house later that day and had a cup of tea and calmly reassured him that I was fine. Otherwise, I was pretty quiet. There was no more George to come home to.

Two days later, Isabella called to say, "Georgie is at Hull's Mortuary in Walnut Creek." My grief calcified into efficiency. I needed to prepay our taxes—which had been easier to think about than my husband being gone—which meant I had to get his death certificate to gain access to his other bank account with more money in it.

Since the certificate was at the mortuary, I drove alone to get it since I had no one to come with me. The mortuary was tucked discreetly on a back street. It looked benign enough, but the driveway had a high concrete lip that scratched the underside of the Consolation as I pulled in. Of course, that was what being cursed looked like.

Isabella had called again a few days later to say, "We are going to bury Georgie's ashes in our backyard under a sundial." There was to be no funeral or memorial service. The sundial seemed an odd choice, counting the minutes for someone who no longer existed and reminding his loved ones of the time that passed in his absence, but I wasn't in any position to comment.

# Debbie Weiss

I don't remember what I said to her, only that it was brief. In retrospect, ignoring George's body to clean out our bedroom makes no sense. I can only guess I sought to erase my memories.

George had died a stranger to me, and I had nothing left for the parents who had lost their only child. I am still ashamed.

*How do you feel about falling in love?* Passionately. I'm just not sure it's possible at middle age.

 *IX. Coda*

What I Really Wanted My Husband to Do When We Found Out He Was Going to Die:

1. Teach me how to program the garden lights. No matter how many tries it took.
2. Finish that damn home theater system so that a technical dummy (i.e., me) could figure it out.
3. Put my name on all the accounts and give me the passwords. Then I wouldn't have had to threaten to sue the bank, benefits, and brokerage companies.
4. Explain how our home computer network worked.
5. Tell me he wouldn't have chosen any other life than the one we had.
7. Tell me how to live without him.
8. Tell me goodbye.

# X. Hooking Up for Dummies

"I FIND YOU VERY ATTRACTIVE. I know I'm a lot younger, but I was friends with benefits with a woman your age and we both had a really good time. Austin 😀"

Sitting at my dining room table on a Sunday morning, I was scrolling through my messages on Plenty of Fish, none of which looked promising, until this one. I was eating the frosting off a slab of carrot cake, rationalizing it was offset by the green tea I was drinking. It had rained the night before.

The sound of rain hitting the windows used to be the coziest thing in the world when I was curled up in bed next to George, but it had become the echo of abandonment, each droplet proclaiming as it broke, "You will die alone."

I checked out Austin's profile. He was an app developer, thirty years old, six feet one inch tall, with huge dark eyes, aquiline features, brown hair down to his shoulders, and rippling, but not overstated, muscles. He described himself as "sapiosexual," meaning he was sexually attracted to intelligence. I had to google that word. We didn't know it when I was young.

*Why not*, I thought, choosing to forget that I probably shouldn't touch him since I didn't know where he'd been.

"Hmmmm, maybe. ☺," I emailed back.

"Awesome! Give me your number."

Despite having known Austin for only five minutes, I gave

it to him. My boundaries apparently had evaporated along with my husband.

"Don't you prefer women your own age?" I texted him after we'd moved off the site. He was a prime young salmon who could have his pick of spawning mates.

"I've always liked older ladies 😃," he texted. Then a minute later, "Plus I just broke up with someone my own age and I could use some fun. 😌"

Perhaps he'd decided to follow Benjamin Franklin's advice to take an older woman as his mistress because she'd be so grateful. All those coffee meetups were starting to seem like an increasingly dreary series of job interviews. I wondered what it would be like to get right down to business with someone terrifically attractive. I might be someone who enjoyed a hookup. I didn't know; I'd never tried one before.

Austin and I met briefly once before the big night to see if we wanted to go through with it. Both of us were on our way home from dates with other people.

"I'm hot for you," he said after climbing into George's Porsche, gesturing toward the bulge in his lap, then putting my hand on it. "I could take it out."

"That's okay. I, um, wanna be surprised," I said. I felt myself blushing, relieved it was so dark he couldn't tell. So this was modern dating. You met the penis before you knew the person.

Twenty minutes later I was on my way home, embarrassed even though all we'd really done was talk. I told myself our pre-date meetup was cool in an "exploring my dark side" kind of way, even though we'd had nothing to say to each other and I didn't really have a dark side, no matter how hard I tried.

I fantasized that Austin and I would become friends, hanging out together in the city and driving around in the souped-up Mustang he'd shown me on his Instagram page.

Pre-widowhood, my greatest skill had been legal writing.

Post-widowhood, it was projecting myself into anyone's life, no matter how unlikely. My expectations weren't so easy to rein in after all.

Sundays used to be George stirring a big pot of risotto Milanese on the stove and putting his arm around me as I stood next to him. The warm scent of saffron used to fill up the kitchen. When the risotto was done, looking as gilded as it did in the cookbook, he'd pour us glasses of the special Barbera we'd bought together at the fancy wine store earlier that day. Then he'd grate the big block of Parmesan over my plate with a flourish.

After dinner I'd start the dishes while he took out the trash, saying, "Save the pots for me." The Man of the House tackling the manly chores. He'd come back inside to serenade me while we cleaned up, singing my favorite song from the Fred Astaire movies we'd watch over and over again, "They Can't Take That Away from Me." As I wiped down the counters, he'd croon as if Astaire himself had just descended into our kitchen.

We might have watched a favorite movie like *Casablanca*. I used to rest my head on his chest, my thigh on top of his, a posture so natural it wouldn't have registered we were touching. Until he was gone.

Now my Sundays were playing Joan Baez's album *Diamonds and Rust* on the turntable. They were "God, I hope one of my groups is meeting soon," "breathe deeply like in yoga," and "wine right at five" kind of days because whenever I looked at the stove, I still saw George standing in front of it stirring that damned pot of risotto.

Then I'd remember his order barring my access to the medical staff at the hospital and make another Manhattan, two parts Maker's Mark Bourbon to one part Dolin Red Vermouth, garnished with two organic cherries in syrup. I sipped my drink and wondered what had caused George to sign that order and what he'd really thought of our marriage and what I really thought of it and why didn't I have any friends I could call on a Sunday afternoon. I'd look around my empty rooms as the bourbon in my glass glinted a ferrous red.

I still couldn't bring myself to get rid of his cookbooks.

Feeling like a carpool mom, I picked Austin up at the train station on the night of our big assignation. At least driving gave me something to do. Once I pulled into my driveway, all I could think about was how I really wished I hadn't done this.

We sipped Chardonnay in the living room. My eyes darted nervously around the stereo speakers and the TV screen and the curio cabinet in the corner. Anywhere but at Austin. I wished I could shrink myself and slide down between the sofa cushions, the cool leather surrounding me, hearing Austin calling out for me, emerging only after he'd given up and gone home.

Finally, he asked, "What's wrong with you?"

"I'm really nervous," I told him. "This is all new to me."

"I'm nervous too," he said. "Think how I felt getting in your car not even knowing where you were going to take me." He'd relaxed a little now that he'd seen I had a normal house instead of a lab designed to harvest valuable body parts for profit.

"I figured the Porsche was such a nice car, the worst thing you'd have to worry about was my politics," I said.

He did not laugh.

This was not exciting. It was two normal people thrust into a weird situation of forced closeness. He seemed to expect me to put the moves on him since I was the older woman. I thought he'd be the one to start things since he was the guy. Sitting on the sofa looking at each other like two eighth graders playing their first game of Spin the Bottle, we were both confused. We barely knew each other, yet asking the usual questions about education or jobs seemed out of place since this was supposed to be sexy. But it wasn't sexy; it was nerve-racking.

"Why don't you take off your shirt?" he said.

"Why don't you take off yours?" I said, like a thirteen-year-old playing her first game of Five Minutes in the Closet.

He pulled his sweater over his head. It was a nice black-and-white striped wool, and I wondered if his mom had bought it for him. Then I wondered if I was older than she was. He had a great torso, but I didn't know what to do with it.

He moved in for a kiss and put my hand in his lap. Did he use this move with women his own age or only with cougars? Maybe he was so young he was still in the phallic phase.

He took a picture of my black-painted fingernails on his crotch and texted it to me as a souvenir of my first, and definitely last, hookup. I pretended to be interested in the photo, but really I was avoiding any more attempts at conversation. We were reduced to looking at a phone.

We walked down the hallway to my bedroom. I walked in front while he grabbed my butt from behind, saying it was "truly awesome, the ass of a much younger woman." But once we got there, he turned shy again, going into the bathroom to take off his clothes and closing the door behind him, which was odd since he had such a great body. It occurred to me that perhaps he wanted to roll on a condom in private, which was probably a good thing since I couldn't picture myself doing it.

Maybe this was his first hookup too—in which case I didn't understand why he'd picked a nice Jewish widow whose profile said she was looking for a relationship, instead of someone who'd listed the acronyms for the sex acts they wanted and that I usually had to look up in the urban dictionary.

Attempting to make out in the living room had been bad enough. Now Austin was just a sliding door away from my bedroom, formerly George's and mine. I was lying in bed wearing my T-shirt and undies and felt like I was undergoing a stress test. I was starring in a film about a sedate, middle-aged widow who was trying to feel alive again by having sex with a stranger, although in actuality she was unraveling. But the original version would have been French and exquisitely nuanced, with Isabelle Huppert as *la Veuve*. I was starring in the clunky American remake.

Austin opened the door to the bathroom wearing only tight black briefs, but when he started to turn down the corner of my duvet, I panicked. "Time to leave. I'm sorry, I can't go through with this," I said, jumping back into my body and leaping out of bed.

Austin wasn't really a player and I wasn't really a cougar. Maybe this was what single people did so they didn't have to be alone at night. He too might have been lonely. He'd texted me every day the week before to ask about my day and tell me about his, chatting about his work meetings and a drinks party he was planning, as if laying the foundation for a friendship instead of a onetime hookup. Or maybe he was acting out his fantasy while I, in my anomie, lacked the boundaries to refuse.

"Are you sure? We were just getting started."

I assured him I was certain. I was worried he'd be mad, but he was already reaching for his sweater. Despite his puzzled expression, perhaps he too was relieved. He hadn't really seemed comfortable once we'd gotten out of the car and he had to move beyond his favorite hand-in-lap move.

I pulled on my jeans and a baggy sweater so I didn't have to put on my bra in front of him. He was already checking the train schedule on his phone. We sped to the station.

"So I guess we won't be doing this again," he said on the ride there.

"Um, no." We were silent for the rest of the drive. How could you have sex with someone you couldn't even talk to? I needed something strong enough to vanquish the raven of loneliness. Black-painted fingernails on a stranger's crotch was just an Instagram photo.

o o o o o

I'd googled Austin before we met, finding his LinkedIn page, online résumé, and Facebook profile. He was who he said he was, but.

This was my nadir, the most disconnected I'd ever been from my body. I'd known from that first moment at the train station a hookup wasn't for me when Austin put my hand in his lap. He'd expected me to jump into action, but it all just felt hilariously awkward. Thank god he didn't go for the head push.

I'd felt like I was talking to a child. All I could think to say to him was to be sure to get to his meetings on time and to serve food along with the drinks at his party so the people didn't get too drunk (I know, a bit hypocritical coming from me). It wasn't that he was unattractive. He was simply the wrong generation.

My dad and I used to play a game we called "How Old are We Today?" If one of us was behaving badly, the other would ask how old they were feeling. If I was missing my mom, I might be seventeen going on ten. When my dad was dating, he seemed like my eighteen-year-old brother discovering girls for the first time. Stressed out over preparing for a work conference, he would turn into a cranky twelve-year-old, albeit one with a PhD in theoretical physics.

*How old are we today?* Younger and dumber at fifty-one than I was at ten when my dad told me not to open the door for strangers.

I was a lot sadder than I'd thought I was if I was willing to try this shit. Having gone straight from my dad to my husband, I was blindsided by living alone. I bemoaned the lack of dear friends to rely on when I needed a Sunday dinner instead of a dive into Plenty of Fish.

I told myself I was intrigued to try something that was previously taboo. Perhaps I wanted to feel attractive and was flattered that I appealed to a handsome, much younger guy. Maybe I was punishing myself for checking out of my husband's death and thought I didn't deserve anything better than a hookup. Or maybe I was punishing George. *See, George, you thought I was done with sex, but I can still want it from this hottie.* Except that I didn't.

I never realized there was such a fine line between erotic exploration and dead husband revenge sex.

I'd already disregarded my instincts by being with Lowell and Denis. A hookup might be the next step to see if sex alone could satisfy the loneliness monster. But it couldn't. My fix for loneliness required actually being seen. This was a failed experiment, but if I was honest with myself, I knew it was going to fail from the start. It just seemed better than spending another dreary Sunday alone, my only human contact being the people who said "hello" to me on my walks. I wish I'd understood then that grief had eaten my judgment.

I last saw Austin in my rearview mirror as he was walking to the train platform and I was pulling away from the curb, shaking with relief. But on the drive home, there were no stars, as if they'd all disappeared. When I got home, I changed the sheets as if to erase the night.

# XI. Remedial Yoga

"LET'S MEET AT THE FARMER'S MARKET today after class," my new yoga instructor Caroline said one Saturday morning. She was my age, with perfect dark bobbed hair, an angelic face, long graceful limbs, and a playlist heavy on Prince.

I agreed, uncertain why she'd asked. I'd been at the studio for about a month and we'd chatted only briefly, determining that I hadn't done much flow yoga in the past, but since I had so much time, being widowed and all, I'd soon be able to catch up to the rest of the intermediate class. But she kept looking over at me during class and saying, "*Mula Bandha*," meaning to contract the pelvic floor so the body felt lighter. It just felt like I was trying not to pee.

Most of my classmates were far more advanced than I was. Their faces glowed but did not drip at the end of class; their breath stayed *ujjayi* calm instead of devolving into panting. They wore cheerful tank tops with stars and moons and "Spiritual Gangster" marching across the front, their yoga pants covered in flowers or tie-dye.

I stuck to my plain blacks and grays, not wanting to stand out. Even my mat was wrong, a cheap waffle-weave thing, too short so I was always readjusting it, while theirs were longer and sleeker, cool brands like Jade and Manduka, the relative merits of which they discussed vigorously and often.

I'd been to the farmer's market only once since George died. When we used to go together, he'd get this maniacal grin while walking down the aisles, spying English peas and announcing gleefully, "Tonight we are having Giuliano Bugialli's risotto *risi e bisi*," or he'd point to one of the stands and proclaim, "Look, zucchini blossoms for that Jeremiah Tower recipe you love so much."

On my one and only solo visit, I'd hurriedly bought an overpriced baked Brie so I could escape all the couples buying healthy produce together. I would be clogging up my arteries alone.

At least this time I was meeting someone, albeit someone impossibly willowy who exuded serenity. As we strolled along, Caroline exclaimed over homegrown tomatoes and leafy bunches of basil, adding some to her basket. I got some too, wanting to be more like her. She bought some cucumbers to have with almond milk to keep her energy up between classes.

I skipped those—I wasn't really that into having energy since it only made me sadder that I had no one to share it with. Pausing at a flower booth, I reached for some blue irises to cheer up my coffee table, then sighed and put them back. George had always bought the flowers.

After shopping, Caroline and I sat on a bench under the trees while she sipped her coffee, her one indulgence, and I ate my chocolate muffin, one of my many, the sunlight warm on our shoulders. Suddenly, her face crumpled.

"I wanted to talk to you today about a man I loved who died," she said, her voice a little higher than usual.

She inhaled deeply, as if relying on her yogic breathing to get through, then told me about meeting the man through mutual friends. It was too soon after her divorce for a real relationship, but he was sparkly and crazy about her, so she began seeing him anyway. After only a short time together, he became ill. She stayed with him until the very end, sleeping in his hospital room so he wouldn't have to be alone as he died.

"I know I helped him to die. It was what I was meant to do," she said, her eyes damp but calm as if she'd weathered a storm. "I want you to know that even though it's not the same, I can understand a little bit of what you've been through."

It wasn't the same at all, but it was an offer of friendship, unlike the usual stories of death people tossed out before scurrying away, as if certain a widow would want to hear about other losses, never considering she might actually need company. After Caroline finished, the air around us was still, as if all the surrounding bustle had been put on pause.

When Caroline touched our temples during *shavasana*, the rest at the end of class, her fingers carried an otherworldly tranquility. I could envision her bringing peace to someone on his deathbed. Hesitantly, I put my arm around her shoulders. Should I? Yes, it was what you did when your new friend was trying not to cry.

"Think of your body as one long line of energy," she said a few weeks later in Thursday night yoga class, again looking over at me as we moved from crescent lunge into warrior three. I wobbled on one leg, trying to think of my arms as wings the way she'd said, but they refused to think of themselves that way. I tottered and fell, a sagging U instead of one long line. I was a defeated vowel.

"A few of us are going out for drinks at the pizzeria next to the studio. You should come too," Laura said as we were rolling up our mats after class.

She was one of the Manduka girls, a full-figured X-ray technician in her early fifties with waves of auburn hair framing wary eyes and an upturned mouth. Maybe Caroline had put her up to it as a good deed. That was the bad part about being vulnerable—people knew your weaknesses.

On one of my late-night visits, my dad had said, as I sat sniveling as we watched old episodes of *The Pallisers*, "This would all be much better for you if you'd made some women friends over the years who you could rely on now."

When I was in college, he'd told me I needed to make friends with the girls in my dorm instead of spending all my time with George. Of course I'd ignored him. My college friendships were never very close since I came home every weekend, and they melted away soon after graduation. But he'd been right.

My mother's friendships looked like trading off on hosting bridge games and dinner parties, but I was too young to know if they ran any deeper. After she died, a divorced friend of hers had tried to date my dad. The woman kept bringing over covered dishes and patting my head, but her smile suggested a different kind of consolation, which seemed pretty gross to a ten-year-old.

My friends in law school were limited to the guys in my study group. Having been raised by a man, I was more comfortable with the task-oriented friendships of men rather than the fluid emotional speak of women. We did not appear weak.

*Say something back to her. You need friends.* I agreed to meet for drinks after class, feeling a little stab of happiness, hoping it wasn't misplaced.

"I need these times with the girls. It's been really hard since my divorce," Laura said later that evening, taking a sip of her Pinot Grigio. "My ex-husband is trying to get alimony from me. And that's after he cheated." That explained the wariness in her eyes.

I'd assumed the Manduka girls were partnered because they all seemed happy, at least during yoga class. It never occurred to me they could be happy on their own, or maybe like me they found bits of relief on their yoga mats, like nubs of caramel in an otherwise stale chocolate bar.

"I'm a widow too," Nancy said after I mentioned George. She smiled wryly, taking a sip of her IPA. "My husband died nine years ago. My women friends have been great. Men, not so much."

Another yogi, Nancy was also my age, a statuesque gardener with shoulder-length blonde curls and downturned lips, but her eyes sparkled as if she were looking for something to laugh about. She was also perfect at arm balances, including the dread flying pigeon.

I'd unofficially awarded myself the title of "Most in Pain," but these women too had known pain. Like me, they were still in pain. But unlike me, they were mothers with college-aged kids. After their divorces, Caroline and Laura had lost their homes and supported their children when their ex-husbands couldn't. Nancy's daughter had learning disabilities and lived in a group home where Nancy was a fierce advocate for her.

I wondered if I'd had kids, whether I would have had the strength to put their needs above mine after losing George, like my father had done for me. He'd canceled a few dates with Jane when I was upset as a teenager. Recently, she'd told me that she never minded. She was just thrilled to have found a man who had his priorities in order.

Had my fictional kids been on their own when George had died, I probably would have moved in with them and never left. "Sorry, my mom says she's too sad to stay home, so she's coming to all my classes with me," I could hear my imaginary daughter telling her college professor, handing me a tissue while answering that yes, I would be accompanying her for the entire year, as if we were starring in some distaff version of *Back to School*.

I watched the customers come in and out of the almost empty pizzeria to pick up their orders to take home and enjoy with their families. The three of us ordered a large Caesar salad to eat there, heavy on the anchovies.

"Yes, ma'am," said the young man serving us when I pointed to what we wanted on the menu. Having just been ma'amed, I felt the endorphins from class dissipate.

Did Nancy and Laura think I looked desiccated by widowhood?

Was I saying the right things to score a repeat invitation? Did they pity me because I had no children of my own to comfort me? I wondered if they'd ever seen me before class with Gene, especially when he was scowling or kissing me for too long in public.

"My divorced friend and I came up with the eight percent rule," Laura said. "Of all the married people we knew, we decided only eight percent of them were actually happy in their marriages." But marriage was so self-contained. I never thought about whether George and I had been happy until he was gone.

"That sounds too small," Nancy said. "I was happily married. But I don't think I'll ever be able to replace him. Every time I meet someone, I think, 'You've got some mighty big shoes to fill.' And they never do." She looked into her drink, her lips turning down even more as if remembering someone she'd rather forget.

"Eight percent seems way too low," I agreed, "but then I was happily married."

Yet happiness for me had come from absence—from not being stressed or having to practice law or doing anything that frightened me. George had picked our meals and organized our home and decided how we spent our time, but sometimes I had gotten sick of grocery shopping for all those recipes and I hated the wires shrouding our living room and I wanted to go away while he wanted to stay home.

But denial and contentment aren't that far apart. You tell yourself you're satisfied with the life you have; you don't really know what anything else would be like. Yet I was starting to think I'd had a lot of practice in deluding myself by the time he got sick.

"I think when it's the right time, the universe will provide us with love," Caroline said, coming to join us after her final class ended. She smiled her usual beatific smile, but her eyes were sad, and I could see the wrinkles in the corners as she no doubt remembered her own lengthy divorce.

I knew now that smile wasn't just yogic serenity but an act of will. She had the faith of a yogi and believed in a universe that provided what you asked of it, so long as you worked hard enough and were pure of heart.

The universe had taken my mom and George way too young. Best to stay out of its way.

The pizzeria had glaring overhead lights and sharp black furniture and the chairs didn't have cushions. It was too harsh a place for sharing confessions. I was ready to go home, afraid I would say something too revealing as the evening wore on. We finished our drinks and hugged each other goodbye, saying we'd do this again soon.

The Manduka girls couldn't have been more welcoming, but I still couldn't stop thinking of junior high when I'd discovered I probably wasn't destined to have girlfriends.

"You are so ugly," said Dawn and Lisa, the cool mean girls, plopping down behind me in seventh-grade algebra and kicking the back of my chair. I felt a sharp yank on my stringy brown hair.

"You should probably just die already," Lisa whispered. "You'll never have a boyfriend."

"Yeah, your mom probably died just to get away from you," said Dawn. I hunched over in my chair, pulling my legs up underneath me.

"Now it looks like she's trying to shove her legs up her twat," said Lisa, giggling.

I could go to the teacher, sitting placidly at her desk while we were supposed to be working on our assignments, but she'd never helped me out in the past. The mean girls would act like we were all friends, and the teacher would just look perplexed, like maybe my mother's death had left me an attention whore.

It was even worse in PE, where Lisa and Dawn had more recruits, girls who'd stare at me while we changed clothes. "She doesn't even have any boobs yet," one of them said. "That's totally the wrong kind of bra," another would chime in. If I failed to serve the volleyball over the net (like that even mattered in real life), they'd glare at me. "She is so fucking useless," another would cackle.

"Ugly Deborah."

"De-Bra." Of course the other girls shunned me too, not wanting to be associated with a pariah.

The junior high school was just a few blocks from my house, but the walk home still felt long. I'd slouch past the Kentucky Fried Chicken, the thrift store, the Western-style Danville Hotel, and the rock quarry, hoping none of the older boys who worked there had noticed me. Turning my key in the front door, I finally felt safe.

Inside, I'd tear off my dad-approved school clothes—a high-necked navy-blue dress. The cool girls all wore Dittos jeans, the seams curving over their butts like horseshoes. My dad would never have gone for that.

I'd pull on my swimsuit, still damp from the shower, hating the silver bamboo wallpaper my mom had chosen and giving the wall a nice hard kick. It added another to the small line of dents I'd made on days like this. I'd go to the kitchen to grab the battered copy of *Steppenwolf* that I'd found in my dad's den, then lay out by the pool, ignoring the list of chores posted on the fridge.

I still had my own evil chore to finish before Dad got home from work. I'd been forging his name on notes to get out of PE, and after that day, it was definitely time for another one. I'd gone to the useless guidance counselor once again to complain, but she'd just said to try to get along with those girls. Even the dead mother card hadn't worked. They could all think I was dying of dysmenorrhea for all I cared.

When I went to college, those bitches would be living in an after-school TV special, burned out at sixteen, struggling to get by on pizza crusts, their boyfriends having dumped them in favor of the good girls, the ones who hadn't put out. But life still sucked, and I doubted whether the fates were really that even-handed. They'd taken my mother and left me with these little sadists, after all.

There had to be something wrong with me, to have my mom die, to have gotten picked on, to have no one to help me with the mean girls even though I was a good student who always followed the rules—at least until I'd started forging notes because the universe was too damn hostile for conventional morality.

A mom would have taken me shopping and helped me to pick out makeup and clothes that made me look like the Dittos-clad, delicately lip-glossed models in *Seventeen*, like the mean girls looked. (Although having read my mom's copy of *Diary of a Teenaged Prom Queen*, she might have just laughed at my requests.)

All I had was my dad saying, "A thirteen-year-old girl does not wear makeup." When I jumped in the pool, the iridescent turquoise eye shadow and black mascara I'd secretly glopped on during my walk to school ran down my face, but it had looked terrible to begin with, like I was trying out for the role of child prostitute. It was my war paint, and I'd been defeated.

I joined Harry Haller in his agony and accepted alienation as the human condition, or at least mine from other thirteen-year-olds. I spent hours floating in the pool, looking up at the sky, in a world with no laundry or bullies, wishing I never had to leave the house, pretending I could have met Hermann Hesse. Dad would have invited him over for dinner, and I would have made my first Sachertorte.

Freud thinks people's personalities are forged during their first few years of life, but I think it happens when puberty attacks. If my mother had lived, maybe I could have seen myself becoming a mom and shepherding my own kid through adolescence. If I hadn't been bullied, maybe I wouldn't have been so certain I was defective. As it was, at fifty-one, I still looked up the mean girls on Facebook and contemplated hiring an assassin.

Thanks to junior high, I never really trusted groups of women, especially women combined with physical activity. Perhaps if I'd made friends over the years instead of having relied on George alone to buoy me up, he wouldn't have thought I was too weak to help him when he got sick. But I couldn't rewrite the past; I could just keep grading myself on it.

Caroline kept saying, "There are no grades in yoga," but there were always grades, whether it was balancing in the crow pose, making partner at a law firm, or even recovering from grief—like the way massages were good but falling into bed with the person giving the massage was bad. So was taking him back after you knew he was damaged. I might be flunking Widowhood 101.

Caroline, Laura, and Nancy were part of a loose tribe of women from the yoga studio. After drinks that Thursday night, I became one of the tribe. Several of them had been single for many years, and I admired them as they planned vacations together and traveled to new places alone and fixed their own broken plumbing and refinished their own furniture.

My phone started pinging with long text threads every time they scheduled a group outing. Nancy usually took the lead, starting with getting thirteen women to agree to one date. Over time there were Yogathons and paddleboard yoga and restorative yoga classes with singing bowls, and even parties for birthdays and hysterectomies where we didn't do any yoga at all.

There were firsts, like the first time one of the yoga girls who lived near me asked if I wanted to carpool to a party with her, and the first time I asked her if she wanted to. There was the first time I asked Nancy out to lunch, just the two of us, despite being intimidated by her stellar arm balances and organizational skills.

There was the first time I had Caroline over for dinner, and she said I was a great hostess even though all I'd done was buy quiche and brownies, which she actually nibbled at. There was my first yoga retreat—three days with the girls in the woods near Yosemite, my otherness melting away like the snow off the pines. The women spoke differently from the men I'd known, with none of the one upmanship the way my dad's friends and the guys from my law firm talked to each other. When Laura texted that she and her boyfriend had broken up, within a few hours Nancy, Caroline, and I met her for dinner. When Caroline was alone on a holiday weekend, we gathered at her apartment for an evening of aura readings and Oreo-encrusted cake.

I too began to speak of my emotions, admitting that sometimes I felt too sad to leave the house instead of trying to appear strong like I did with my other groups: "Yup, widowhood's been great, dropped a few pounds, and plenty of time to replant those flower beds!" Being willing to appear weak had become a strength.

George and I had dinner together almost every night, and I never would have left him to go out with the girls, much less abandon him for an entire weekend to attend a yoga retreat. It made me sad that his loss was the catalyst that allowed me to give that sad, slumping twelve-year-old, her arms crossed protectively over her training-bra-clad chest, a big hug goodbye and, finally, to let her go.

We'd linger in the studio after Caroline's Saturday morning class, sitting on the blond wood floor, chatting away as cars pulled in and out of the parking lot and sunlight streamed through the windows. My new friendships were as sweet as a sixteen-year-old girl's room decorated with painted fans, silver-embroidered pillows, lacquered parasols, and Carole King's *Tapestry* playing on the stereo.

I thought perhaps this life too could be good.

# XII. When Men Become Rooms

"I THINK WE NEED TO DO THIS ANOTHER TIME," I said to Francis at the start of the phone call we'd scheduled after he contacted me online. "I'm in a really bad mood."

It was another one of those Sundays. I no longer ran over to my dad's house on Sunday nights, but my loss still pulsed a bloody crimson when I was home alone hearing my next-door neighbors having a party, although sometimes it receded to a shell-like pink after an outing with my yoga girls.

"But this is the best time to talk because I get the real you," Francis said. Who wanted that?

"I just hate the whole dating thing right now," I said. "Don't you ever get that way?"

"I don't have to. I haven't found anyone promising lately so I'm not wasting my time. I'm happy on my own. I just adopted an adorable Labrador rescue dog. We're making butternut squash soup tonight, then we're going to watch a movie together, aren't we?" he said. His voice lilted as he addressed his last sentence to the dog.

Francis was five feet ten inches tall, a bit stocky with glowing olive skin, graying black hair, a well-trimmed beard, and a smile that radiated contentment. He looked like someone who made his own soup. A paralegal living in Oakland who ran a catering business on the side, he'd been divorced many years. He had two adult kids and a clutch of close friends.

I'd answered his message on OkCupid because he seemed happy. While we were talking, I checked out his Facebook page, which showed him romping on the beach with his dog, looking just as happy as he sounded over the phone. I wanted to be more like Francis.

So many guys' profiles started out, "My third live-in girlfriend just left me and she took the cat." Or they warned, "Do not contact me if you're not over your ex or you need a sugar daddy or you've lost your lease." Or they were trying out some alternative lifestyle involving tantric bondage and extreme composting that I didn't want to know about.

I told Francis I wasn't into cooking, but he said, "How do you know you don't like to cook? Did anyone ever try to teach you? What do you like to eat?"

"Everything," I answered, leaving out, "so long as I don't have to eat it alone." I also left out that I still feared the kitchen's secret death powers.

"What if I come over to your house on Saturday night and we make paella together? I'll bring the ingredients. You get some wine and snacks to keep us going while we cook," he said.

"You're offering to give up your Saturday night to make me paella?" I said just to be sure.

"That's right," said Francis. "I'd love to cook with you. But you'll be doing most of the work. I'll be teaching you."

I accepted gratefully.

"So you said on the phone that you're seeing a few guys, but you're not serious about any of them," Francis said that Saturday evening as he showed me how to devein the shrimp.

He'd come bearing a grocery bag overflowing with paella ingredients, a carrying case with his own knives, and a bag with two white chef's aprons inside. He pulled them out, tying one around his waist, then helping me to tie mine.

"That's right," I said. "That's why I'm free tonight." I stopped myself from saying deveining the shrimp had been George's job. I was too embarrassed to tell Francis that George had used a special extra-sharp knife I had not been allowed to touch—not that I'd wanted to.

I could imagine Francis hesitating for a moment, not wanting to criticize my late husband, but finally saying that was ridiculous and that he should have taught me. I thought of myself as an incompetent sous chef, limited to the tasks George had assigned me, but I took Francis's knife and ran it along the back of a shrimp, pulling out the dark gray spine. It wasn't difficult, but I didn't see the point without having someone to share the finished result with.

"Why don't you just hold out for the right person instead of wasting your time?" said Francis, slicing the fish into even pieces, then showing me how to hold both the knife and the fish so that neither of them slipped. He watched as I tried to make my slices as thin and uniform as his. Though I matched neither his skill nor his equilibrium, they turned out fine. He smiled at me as if to say, "See, that wasn't so hard after all."

Why hadn't my husband taught me how to use all the knives? Probably because I had never asked. I had been intimidated by their sharpness. But a sharp knife is less dangerous than a dull one.

"I'm not even sure who the right person would be," I said.

"I'm not sure I've met the right person yet either," said Francis, looking down, suddenly shy. "But I can usually tell from the start whether we have a future. And if I don't see a future, I'm out of there." He added some saffron to the pot of broth on the stove, opening his hand as if to say "presto" and make all his bad dates magically disappear.

"Well, you know I'm just dating around for now," I said, not wanting to lead him on. He lived forty-five minutes away and had to hire a dog sitter for the evening. He wouldn't have organized a paella fest for someone he didn't see a future with.

"Never believe you can't cook," he said as he added the onions to the pot, but I sensed he wanted to say something more.

We hovered over the stove and put in the rice, fish, prawns, mussels, and tomatoes in turn and let each cook for the prescribed amount of time. Our mouths watered as the kitchen started to smell of saffron and garlic, and we nibbled on the almonds, olives, and Manchego I'd bought to tide us over. Francis's smile lit up the room.

I beamed back, surprised to see my kitchen come alive again, the ingredients scattered across the countertop like a high-end grocery store. My stove simmering once again with something good.

Francis set the table with George's favorite stoneware bowls. Finally, we whipped off our aprons and sat at the dining room table, now transformed into *Chez* Francis, savoring the flavors of seafood and broth and crooning over its perfection.

"You deserve the best," Francis said, putting down his fork and looking pointedly at me. "At some point you'll stop compromising."

*So that's what he wanted to say before*, I thought. I wondered if he meant that he was the best and he was willing to wait until I saw it too.

After dinner, he put the leftover paella in the fridge, refusing to take any home with him. He said I'd have enough food for the week, as if he'd already figured out I ate badly when I was alone. I thanked him a little too profusely, overwhelmed by his thoughtfulness.

He stood over the sink and scrubbed the pots, the water splashing on his tomato-stained apron. As he talked about adopting his dog from the rescue facility, the sadness was released from my kitchen. It had been replaced by the scent of saffron.

It was the best night I'd had since George died.

"Would you like to learn to make Beef Bourguignon next Saturday?" he asked as he was leaving, putting down his knife case to give me a long hug goodbye. For once, I had something to look forward to on a weekend besides coffee with a strange man followed by takeout with Nancy Botwin.

For my second lesson, Francis surprised me by bringing over little dishes of crème brûlée, showing me how to caramelize the tops with a mini blow torch just like the chefs on TV. We spent another perfect night cooking. The beef turned out velvety and rich, and the crème brûlée tasted like caramelized bliss. Francis was a serious instructor, but he lit up my kitchen and left me with a kiss on the cheek, food for the week, and a warmth that penetrated my icicle heart.

I had so many leftovers that I brought some over to my dad's the next day.

"We like Francis," my dad said, his spoon piercing the honey-colored crust on the crème brûlée.

"I made that crust," I told him proudly.

"For this I paid for law school?"

"You've got custard in your beard."

"You look more relaxed than I've seen you in months," he said. That was because the kitchen's secret death powers were weakening.

The next time I brought him leftovers, he asked, "Have you given any thought to marrying Francis?"

But I worried I was using him.

Francis and I talked about almost everything—how to handle a friend who was taking him for granted, a bad coffee date he'd had, and even how much I missed George. Most of the other men I'd dated just assumed I'd be whatever they needed, a therapist for reliving past loves, or a girl Friday who lived to serve, or a chick who was down to fuck on short notice.

But Francis was different. He paused in the middle of his stories to see if I was interested and asked me questions when I told him my own stories.

I told Francis we could only be friends because I liked him too much. Once you started dating someone, he became temporary. Francis said he understood, but I knew at some point he was going to want to do more than bake.

I watched him stir a pan of mushroom duxelles on the stove, admiring him, but feeling no desire for him physically. I could see us living together platonically, hosting dinner parties for my yoga girls, making a St. Honoré cake for dessert, chatting about a new Bundt mold we needed to buy, but I couldn't see us together in bed.

One night he kissed me deeply in the darkness before we were about to start a movie, opening my mouth with his own. I went blank. "Are you all right?" he asked.

I assured him I was, liking him just as much as ever but feeling as if I'd just used someone else's toothbrush. Maybe I wasn't attracted to him because there was something feminine about him. He had the empathy I'd so missed in the other men I'd dated. But his voice was high-pitched and he moved in a way that wasn't traditionally masculine, like the way George moved.

Or perhaps it was the way he watched me intently as if to see when I was going to come to my senses and stop seeing other men. I wanted to tell him I was hiding the bad parts, the unresolved guilt and incessant neediness, like the way I hid my imperfections by using more concealer after a makeup artist had advised me when I went for a makeover.

"Good for me" and "sexual attraction" had failed to converge. And having reawakened my desire, I didn't want to put it back to sleep, even if I could have. But I've always wondered if I would have felt differently about Francis had my grief been more resolved when we met, and if, when he looked into my eyes, I could have looked back into his without flinching.

o o o o o

"Would you like a tour of my ranch? I could make dinner and show you around," texted Buck, a cowboy and songwriter I'd met for coffee more than a month ago.

He had a fringe of blond hair peeking out from under a cowboy hat, a lanky six-foot-three-inch frame hardened by farm work, and a sexy sidelong look delivered by dark, slightly beady, marble-like eyes. During our initial coffee date he'd been so quiet I never expected to hear from him again, even though he'd treated me to that look several times, apparently in lieu of words.

As I drove over to the ranch, the backroads stretched out before me like a ribbon. I arrived just as the sun was setting over the hills, bathing everything a glowing auburn.

Buck poured us each a glass of red wine and took me on a tour. The ranch looked like the movie set of an old Western, with antique farm equipment long unused, whitewashed cottages available to rent on Airbnb, and a recording studio tucked into one of the old barns. The entire place was available for weddings and photo shoots.

Back in his own cottage, Buck sautéed chicken for fajitas while I stood next to him chopping mushrooms. He was in a red-and-blue plaid shirt, and I wore a black V-necked shirt. I felt like our arms were touching even though they weren't. Cooking a meal with someone you barely know creates a false sense of intimacy.

Over dinner at his battered wooden table, he kept our wine glasses full while we talked about Gene Prine, Alan Watts, and the intersection of consciousness with quantum physics. I tried to keep up, mesmerized by that sidelong look, and wondered if this was a seduction scene or one of those romantic movies that were all conversation.

"We could sit outside," he said after dinner. "I put a bonfire together." I felt the camera move in for a close-up as we sat in camping chairs under the pine trees and listened to the embers crackle. He went inside to get a second bottle of red wine. When I protested that I had to drive home, he said I could stay over in one of the guest cottages. I agreed that I could, and wondered if he'd come join me.

"If you added up the length of my three marriages, they'd be as long as your one relationship," he said with a wry laugh when he returned with the second bottle.

"Life never turns out the way we expect," I said carefully, feeling the fire's warmth on my face.

"I think it's wrong to be stuck with just one person. I'm done with that. I need to be free without any commitments," he said, pouring us each another glass of wine. "I was feeling pretty trapped by the end of my last marriage."

"I get it," I said. "I was with my husband for so long these are my college years to experiment." I didn't add that it was only a phase—that eventually I hoped to find real love with one person. But that wasn't the stuff of first-date chitchat, especially with someone who fancied himself a libertine.

"I'm seeing another lady who's also a widow, but I'm not into monogamy or possessiveness. I consider myself free to see other people," he said.

So he was laying down his terms: if we got together, I'd have to share. But we'd only just met, and I was seeing other people too.

"I totally get the detachment thing," I said. "I just want to have fun for now."

There, we'd set out our parameters: freedom first, no obligations, live for today, and a bunch of other clichés born of wine and, in my case, wanting to seem cool. Our talk of quantum physics hadn't been very impressive either. We stared into the fire as if it could tell us what to do next.

Suddenly, he leaned over with a mouth full of red wine and kissed me so that it poured from his mouth into mine. Thankfully

I managed to swallow, so it didn't spill down the front of my shirt. I pretended not to be surprised, babbling on as if nothing had happened. As we talked, I got a few more of those messy kisses that sent sparks flying through my rib cage.

He looked at me seriously as if to confirm that I understood commitment wasn't part of the bargain, then he picked me up and carried me effortlessly to the bedroom, our mediocre dialogue turning into a sexy fadeout. Putting my arms around his neck, I smelled hay, spicy cologne, and studied nonchalance.

Buck was a caveman, tearing off my clothes, tossing me on the bed, and inhaling me all at once. I was acting out a fantasy I'd never even known I had. I'd been with so few men I didn't know what I liked. Had I told Buck he was only the fourth man I'd ever been with, he probably would have run, afraid I'd lay claim to his freedom. I lay awake most of the night, imagining I was in the old West, waiting for the sun to rise, and feeling way too exposed.

When I got home the next morning, I had a huge grin on my face and purple hickeys on my neck and thigh. I photographed them as a souvenir of my belated youth, unable to stop humming the Georgia Satellites' song "Keep Your Hands to Yourself," giggling over words about cows and free milk. I was the cow and I'd given away the milk for free. I burrowed in my bed and tried to absorb the newness of it all. I was still smiling when I went to writing group later that day.

"Why do you look like the cat who ate the canary, although I think I have some idea," Delilah said with a mock innocent smile when I arrived. She widened her big green eyes so that she too looked like a beautiful cat, albeit a slightly surprised one.

I kept picturing Buck and I riding horses over the tawny hills behind the ranch, then going for a romp in the hay, even though I hadn't been on a horse since I was nine and that was just riding around in a circle, the horse firmly tethered to a ring in the middle, and hay was probably really scratchy. Still, I wanted to be a cowgirl. Even though Buck would probably never call me again since I'd already given away the cookie.

"I was a bad girl," I told my yoga friends over Thursday night drinks. "I slept with a guy on the first date."

"It's practically a rite of passage," said Nancy, her lips turning up as if she was recalling a private memory. "A lot of women have one-night stands after the end of a long marriage. Just don't read anything into it. Take it for what it was."

"I had some good times after my divorce," said Laura with a secret little smile, her lips turning up even more. But Caroline just stayed silent, and I knew she was biting her tongue to stop from advising me to hold out for love.

A few days later I got a text from Buck: "Redheads are addictive. Do you want to get together again?"

This time he came over to my house bringing wine and popcorn. I supplied the home theater system and my neurosis.

After another overnight at the ranch spent hot tubbing into the early morning hours, I left without my thong, unable to find it in the tangled bedding. I congratulated myself on finally living out my madcap college years. But my instincts told me I was going to get hurt.

Buck was a challenge—the kind of guy I never would have gotten in high school—but his cowboy machismo and emotional ice weren't for me. I couldn't really be detached about someone I was sleeping with. It just wasn't my nature.

I was living in two different worlds with Buck and Francis, one clinging to freedom and the other seeking love. I was getting ravished one night and then nurtured the next. I wanted both of them, and something more, something I was afraid to admit was love because that would have made me vulnerable. Worse, in order to accept love, I had to believe I was worthy of it, and that's where my guilt came in.

○ ○ ○ ○ ○

"You are by far the most beautiful and captivating woman I've met for some time," David said ten minutes into our first date, a weeknight dinner at Bridges. He managed to look both at me and through me at the same time.

I refrained from saying, "Then you haven't gotten out much." It was the kind of joke George would have made.

David was five feet ten inches tall, in his early sixties, an architect with his own firm who spent most of his time working. Dapper in a black suit and thick black-rimmed glasses, he was devoid of any distinguishing features save for a red face, as if everything made him blush.

"My work and my two grown kids are the two pillars of my life. A relationship would be the third," he said. So architects really did speak in terms of structures.

I ordered a Hendrick's martini. He ordered one too, noting we had the same favorite drink as if we were destined to be together. But I had a feeling he probably would have asked for an extra-sour kumquat daiquiri, heavy on the whipped cream, if that's what I'd ordered.

"I want to have one last great romance before I fizzle out," he said, sipping his drink. "It would be my last relationship."

We agreed to split a hamachi appetizer, both deciding on the grilled salmon with quinoa as our entrees, signaling our health consciousness. But it all felt terribly fraught with peril for a first date. We talked about the proper curriculum for liberal arts colleges, both agreeing a little too fervently that calculus should be a requirement even for English majors.

"I find you attractive in so many ways," he said suddenly.

"I have a lot of flaws," I said weakly. "I don't like to travel far for dates, or drive at night, and . . ." I couldn't continue. David was looking at me as hopefully as if he'd just discovered a new kind of truss. At some point his giddy infatuation was bound to deflate. That's what happened when you filled in the blanks with what you wanted them to be.

"What are you looking for?" he asked.

"I'm still trying to figure that out," I said. "Of course, who wants to live without love?" Too late I realized that in my effort not to sound shallow, I instead sounded soppily romantic.

"It is terrible to live without love," he agreed, his cheeks flushing even more.

After the plates were cleared, he ordered us each a second martini, then reached across the table for my hand, clasping it a little too tightly. "Are you a bit of a princess?" he asked. "But I already know the answer to that." We were both half-Hungarian Jews whose families used to live in Brooklyn. Despite our stilted conversation, he might have a genetic window into my soul, but I was pretty sure he didn't really see me.

"I used to be."

"Jewelry? I want to know what I'm in for."

"I have all of that stuff. Now, I want to have experiences," I heard myself say smoothly as if I were reading my lines off a teleprompter.

I guessed jewelry was how he referred to commitment. It was way too soon for either, but he'd said it himself: he hadn't met anyone promising for a long time, so he'd decided I was the one. After all his searching, someone had to be.

As I looked at him across the table, he reminded me of a baby bird, its heart beating visibly in its little feathered chest. I agreed to see him again because he seemed so right on paper and I was so far from being three-dimensional.

For our second date he made me dinner at his Craftsman-style house high in the Berkeley Hills. "You can write in here once you start staying over," he said, showing me his spare office during the tour of his home.

I felt a chill, not knowing it had already been decided. His home was lovely, with thick white walks and dark wood beams, but he moved around it lugubriously as if he were covered in moss.

Over predinner martinis on his deck, he stared at me intensely but had little to say other than commenting that the sunset wasn't very good that night, as if he should have ordered a different one.

After many minutes of silence, he said, "You're wonderful." I, in turn, could think of nothing to say back to him. It was as if we'd both misplaced our personalities, or our screenwriter had taken the night off.

On our third date, he said it was time we had sex. It seemed right. We were both stable, liberal Jewish professionals. That, and we'd both had several martinis. I didn't really want to, though, never having felt comfortable with him, but I disregarded those thoughts.

He seemed really nervous, leaving on most of his clothes, touching me as if I were an urgent to-do item he needed to check off his list. Perhaps he too was disregarding his instincts in order to play the role he thought he should. As he hovered over me, I saw us from above, contorted as if we were playing a game of Twister.

I was getting used to taking off my clothes for strange men.

"You don't have to settle. You deserve the best," Francis said each time I saw him over homemade chocolate tarts or Hungarian goulash or a well-curated plate of takeout sushi. But he didn't have to settle either, and he knew it; he deserved to be with someone who was in love with him.

I had procured babysitters for all the rooms in my house: Francis in the kitchen, Buck in the bedroom, and David in the living room, where we had tortured conversations before he pounced at me. I didn't know how to live in my empty space other than to fill it with men. I was even seeing Denis again after he'd surprised me with a romantic seaside overnight during which he mentioned neither getting tested nor being exclusive. But I was just using him to avoid being alone.

Life had become surreal. I was wallowing in my poofy bed, stockpiling men so I wouldn't be alone in case one of them defected. It was like buying the uber carton of toilet paper on Amazon even though you were the only person living at your house.

One widow emailed me through my blog, saying, "The worst thing about being single is waking up in the middle of the night, feeling overwhelmingly anxious and having no one in bed next to you." Exactly. But I was too removed to notice that having the wrong person in bed next to you was even worse.

# XIII. Red Flags I Never Should Have Ignored

1. Acted like my time was worth less than his
2. Always had to be right
3. Anger issues
4. Asked me to pay without checking beforehand
5. Blamed me for his past problems with women
6. Couldn't handle my talking about George
7. Danville bashing
8. Debbie bashing
9. Depressed
10. Didn't care about his health
11. Didn't appreciate women his own age
12. Expected me to fix him
13. Excessive drinking
14. Ex bashing
15. Inability to compromise
16. Kept changing meeting times and canceling
17. Monogamy bashing
18. Narcissistic
19. Never satisfied
20. No time for a relationship
21. Not over his exes
22. Overly critical

23. Overly possessive
24. Put his needs above mine
25. Put no time into the relationship
26. Rude to others
27. Selfish in bed
28. Stingy
29. Stuck in his ways
30. Took his bad moods out on me
31. Tried to change me into a doormat
32. Wanted a premature commitment
33. Wanted to split meals but was a picky eater
34. Wouldn't come to my place
35. Aspirin is not a food group

# XIV. Knees Together

"YOU'RE AN ALPHA FEMALE. You're having trouble findin' guys 'cause they're not alpha males. Women want what's down here," Buck said, slurring his words together during another movie night at my house. He'd already chugged a bottle and a half of Cabernet, then lain back on the couch, patting his dick so often he might have been masturbating.

I was speechless.

"I could have sex with a lot more women if I wanted to," he said a few minutes later. "Last month, this Western wear company shot their ad campaign at the ranch and there was this twenty-four-year-old model I could've fucked. I turned her down because she was too young, but she wanted me."

Then he passed out, the alpha male, all long limbs akimbo. His flannel-clad arm snaked across the back of my sofa, his cowboy boots sat by the fireplace, and his mouth was finally, mercifully silent.

"You're pedantic and you're a dork, but you have a good heart," he said, waking up a half hour later, still in a drunken haze.

Ouch. In one night, actually one nap, I'd gone from hot to dorky. Maybe it was because on our first date I'd talked about quantum physics, but it was probably because he could see through my pretend coolness to the big ugly crush lurking underneath.

In high school, when our freshman English teacher couldn't recall a word meaning inherently contradictory, I'd spoken up proudly, offering the word in question, "oxymoron," and causing my classmates to stare. Back then, I couldn't wait to move on to an advanced English class so I'd no longer be surrounded by empty desks. I thought I'd left my high school self behind, but she was still there, wounded after a disastrous date with one of the cool guys.

"Oxymoron," a figure of speech in which seemingly contradictory terms appear in conjunction, like "painless dating."

Realizing what he'd just said, Buck apologized, but it was too late. Now I knew what he really thought of me. The worst part had been the "good heart" comment. I let him sleep it off on the couch, grateful to hear the door slam an hour later as he shambled off to his truck.

He texted me during the week asking to get together again, but I just couldn't. If I saw him, those deadly words would be all I would hear. I wanted to reclaim my dignity, or at least impugn his own.

I texted back, "You got all Don Draper on me the other night. After saying you could've fucked a twenty-four-year-old model, you passed out drunk."

"Poor old Debbie, jealous of a twenty-four-year-old girl," he texted.

Not exactly, but the way he'd talked about her had made him seem ugly and insecure. Worse, he wasn't that far off. I wasn't jealous of the model, but I was jealous of his other lover, who he'd previously told me was also a widow.

He'd told me she liked bondage and she wore the same kind of underwear I did, joking that it must be a widow thing, like being widowed meant wearing black thongs instead of wondering how much longer you wanted to keep on living without your husband. I'd just laughed, not wanting to seem oversensitive, but he made she and I sound like fungible fuck buddies, an ugly expression I hadn't known when I was married.

He'd also told me she was very wealthy and wanted to take him on vacation with her. I pictured him staying at her house in Hawaii, falling in love with her over coconut cream eggs Benedict, spending far more nights with her than he did with me, finally becoming her boyfriend.

I wondered if he made her breakfast on the nights she stayed over. He'd never made me breakfast or even offered to. He just pulled on his coveralls early the next morning and said he had to get to work. Either she and I were interchangeable, or he liked her better because she had more to offer.

Now I knew; I was too analytical for non-monogamy.

"I want my thong back," I texted him.

A few seconds later I received his response. "No, I'm keeping it as your punishment. Sincerely, Don Draper."

There was sexual freedom in theory. Then there was being sexually free with a prick.

I'd been seeing a lover who didn't like me very much. After his drunken ramblings during our last date, I doubted he liked women in general very much. Worst of all, I hadn't been able to tell.

He was probably twirling my thong around his finger, putting it in a drawer with who knew how many others, his beady little eyes scrunched up with laughter. I'd always thought they looked a little hollow. I should have listened to my dad when he'd said "knees together" every time I left the house.

*Could you date a misogynist?* Why didn't they come with hazard warnings?

"I know you're unavailable sometimes because you're seeing other people," Denis said the next time he called, wanting to get together.

"I never lied. I told you I need someone who's around more," I said.

Denis was so overloaded there was barely room in his life left for him, not to mention a possible partner. He should have probably just gotten into sexting and been done with it.

"I've never been in a relationship with someone where I haven't gotten closer to that person as we've spent more time together," he said. Then he added ponderously, "And we *are* in a relationship."

But you probably weren't in a relationship if you had to remind the other person that you were.

"Is it my fault you don't feel closer?" I said.

He offered only scattered dates at odd times, checking his watch after sex, then scurrying away like a fugitive, saying he had to get home to his kids, leaving me to return to my bed feeling faintly corrupted. That wasn't a relationship; it was being on call.

"I want *real* intimacy," he said, as he had several times before.

But someone who needed to modify the word "intimacy" with the word "real" probably had a history of faking it. To me there was only one kind of intimacy, unmodified, and it was the kind I'd had with George, which had lasted our entire lives, and it came from being there for each other.

It was almost the holidays. I'd found a dead robin in my planter, perfectly intact, its body frozen, its soft brown wings spread as if in flight, its black eyes opaque and vacant. It was the man's job to get rid of the dead animals. The next day I steeled myself, scooped the robin up with a shovel, and tossed it into the landscaping bin. It was nothing really, but I kept seeing its little face long afterward.

If I ever felt inconsolably sad, like when my dad got sick, George would sit next to me, our arms touching, silent, and he would just look at me and offer sympathy. He wouldn't leave, even after a really long time. Even when I said he should go, that there was nothing he could do.

I knew he would stay for whatever I was going through; he

couldn't bear not to be together, even if all he could do was watch. It was one of the greatest gifts he ever gave me. Robin's eyes, George's eyes.

My world had turned icy without him.

Now that I was alone, intimacy to me meant being able to tell someone how I really felt, like someone was squeezing my lungs so hard I could barely breathe. The raven of loneliness had returned with the holidays, and my frenzied dating schedule was no longer enough to keep it at bay.

"I don't think I can go through November and December seeing someone without love," I told Denis.

Living without love was starting to unnerve me. It hit me when I was walking to my car after evening yoga or buying frost cloths to cover my plants. I might hole up in my house for the winter and never again leave. Like the robin, I too would probably die alone.

"I hear you," said Denis. But I knew he didn't.

"I'm thinking of swearing off dating until after the holidays," I said.

"I hear you."

"Look, you say you want real intimacy," I said, finally getting to the point. "Here's the real problem. I don't want to spend Thanksgiving Day alone." I hung up quickly, horrified that I'd just sounded vulnerable.

Only the week before, I'd thrown my phone across the room trying to juggle my crowded social schedule, but unless I made plans, I'd be spending my second widowed Thanksgiving alone. I always had to make plans, whether it was finding someone to eat with, or talk to, or curl up with at night. And if it was someone to curl up with, it had to be someone who mattered, or more precisely, someone to whom I mattered.

My college years had lasted less than four months, but already I was sick of them.

Over the next two weeks, Denis kept texting, asking why I wouldn't see him, rather melodramatically saying the world didn't make sense, meaning *I* didn't make sense, and not so subtly sending me a video of Louis Armstrong singing about spending one last night together. Denis professed to be a feminist, yet he was trying to hound me into seeing him.

By now I'd dated several men who expounded at length whenever we disagreed, often using my limited life experience against me as if I were too naive to understand them. But if I wanted people to talk over me, I would have kept practicing law.

Bowling over someone's arguments might work in a court-room, but not with a friend, or worse, someone you were sleeping with. I doubted he'd tolerate my doing the same, listening to me expound that his short, failed marriage meant he didn't under-stand commitment, or lawyersplaining how I thought he'd mishandled his career.

I kept telling Denis that if we were in a relationship, he'd include me in his Thanksgiving plans. His parents were flying in from New York to spend the holiday with him and his teenagers at a rented farmhouse. He'd previously said that real intimacy meant we could tell each other anything.

"I wouldn't want my family to know I'm seeing someone I met through an online dating site," Denis said wearily when it was clear I wasn't going to give up. "Besides, there couldn't be any intimacy between us when I'm with my family."

Ah, he was referring to physical intimacy as opposed to "real." He didn't need a modifier for that kind. Perhaps I'd made a mistake in thinking I could separate the two.

"I can control myself," I singsonged like an irritated teenager. And why would his parents have to know we met online, unless he told them?

"What would I tell my parents?" he said.

"Tell them I'm a recent widow who needs a family to celebrate the holiday with," I said slowly and deliberately.

Perhaps if we hadn't had sex and he had still been pursuing me, I would have been an acceptable friend to introduce to his family. But people treated their dates far worse than they treated their friends. There seemed to be almost no overlap between the two.

"What if we spent the weekend before Thanksgiving together?" he said. So he could spend a couple of days getting his rocks off, yet remain blissfully unconcerned that I'd be spending the holiday alone.

I'd become the girl in high school the popular guy did in his Trans Am but didn't take to the prom. I guess good girls still didn't. Even if they were fifty-one-year-old women having what they thought was grown-up sex with middle-aged men. From married princess to pork-subsidizing vagina.

I never saw Denis again.

*Could you date someone who didn't care about you? Res Ipsa Loquitur*: The thing speaks for itself.

But to be fair—Denis got to decide who his kids spent time with, just like he got to decide when he had to go home to them. He seemed to have them far more than half the time, the eldest eighteen and the youngest thirteen.

With my nocturnal dad, I'd gotten myself off to school by myself at thirteen. We'd often eaten dinner with the women he was dating no matter what they did when I wasn't around. They had just been friends who were fun to talk to and wore sexy Bohemian tops and hip-hugger jeans he'd never let me wear. One of them had even taken me to get my stringy hair cut and styled.

Other than becoming an attorney, I'd turned out okay. But Denis's choices were his alone.

I'd learned that I couldn't date men with school-age kids. I needed more than a half-time relationship. If I too had had children, perhaps we could have tried to mesh schedules, but I was a maladjusted only child who wasn't used to sharing.

My version of detachment required an offer to spend the night after sex and to have breakfast together the next day. Even if you didn't love someone, you should at least care enough not to send them home hungry after getting naked together.

I needed someone who'd offer to scoop up a dead animal if that's what really mattered to me. Otherwise, I'd just feel even more alone. But I had a feeling I'd be scooping up my own dead animals for a while.

Knees together.

I ended things with David too. On one of his visits to my house he said, "You should get a king-size bed. You aren't a little girl anymore," as if he were certain he'd be spending lots of time in it.

*No, I'm not,* I thought but didn't say. *I've seen my spouse through cancer. You haven't.* He wasn't so complimentary anymore, now that his infatuation had worn off.

I had a vision of my future: One, two, then five years would pass and I'd still be emailing with men named RubberDucky37 and RacerXXX, picking them up and discarding them like a never-ending game of poker, cruising around the Bay Area to meet them, but never having anyone to come home to.

My life had become a giant taste test, but nothing tasted right. It was like squirting dessert topping out of a can instead of whipping up fresh cream, then adding the sugar and vanilla. Ersatz intimacy instead of real.

I'd been so disconnected from most of the men I had dated, yet I'd just closed my eyes and gotten into bed, or at least agreed to a second date. I'd rationalized that I was experimenting, but those guys never felt right to me in the first place. It was like continuing to try non-dairy gelatinous dessert toppings when you already knew you didn't like them.

I took down my OkCupid profile. My dating experiences had left me feeling overly pawed, but it was better than remaining numb to the touch of the wrong hands.

"Are you sure?" the automated message asked. "Could you take a minute to explain why?" *Because dating was like being in a sci-fi movie where the alien finally runs out of enough energy to stay disguised as a human being.*

You meet a man and hope it's love because you both order Manhattans made with Angostura, not Peychaud, bitters, and you love the first and fourth *Evil Dead* movies, but not the second and third. He starts out passionate and, even more importantly, considerate.

Then he expects you to become his therapist, or administrative assistant, or every other Wednesday night lay, or the one who fixes him after all the damage the other women allegedly caused but which was really his own fault, and you wind up settling for a relationship as compartmentalized as a file cabinet and as passionate as indigestion.

Dating was not supposed to be a metaphorical head push and the bill for a plate of something I never ordered—meretricious blonde, or withholding mother, or self-serving ham. But from what I could tell, middle-aged dating was about reliving the past. The problem wasn't that we spoke different love languages; it was that we were incapable of understanding each other because we were hearing the words through our past partner's mouths.

The men I met often didn't seem to be talking to me, but to their exes, as if I were wearing another woman's face, the one who never cooked them dinner or demanded too much time or left them for some guy at the gym. That's why so many of them had never bothered to ask me questions about myself. It hadn't mattered. They were never going to hear me anyway.

As his parting salvo, Denis had informed me that his last girl-friend—whom he was crazy about but who failed to make time for him—dumped him just before Thanksgiving the previous year. Ostensibly, he wanted me to know other people felt sad over the holidays too—tactlessly equating a short fling with a long marriage—but really, he was letting me know I was the object of misplaced revenge.

Buck had been overwhelmed by his ex-wives' (probably quite reasonable) demands, so now he offered nothing but shooing out in the morning and drunken insults at night. With his repeated excoriations, Lowell was speaking not only to me but to all his past girlfriends.

I finally figured it out. Almost all my relationships had been adversarial. Dating was a power struggle. Once the pursuit was over, I lost my power. Then it was about how little could the men give and still get laid. How much emotional labor could they exact while not offering any empathy in return because, you know, listening to me was kinda boring, and they'd already been through so much with their ex-wives.

Why offer to treat me to anything when we were so unin-vested that we might never see each other again? They'd been invested before, and look how that turned out.

Unless I withdrew. Then they had to be nice again, but by then it was too late. I'd seen the truth. The winner of the game was the one who put in the least and got out the most. Which was antithetical to everything I knew about love.

Growing up with my dad and George, I thought men were sup-posed to be protective of women, and that they would care about them more, not less, after they had sex. But sex seemed to come with contempt, perhaps subtle and disguised as constructive crit-icism or modernity or non-monogamy or lack of time, but it still quacked like a sickly duck. I needed to expect more from the men I dated, and goddammit, they needed to expect more of themselves.

I took the blowups of my profile photos off my office shelves and stashed them in a drawer. The grinning redhead in the pictures wasn't me; she never had been. I felt like I'd skinned my elbows. I could hide them under a long-sleeved shirt, but they still stung like a motherfucker. And it hurt even more because it was my fault for disregarding my instincts in the first place. Forget detachment. I was a middle-aged romantic, which meant that I was a self-defeating oxymoron.

"Hey, Francis, I don't want to intrude, but I'm kind of alone this Thanksgiving," I said with a fake little laugh, calling the one man who was different and clutching my phone way too hard. I hadn't seen him in a while.

I imagined spending the holiday by myself, going to morning yoga, lying that I had plans if anyone asked, going for a walk, coming home to watch TV, getting drunk on red wine because I needed so badly to fall asleep. Then I'd wake around four in the morning, knowing the next day wouldn't be any different from the one before.

"Then come spend the day with us," Francis said with a grin I could hear through the phone, referring as usual to himself and his dog. The compressed feeling around my lungs started to give a little.

Loneliness = shame.

On Thanksgiving morning, he gave me a tour of his bright little bungalow in Oakland, asking "okay?" a couple of times, as if checking to be sure I could be comfortable there. His lab, Winston, kept sniffing around my feet, then scampering away when I tried to pet him.

We spent most of the day in his orange-painted kitchen with its rows of hanging pots and blue-and-white painted tiles. I made his complicated stuffing recipe and chopped three types of mushrooms and two kinds of sausage while he made everything else.

We stood with our shoulders touching at the stove, he stirring two pots while I stirred one. Condensation fogged the windows, mingling with his hopefulness and my regret.

When everything was cooking, we sat down at his well-used wooden table, sipping the red wine I'd brought and nibbling goat cheese on a fresh baguette. The way Francis looked at me told me everything. He would have scooped the dead robin out of my planter, even if he'd had to hire a dog sitter. But for me it was just playacting, sitting with him at his table, then joining him and his dog on their nightly walk, looking like one of those couples I dreaded seeing on my own solitary treks.

He and I could only be friends, and he wanted to find love. I envied the woman who would become his girlfriend.

Winston was getting used to me. He sat at my feet at the table, with his silky fur brushing against my leg.

"He really likes you; he's usually scared of new people," Francis said, then whispered as if the dog could understand. "When I adopted him, they told me he'd had some really bad experiences."

I could relate.

I'd made sure to be very still and quiet when I sat down. When Winston approached, I put out my palm for him to sniff. When that was okay, I patted him slowly with just a few gentle strokes, nothing too eager. I was using my dating skills. Now I just had to learn to sit still when I was by myself.

Knees together.

# XV. Post-Dated

WHAT I LEARNED FROM DATING WITH DETACHMENT:

1. Life without George might not be worth living.
2. I only wanted to be with other unhappy people so that my life seemed okay by comparison.
3. Sex might be a food group.
4. Love was definitely a food group.
5. Detachment was junk food.
6. I was starving.

# XVI. The Telephone Pole

"WHAT IF I TOLD YOU I WAS GOING TO SEE Todd Rundgren at the Fillmore on Thursday night? Max," said a new text on my phone. A few minutes later I got a second. "I hope you haven't forgotten who I am."

I looked up from my *Grey's Anatomy* marathon and my martini—two shots of Hendrick's Gin, half a cap of vermouth, and three blue-cheese-stuffed olives—and tried not to think about having blue cheese burgers with Gene. I was bored with watching surgeons who looked like professional models having PG-rated sex. It was mid-December and I'd been offline for a month. My bed used to have men in it. Now it had those little foil wrappers from the Lindt chocolate truffles.

Other than a few texts from Francis, my phone had been frighteningly quiet. When I was married, I barely ever checked my phone; life with George just happened. Now my phone kept me tethered to the rest of the world.

Two weeks before Christmas, I'd thrown my first party ever in honor of Laura's birthday, after she complained she never got to have one because the date fell so close to Christmas. I wound up with twenty-two yeses to my first Facebook-issued invitations and set about arranging red-berried nandina in vases, putting out battery-operated candles to avoid any risk of fire, and buying wine with names like Bitch and Girly Girl.

Nancy came over early to help me set up. She brought her special smoked salmon dip and reassured me that people really would show up. She told me I was right to include the people I didn't know from Laura's guest list. That was how to make new friends, she said, undoubtedly echoing her advice to her own kids back in grade school.

The yoga girls all came, bringing tomato bruschetta, vegetarian pizza, and strawberries with crème fraiche—enough food for three parties. They stayed late into the night, chatting away, then sat close together for a group photo. Over my insincere protests, Caroline stayed even later to do all the dishes.

"You feel like a sister to me," she said, her eyes glistening as she wrapped me in a long hug, rocking us back and forth.

"I feel the same about you," I said, blinking hard. She and I were so different. She was from a lackadaisical family, while I had grown up with my overprotective dad. She had the mystical faith of a yogi. I believed in entropy.

"When we get old, let's all live in little houses next door to one another," she said, pulling on the motorcycle boots she'd left by the door. Her face was even more beautiful through her tears. It was a night that threatened to dissolve my cynicism.

But a week later, my holiday misery had settled over me like a mildewed blanket. My girlfriends were busy with their families, and my writing group had disbanded for weeks. I even considered going back online, but had been warned by Laura that all the sane daters took their profiles down until after New Year's, fearing an onslaught of holiday zombies.

My Facebook feed was full of photos of holiday dinner parties hosted by women accessorized by husbands and hashtags: #happilymarried and #husbandbestfriend. I hated them, even if several had come to my party and brought dishes containing real crab.

⊙ ⊙ ⊙ ⊙ ⊙

Max was another arrow shot from OkCupid, but I hadn't heard from him in over a month. A telephone repairman, he was sixty but looked much younger, six feet tall and slender with spiky dark gray hair, tawny, weathered skin, high cheekbones, green eyes, and long, ropey muscles from climbing poles all day. He was even cuter than Doctor Owen Hunt on *Grey's Anatomy*.

During our initial coffee date, he told me he'd been the lead guitarist for some bands in Chicago during his youth. He'd even recorded a demo tape, but lost it years ago.

Then he took me for a ride in his ancient roadster. I had to drown out my dad's voice forbidding me to go because it didn't have a roll bar. Max sped confidently, if a little too quickly, through the hills, accelerating into the curves. His long, slender fingers moved over the shift knob while I admired his handsome, if slightly dissipated, profile. He'd obviously lived a lot more than I had.

We met for drinks the following week, but when I arrived, he was betting on football and drinking his third Jameson Whiskey, his eyes glued to the TV. He kept asking me, "Who do you think will win? The Seahawks?" I kept telling him I didn't follow any sports.

"Not even football?" he asked.

"Not even," I said, probably confirming his worst fears.

Against my better judgment, I went to his house afterward— he was that great looking. But once I was there, he fielded calls from an ex-girlfriend who wanted to come over. He was a hot mess, but I could see why she still wanted him. He lived behind an auto row in an old wooden house ruled over by a cranky ancient cat, the bedrooms were stuffed with music equipment, and a huge TV dominated the living room.

He played me a few songs on his guitar, then looked into my eyes, those long fingers roaming over the strings, and asked, "Do you want to go to my room and smoke some pot?"

He was a post-middle-aged Jeff Spicoli, the stoner guy from *Fast Times at Ridgemont High*. I said I had to go home.

When he called to ask me out again, I said we were too different. As I clumsily tried to explain to him what those differences were—*don't say Spicoli, don't say Spicoli*—he hung up without even saying goodbye. Contacting me six weeks later to say he was going to see Todd Rundgren seemed like a non sequitur.

"That sounds like fun," I typed back.

"Does that mean you want to go with me?"

I knew Max was wrong for me, but boredom and loneliness had eaten my judgment. I was sick of being alone night after night watching *Grey's* and pretending that I was dating Doctor Hunt. Perhaps Max with his easy physicality and apparently simple needs would be easier than the other men I'd dated, and I'd be spared the demands for *real* intimacy and pointers about my faults. Clearly, he had enough of his own.

I agreed to go to the concert with him. I'd listened over and over again to Rundgren's *Hermit of Mink Hollow* in high school, especially its hit single "Can We Still Be Friends." If my date with Max went badly, we'd already have our breakup song.

"Why?" he texted, no doubt thinking of my prior rejection.

"Because I love Todd Rundgren and I think you're cute."

The last time I'd been to the Fillmore, I was twenty-seven and accompanying George on his yearly pilgrimage to see the Ramones. He had come to find me in the balcony, his eyes gleaming, excited to tell me how close he'd gotten to the stage. My husband the adorable wannabe punk, my husband the dying wisps of skin and bone, both now inseparable.

This time, as Rundgren's band started to play *Muskrat Love*,

Max put some pot in his pipe and lit up, rubbed my back, then reached around to hold me. When I leaned against him, my memories faded.

Suddenly, snuggling muskrats seemed cool. The lyrics about shimmying had to be a euphemism for sex; it's just that rodent sex is gross. I was a high school senior again, except this time I was dating a stoner instead of one of the nice boys from the audiovisual squad.

As I was leaving the restroom, the woman I'd been chatting with asked who my date was. "What a great-looking guy," she said when I pointed to Max. He was wearing aviator-style sunglasses and a vintage pin-striped jacket with black slacks and work boots, his hair spiked just so. Noticing us looking at him, he gave us a smile, raising two fingers in a Sinatra-like salute. I melted just a little.

"Hey baby, want to go with me to Harvey's Casino in Lake Tahoe next week? It'd be for three days, four if we're having a good time. There's a great blues band playing. The casino pays for it all," Max texted two weeks after the Rundgren concert.

I considered. I certainly hadn't known him long enough to be sharing a hotel room. But by now I'd been to his house and seen him working in his garden, pruning his cherry tree and weeding his flower beds. I could picture him coming over to my place to scoop up a dead animal, bringing his own shovel in case I didn't have one, and teasing me about my squeamishness. But secretly, he would be proud to be of help.

"So, does this mean you aren't seeing anyone else anymore?" he asked the first time after we made love, defying the unspoken rule that you had to be with someone for a while before you could ask them about other people. But I didn't think he knew those rules.

I said we could still date other people, wanting to seem like a modern woman, even though neither of us was actually seeing anybody else. He'd dressed hurriedly and left without saying goodbye, but despite that, I was touched. He'd rushed through sex too, but being together must have meant something to him. He was old-fashioned. I was beginning to think I was too, no matter how hard I tried not to be.

I learned that Max had left Chicago in his twenties to follow a dancer he'd fallen in love with, and had worked in Lake Tahoe as a day trader while she had danced in the casinos. They had eventually broken up because she was always on the road. After that, he had worked as a mobile chemist driving around California doing environmental testing. Finally, in his forties, he had ridden his motorcycle to Oakland, found some musicians to jam with, and never left the Bay Area. He later sold the motorcycle after yet another in a series of accidents.

I could tell he wasn't a grown-up; he described a life spent bouncing around with little purpose, but at the time it didn't seem to matter. I was moved when he thumbed through George's record collection, noticed George owned almost every single Beatles album, and said, "I would've really liked him."

"Why is the trip free?" I asked.

"I've played a lot of high-stakes blackjack there over the years," he said with a wry smile.

"You know, it could cost a lot more than a free room if you lose."

"C'mon, baby, I don't want to hear that. Just say you'll go."

Max was a gambler. He believed fate controlled the roll of the dice or the deal of the cards, deciding if he was a good guy who deserved to win, especially if he was already in the hole for a lot of money. But cards have no memory or morality, and each deal or throw is unrelated to the ones before.

Dating is a lot like gambling in its suspension of disbelief. I agreed to go with him to Lake Tahoe.

At the casino, he was greeted with offers of free massages and meals, his usual bottle of Jameson delivered to his suite, and yes, a nice bottle of Cabernet for his girlfriend as well. We changed into swimsuits and fluffy hotel bathrobes and ordered piña coladas, sipping them in the hotel hot tub against a backdrop of white-capped mountains. My drink tasted of creamy coconut and new adventure.

We walked through snowy meadows under tall pine trees, practically the only people there, the whiteness as blinding as a benediction. It was my first trip with a man who wasn't my husband, and the fates weren't even punishing me for it. Max steadied me as we trudged through the snow, having an uncanny ability to stay on his feet while I skittered around.

The casino, with its hyperactive gambling floor and dealers who greeted Max by name, was just the right degree of dissolute, and we were its homecoming couple. Several women nodded at me as if acknowledging my good taste in men. "How old are we today? Sixteen?" I could hear Dad asking.

"Probable gambling and pot addictions," I could hear my writing pal Will warning me. But I drowned them out, listening to Aimee Mann's "Save Me," one of the songs on Max's playlist for when we made love, never thinking that the title should have scared me a little.

"I get really excited, but you change it up so fast when we make love, I don't, um, you know," I explained to Max one night, feeling myself blushing scarlet, squirming in my casino bathrobe. "I need you to slow down. I'm getting kind of, uh, frustrated." My last words dwindled to a whisper.

Our bodies matched perfectly, but he moved too quickly, like sex was something embarrassing to finish up, and I was too inexperienced to know how to re-orchestrate him. "You haven't been, um . . . I've never thought about that before," he said, his voice trailing off, looking rather embarrassed himself. "You're the first woman I've been with who's ever brought that up."

I might be a modern woman after all, enrolled in How to Retrain Your Man. After that, sex went from rubbery scrambled eggs to a rich, fluffy soufflé. "Nice and slow, right, baby?" Max would say as if he'd figured out the answer to a particularly tricky puzzle.

Our first two nights in Tahoe I slept little, waking when the sky was still dark, Max asleep next to me. The third day, as we stood outside the little History Museum, a few stray snowflakes falling around us, he said, "I love you." He quickly added, "It's too soon. I just wanted to say that to someone here." But I understood; he was a romantic.

He might have been funky and a little broken down, but by the end of our trip, he was starting to feel a tiny bit like home. His manners weren't great, but I hadn't yet caught a whiff of contempt.

We stayed in Tahoe all four nights, spending most of our time in the room with movies on demand and snow blustering outside. I was finally starring in my own rom com instead of a horror movie.

"You're really all right?" Dad asked when I visited him a few days before Christmas. He peered at me in disbelief, then took a sip of his green tea, offering me a red bean mochi he'd ordered on Amazon.

Jane had decorated the house for the holidays. She'd hung our old red chili pepper ornaments from the lampshades, put the ceramic Santas and snow globes from her Midwestern childhood on the tables, and covered the mantel in tiny white lights.

I emptied my faded green felt stocking, a relic of my mom's time, most of its choo-choo train cars and candy canes long gone, but my dad still filled it every year with chocolate truffles for Christmas and gelt for Chanukah, along with a check to do something fun. But I didn't know what that might be without George to do it with.

"I'm really fine and I've got good news. An Australian magazine called *Mamamia* is going to publish one of my blog posts on their website," I said, biting into the mochi. I was grateful it was sweet instead of Sriracha flavored.

Ironically, I'd hated that post in which my blogging persona, The Hungover Widow, had suggested surviving the holidays by taking long walks and extra yoga classes. She reminded widowed readers that while things would never look the same as when we were married, we just had to refocus the lens. Fatuous bitch. To me, the words "wellness" and "widowhood" didn't even belong in the same sentence.

When the magazine had contacted me, all I could think was how much I wanted to tell George about it, to hear him say he was wrong about my not being a good writer—he always knew I could do whatever I set my mind to. We would have gone to Oliveto, our all-time favorite restaurant, to celebrate and gotten a special bottle of wine and a piece of hazelnut chocolate cake to go, to eat later in bed.

For the rest of my life, I was going to be celebrating whatever triumphs I had alone. And even if I ever did find someone new, the person I most wanted to share them with was gone.

"I could tell things were better since I haven't seen you a lot lately," my dad said. "Not that you need to come see me. I'm fine. I never want you to feel obligated. You should feel free to take all the time you need to . . ."

"Actually, I haven't been around much because I have a new boyfriend," I said, stopping him before he got all Jewish mother on me. "Max and I have been spending so much time together I almost forgot it was the holidays." I'd spared Dad the late-night visits and phone calls of the year before, the crinkles around his eyes relaxed instead of scrunched with worry.

"Whoever this Max is, I like him. Honestly, I was dreading this season. You know you're always welcome here, but it's much better if you don't *need* to come over," he said. We were so much lighter this year than the year before when I'd sucked up what little energy he did have, like a grub burrowing in the ground to escape the cold.

"Max left home at fifteen," I said. "He had to drop out of junior college to support himself. He works as a telephone repairman now, but he's been a chemist, a day trader, and a lot of other things. I don't think you'd really relate to him."

But Dad stopped me, saying, "If he makes you happy, that's all I care about. Thank the Telephone Pole for me, but don't tell him I gave him that nickname."

"Knees together," Dad called out as usual as I was leaving.

As with so many things, I should have listened to him.

"I hope he's good enough for you," Francis said when I told him about Max over Christmas brunch. Of all the guys I'd dated, Francis was the only one who ever really listened to me. He'd invited me to brunch weeks before so that I didn't have to worry about being alone on Christmas Day itself.

He took a sip from the Bloody Mary he'd meticulously constructed at the do-it-yourself drinks bar. I'd thrown my own Bloody Mary together hastily, eager to start eating, never thinking my inability to tolerate delayed gratification might apply to my taste in men as well.

Francis and I could be friends only so long as neither of us was seriously seeing anyone else. We'd spent Saturday nights together because we liked each other best, leaving open the possibility I'd finally come to my senses and choose him. But at brunch, it was obvious that I'd chosen Max.

So after Christmas, Francis faded away. I missed him and knew he was better for me than Max, but Max's and my eyes were almost the same shade of green, and when we looked into them, neither of us wanted to be with anyone else.

We were spending so many lazy afternoons in bed watching movies and holding each other I no longer heard the flap of the raven's wings. After all my frenzied dating, it was a balm, even if Max was usually stoned and often drove with a cup with whiskey in the cup holder.

On New Year's Eve, Max set up a tent on my living room floor, putting a double sleeping bag inside, designating it the neutral zone in my super-neat house. At midnight, we climbed into the tent and kissed, trying out the sleeping bags before running to the bedroom to escape the cold.

Perhaps these moments could start to add up to a real life, or at least give me enough butterflies in my stomach to soothe my savaged heart.

# XVII. White Trashed

A FEW MONTHS LATER, I went to see Max after my Thursday afternoon writing class. I was being the good girl, checking up on her delinquent boyfriend. He'd been off work on disability the past few months with a strained shoulder.

I went around to the backyard and flopped into the worn rope hammock under the cherry tree surrounded by banks of white calla lilies and purple lantana. He made me a gin and tonic garnished with a Meyer lemon from his overburdened tree. Whatever Max's faults, his garden certainly loved him.

I'd had three more articles published: an essay about uncertainty in a small literary magazine, another called "I Was an Online Dating Addict" in the e-magazine Xojane, and a third called "Tripping Over Our Own Baggage" about middle-aged singles' inability to change in The Huffington Post.

Max's laconic "Congratulations, baby" meant more to me than it should have, but he bought us a bottle of Prosecco, and I was thrilled to have a boyfriend to celebrate with. Perhaps writing was something I could look to in the future, but for now I was slacking, shutting off my brain with my hot stoner guy.

Max was like an old British sports car, great lines and fun to drive, but he could be temperamental and unpredictable. Hearing certain songs or spending too much time alone sent him spiraling into his past, thinking about friends who had died, and bands that had dissolved, and cross-country moves that had never panned out.

"I want to play you a new song I wrote," he said with a laugh, looking down shyly. "It's a true story about losing my socks in bed with a girl named Debbie."

He lit up a joint, inhaling deeply before passing it to me, then reached for his guitar to play the first song anyone had ever written for me. He sang in a voice destroyed by years of cigarettes even though he'd quit smoking long ago—a sexy rasp promising passion but also chaos. I tried to stop editing his lyrics in my head to make them better fit the melody.

"Didn't get much else done today," he said with a sigh after he finished. "I got some blow last night, not that much, but once I got started, I really went through it."

He'd called me late the night before from the West Oakland off-ramp after he'd gone to hear a speed metal band play at Eli's Mile High Club. He told me he loved me, and he knew that there were things about him I liked or even loved, but said that I didn't really love him back. I told him sometimes you loved someone because of their faults.

I loved Max because in him I saw a loneliness as desperate as my own. But I also worried he was too childlike and impulsive. His untreated ADHD fragmented his thoughts and made it hard for us to communicate. Case in point: last night's phone call with his sad accusations and my careful avoidance. He was definitely a little damaged (not that I wasn't).

"It doesn't travel well," I said, repeating the phrase my college friends used to say when they'd bought cocaine to do over the weekend but wound up doing it all the first day.

Having coke meant he'd met a dealer outside of Eli's and made his purchase in public—too reckless for me—but I reassured myself he'd just partied a little too much. Lots of people did blow.

He had other flaws too. A few weeks after we started dating, I noticed he tried very hard to avoid spending money. We each had enough to last many years—he inherited his from his insanely frugal parents—but he hated to part with any of it, except when he was gambling.

He picked cheap restaurants when it was his turn to get dinner, drank at home but not when we went out, and winced when I did. He'd ask whether it was my turn to pay for dinner when by my memory it was actually his. I was happy to trade off paying for meals, but not when he tried to weasel out of his turn. I rationalized I'd grown up spoiled—as he kept reminding me—but I was still tired of eating bad food.

We'd tried what was supposed to be a romantic overnight in Monterey, but he'd insisted on picking the hotel, so we wound up staying next to a porn shop. After that, I'd decided I didn't need to go away for any overnights other than the free ones he got from the casino, but I was starting to make too many excuses for not getting what I wanted.

"There's still a little coke left, if you want some," Max said after he finished singing and we went to his bedroom.

Every available surface was covered in piles of CDs, from the Dead Boys to Donovan, some in a CD stand capped by a bright green alligator's head. His walls were hung with guitars and a battered but lovely sitar. I cringed at the mess on his nightstand—M&Ms, a whiskey bottle, playing cards, a plastic skeleton, and a battered notebook filled with his song lyrics.

When he'd first spotted the sleek aluminum key case hanging on my kitchen wall, each key resting predictably on its own little hook, he just sighed. He drove me crazy losing his own keys, but obviously he thought my solution was overkill. He seemed to think there was something aggressively hostile about having everything in its place.

But when I stretched out on his bed and he rubbed my back, I felt my bones relax. I did a few small lines of coke and put a little under my gum to feel the numbness.

"I love you," he said after we made love, our long bodies stretched out on his red paisley sheets. The bed felt like warm silk even if it did have cookie crumbs in it.

"It doesn't count if you say it right afterward," I said, taking a hit from the joint he offered.

*Tempus fugit*, my ghost whispered as she passed by, running off to do something so interesting I couldn't even imagine what it was.

My girlfriends weren't faring much better. Over post-yoga drinks one Thursday night, Nancy said, her lips turning down even farther than usual, "My guy's really cheap even though he's rich. He expects me to cook dinner, and when we do go out, he leaves the check sitting on the table so long I finally get sick of waiting for him and pick it up myself. He's even been hinting about moving into my house! It's been almost a year and I need to break it off."

She'd said the same thing about him, a phlegmatic attorney eight years her senior, many times before. He was the one thing she wasn't proactive about.

"Then there's my guy," Caroline said with a hollow laugh. "He's practically homeless these days."

She was dating a quixotic real estate developer with grandiose plans, always thinking the next one was going to make his fortune. Caroline got by on a yoga teacher's salary, and she had two kids, yet this guy had the nerve to borrow money from her, all the while proclaiming he wanted to marry her. It may have been true, but he clearly didn't have her best interests at heart.

Laura remained silent, but she'd spent our last yoga retreat with the phone clamped to her ear, listening silently while her boyfriend spewed what was supposed to be constructive criticism. There was certainly a lot of it. Apparently, he saw faults in her that none of us had ever seen.

"What are you going to do about Max?" Nancy asked. By now, they'd all heard me complain ad nauseam about his cheapness.

"I don't know. We're driving each other crazy," I said. "We're going to Tahoe again this weekend, but he usually spends one day hungover from gambling the night before." I was trying to ignore his addictions, my powers of denial again kicking into high gear. If I could ignore my husband's Stage IV cancer, it was nothing to turn a blind eye to Max's faults.

"My therapist said that if you can't see staying with a guy for the rest of your life, you're just wasting your love energy being with him," Laura said.

"It's not like any of us are finding guys we want to spend the rest of our lives with," I said, thinking back to my days of dating with detachment.

"My therapist also said we have only a finite amount of love energy to give over our lifetimes," Laura said.

"I haven't wanted to say this," said Caroline, looking over at me with a pinched little frown, "but he's not good enough for you." A true yogi, she almost never said anything negative about anyone. This must have cost her.

"Maybe we should just date each other," Nancy said, probably thinking of her own marriage to a good man.

It made sense. By now, I'd heard Caroline sigh that she was getting wrinkles, and I had watched Nancy pinch her stomach and say she was gaining weight. Laura changed her hairstyle so often that sometimes I needed a minute to recognize her. To a one, my prior dates had acted as if they were prizes, never mentioning any of their flaws.

My research showed that men made up about fifty-two percent of online dating users compared to forty-eight percent women. Yet so many men acted like middle-aged women should be grateful for whatever attention we could get, like used Buicks waiting to have our tires kicked and get taken for a test drive, while the guys could be driving younger models they found at Forever 21.

We'd all been confused by indifferent men who wondered when we might happen to be nearby, asking us to meet them at their local watering holes with no bridging the distance. And we'd tired of guys who texted endlessly, saying they were too busy to meet or offering only one day's notice. At our age, misplaced retribution so often looked like lassitude.

If dating in our youth was about falling in love, dating in middle-age was about what we could tolerate. Nancy's guy probably thought he gave too much in his prior relationship and now he was going to let a woman do for him, and Laura's man felt he wasn't allowed to speak his mind in the past, so he wasn't about to let that happen again. If so, then Denis had been right—they were all broken. Or, like love energy, empathy too was finite, while revenge sprang eternal.

"I used this meme for my latest blog post: Dating as an adult is like going to the dump and looking around for the least broken and disgusting thing," I said.

"Yup," the three of them said, speaking as one.

A few days later, I called Max in despair. The guest room toilet was leaking, and I was on my third plumber, having gone through two who wanted to replace the entire toilet. They claimed this one was too old, the parts too hard to find. One had even given me a quote to remodel the entire bathroom, not that I'd asked.

Once things started to fall apart, you never knew what might go wrong. George always fixed everything.

"Sell the house!" my dad and I used to joke whenever something broke down, but we'd had each other to rely on. I'd stay home to wait for the repairman while he'd go for takeout from our favorite Indian place so we could have dinner after the man left.

Hearing how stressed I sounded, Max told me to hold off

on calling another plumber. He came over later that evening, checked out the toilet, then went to Home Depot and returned with a new flapper contraption. After shaving it down a little with one of George's rasps when it turned out to be too tall, he installed it in place in the tank.

He had never looked hotter than when he was hunched over the toilet installing that rubber doohickey—not when he was playing "Angie" on his guitar, or wearing his paisley jacket and work boots at the Fillmore, or even when he rolled over next to me in bed.

"See, it works and I saved you the price of a plumber," he said as he finished up, flushing the toilet with a big "Ta-da!"

He was speaking my love language. I'd finally found someone who could keep the raven at bay, whom I could rely on when things went wrong—a very important trait to someone who suffered from anxiety, and a quality sorely lacking in the other men I'd dated. I could imagine one of them coming to see me, the water from some plumbing disaster pooling around our feet while he tried desperately to get laid—he'd had to come all the way to Danville, after all—eventually telling me I might want to get that checked out as he headed for the door.

"I love you," I whispered to Max when we went to bed that night.

"I love you too," Max said, his arm tightening around me.

"Hey, baby, I need to stay here awhile," said Max, four months later on the Saturday of Memorial Day weekend.

He was sitting at one of the high-stakes blackjack tables at Harvey's Casino in Tahoe. At midnight I'd wandered over from the Diamond Club, the free bar for elite gamblers, to check on him since he'd been gone for over an hour. The bartender there had offered to set me up with a couple of guys if Max and I didn't work out.

"Gamblers and normal people don't usually last," she'd said with a knowing sigh.

I told Max I was going up to the room. He said he'd be up soon, but he was already switching tables, introducing himself to the other players as "Mad Max," the false cheer coating his mouth like an over-sweet liqueur. Switching tables meant he was trying to change his luck.

I woke up often during the night, hoping he hadn't lost too much even though it might finally have gotten him to stop gambling. He was back at work and came home at night with the exhaustion of a sixty-one-year-old man who climbed telephone poles all day.

I heard the door open around three in the morning. "Hey, baby, can you believe it, I won four thousand dollars. I was in the hole for seven, but I worked my way back up, little bets at a time, that's how to do it. Nothing too greedy."

"Congratulations, I guess. Though you know how I feel about your gambling," I said. "You promised me you'd set a thousand-dollar limit."

"Yeah, I know, but one thousand became two and then . . . Anyway, I gotta sleep," he said, his voice already fading. I could smell the whiskey and coffee on his breath when he leaned over to kiss me goodnight. "I'll make it up to you tonight. I'll take you someplace for dinner outside the casino. Someplace nice."

He slept into the afternoon while I went hiking on the trail that ran behind the casino, breathing in the thin air, trying not to slide on the last of the snow, and wondering what I was doing there. We were finding out we had little in common other than a mutual love of make-up sex, Hermann Hesse, Wang Chung, and the same pizza toppings (pesto, spinach, and mushrooms).

But the make up sex was so good that every time we argued, we agreed to try harder, even though neither of us could say exactly how we were going to do that. We oscillated back and forth like angry pendulums, breaking up, then getting back together. It left me little time to think of anything else—exactly how I wanted it to be.

Before we left for dinner that night, Max and I each had two drinks at the Diamond Club, Jameson on the rocks for him and Bloody Marys for me. We walked over to the nearby shopping plaza. The fire pits were surrounded by revelers, and the neon-colored playground was overflowing with children.

We settled on an upscale Hawaiian restaurant, where the dining room was set with white tablecloths and orchids. It was all blissfully quiet after the bustle outside.

"It's your kind of place," Max said, the kind he usually found "too hoity toity" for him—an adjective he often used to describe my tastes—where they asked if you wanted your water still, sparkling, or tap.

Our server came over to reel off a list of the specials. Even though we'd barely looked at the menu, Max said without asking me, "We'll split the entree special, the seafood risotto."

I bit my lip to keep quiet. Risotto required a lot of stovetop stirring, which most restaurants didn't have time to do, usually resulting in a soupy mixture instead of the crisp texture of a true risotto. And it should be made with arborio instead of regular rice, but saying anything would have sounded hoity toity.

"Something to drink with that?" asked our server.

"Just water," answered my dream date. "See, that was decisive, and it cost a lot less than ordering a bunch of other stuff."

"Maybe we could split a small sake?" I suggested. Actually, I preferred a large, but didn't want to appear greedy since Max was paying for dinner. I was making yet another excuse not to get what I wanted.

"We can get free drinks at the casino," he said huffily. "We'll be back there in a half hour." Max did not believe in leisurely dining. It was yet another trait of his that was starting to grate on me.

"If I want a drink, I can just pay for it myself," I said, hearing the strain in my voice.

"Why do you have to go and do that?" he suddenly screeched, his voice way too loud in the quiet room. He jumped up and paced back and forth across the floor before coming to stand beside me at the table.

I froze, looking down, my shoulders hunched as if expecting a blow. He should have been in a good mood from his winnings.

"I have to get out of here," he muttered. "You stay here. I'll just go." The other diners were probably staring at us, but I was too embarrassed to look up to find out.

"Just sit down," I said, still looking down, afraid to make eye contact with him. "I'm sorry. Calm down. Sit down." Going to a fancy restaurant with a cheap, strung-out date had been a recipe for disaster.

The George-o-meter had red-lined to "Run," but I was frozen in my chair. If I'd just won $4,000 at blackjack, I would have been happy to spring for a few drinks. It was karma. Like the way that after your husband died of cancer, you deserved a sweet boyfriend, not a professional gambler who turned apoplectic over the cost of a drink.

"I was trying to show you a good time, to take you out," he said, finally sitting down, shaking with nerves. "And you had to go and make me feel small. We could have just gotten drinks back at the casino."

Max's winnings this past year had come to $23,000, proving yet again that karma was a joke.

"I'm sorry, let's just eat and go." Max wasn't used to paying for drinks in Tahoe. They were free in the casinos, so people rarely ordered them in restaurants. But why go out—or be with some-one, for that matter—if you couldn't have what you wanted?

We waited in silence for our food to arrive, soupy rice garnished with pallid bits of seafood and an edible flower. It tasted fine at first but with an underlying fishiness that bled through, just like us.

The couple at the next table were chatting and pointing at the cocktail menu, probably picking out rage-free drinks and waiting for us to leave so they could talk about us, wishing we were already gone so they could enjoy the rest of their meal in peace.

Max scarfed his risotto like he was beating out a pack of starving wolves. I said nothing and pushed the rice around on my plate, nauseated by the smell. I wondered how we could have come to this when he had professed to love me, but I had failed to see that all the signs were already there.

He paid the check, then stalked off ahead when we left the restaurant. I sat down on a bench nearby, trying to figure out what to do next. We'd driven up in his car, and it was too late to rent one. I doubted I'd be able to find an Uber driver willing to make the three-hour trip home. I could have tried to find the bus schedule online but might have wound up waiting for hours at the terminal.

"All you had to do was hold off until we got back to the casino. You could have had a drink there. You didn't have to go and make me feel small," Max said, coming to sit beside me. "If you want a drink, you should offer to pay for the whole meal. Don't just say you'll pay for your own drink."

I shrank away from him and refrained from saying that by his logic, if I ever wanted a drink, I'd be stuck paying for the entire tab even if he'd invited me out in the first place.

"I want to go home," I said, meaning Danville, not the casino with its acrid air, unmoving slot jockeys, and acres of broken hope. I saw myself older and exhausted, white roots showing through red hair, blowzy from all the free drinks, trailing behind an aged Max as he strode through the casino, his face contorted in rage, mine twisted in supplication.

Just the day before, I'd been thrilled to be going away for the weekend. When my yoga girls asked what I was doing for Memorial Day, I told them Max and I were going to Tahoe again, just like we were a real couple. Except that we weren't. We were a gambling addict and a woman way too afraid of being alone.

I got up and started walking back to the hotel in the fading sunshine. Max walked beside me, ranting on, gesticulating wildly, those long fingers I used to love flying in my face.

"Shut the fuck up! I didn't do anything wrong," I heard myself yell, my two Bloody Marys finally kicking in.

A few people looked over at us, and one young mother jerked her stroller as far away from me as possible, but we weren't worth looking at. We were just white trash airing our dirty laundry in the early evening calm.

Back at the casino Max left to go walk around, saying he had to cool off and singing a snippet of a song he often sang, Willie Nelson's "If I Were the Man You Wanted," which is, in fact, about being quite the opposite.

For the first time, I realized it was his manifesto.

By now, Laura had dumped her perennially dissatisfied boyfriend. Her phone was no longer clamped to her ear, and her lips were once again upturned without having to listen to his stream of poison. Nancy had broken up with her manipulative lawyer, finally realizing she was much happier without him.

Even Caroline, with her forgiving nature, had put her man on probation and stopped seeing him until he stopped risking so much money. Her face was once again serene after she'd stopped letting him stay at her apartment.

Max had all those faults and more, yet I couldn't follow their advice and end it. I was still listening to him complain whenever

I ordered a drink or told him it was his turn to pay, at least emotionally. Laura said that her therapist would have fired me for wasting my love energy.

I listened to their advice, assuring them I'd end it soon but telling them that I just needed to wait for the right time, when the days were longer, or after his birthday or after mine. But then I'd continue on just as before.

Perhaps my girlfriends were stronger because they were used to living on their own. Nancy had met her husband in her mid-thirties. After their daughter was born with learning disabilities, they'd traded off caring for her, so Nancy had had her own support network, not to mention being able to do many of her own home repairs.

Caroline had essentially raised herself and then had gone on to raise her children when her husband proved to be unstable. I'd always had my dad and George to fall back on, so I never developed my self-reliance muscle.

I could blame my staying with Max on the declining quality of middle-aged men, but really, my love language was need. I required a man with lots of time for me, which pretty much ruled out many men with interesting lives of their own.

I'd been to a synagogue fundraiser where most of the other women were married. Their husbands had bought their drinks for them while I stood in line for the bar by myself, the sole uncoupled polymer molecule, wearing a black tuxedo-style pantsuit since I had to be my own date. Several of the men studiously avoided talking to me, as if I radiated desperation.

I'd also seen the impressed look on my yoga girls' faces when I'd turned up at a house party with Max, causing Laura to whisper, "He might not be too bright, but he's hot." Like many men before me, sometimes I needed arm candy to venture out in the world.

I didn't want to go back online. Even if I had gotten on one of those elite sites that prescreened everyone, I probably would have found a guy who'd expect me to meet him in Gstaad, ask me to pay for half the white truffle plate he'd ordered, then tell me he didn't find me nurturing enough to adopt a standard poodle together. And he still wouldn't be able to think in the abstract.

I needed Max to make me—the quitter lawyer, Manhattan guzzler, defeated society girlfriend, failed zipless fucker, undetachable dater, unemployed slacker, wannabe stoner, lost lamb—look good by comparison. He was so unlike George that he didn't stir up any memories. And having failed George, I didn't plan on having much of a future anyway.

I'd found a toxic love. It was like choosing food way past its expiration date.

But this time he'd gone over the edge. For the first time, I was trapped with him, like that night with Gene when he refused to leave my house. I had to accept that Max wasn't just addicted but mentally ill. *Hey, baby, meet me at Diamond Club.* Both his parents had been hoarders and two of his five siblings had committed suicide.

I'd been seeing only shadows where there was opacity, failing to recognize that all his quirks were symptoms of a far greater disease. Maybe if I hadn't been trying so hard to obliterate my brain, I would have realized sooner how troubled he was. I finally dropped off to sleep, huddled as far over as possible to my side of the bed.

When I woke up the next morning, Max was back, saying we should go out to eat, acting as if nothing had happened. He even asked if I wanted a Bloody Mary with breakfast, knowing he'd have to pay for it. I noticed he had a small cut on his chin from shaving, a fragment of Kleenex still clinging to it, but I wasn't about to tell him about it

I just kept running to the restroom, wondering why my stomach hurt so badly and I kept having to pee. Since I needed him to get home, my anger had become a luxury.

After breakfast, he bought us tickets for the gondola that ran up the mountain, ignoring my requests to start heading back. The tickets cost $50 each, so I figured he was trying to make amends. At each of the stops, I had to run for the restroom, attributing the weird stabbing pain in my stomach to yesterday's incident. But on the third stop I noticed blood in the toilet.

After an agonizingly slow ride down, I spent the next two hours on the phone with a Kaiser advice nurse and found out that I had my first urinary tract infection. I struggled to find a pharmacy on our way home that was open on Memorial Day. While I'd been rationalizing why I stayed with Max, my body had been rebelling, too stressed to keep tolerating what he was serving.

"I still think I was right about those drinks," he said as we were driving to the pharmacy on our way home from Tahoe.

"I'm in pain. I can't talk about this," I said. For once he was quiet. I checked off the miles on my phone. *Keep the peace until you can get out.* He looked embarrassed, like this was too much female stuff for him to deal with.

"Call me," he said when he dropped me off three hours and fifty-three minutes later, the drive having dragged on like a never-ending algebra class. "I could come over later and cheer you up." He must have been worried about losing me if he was offering to come over when we couldn't even have sex.

"I blame you for this," I said, going inside and locking the door behind me.

# ❦ XVIII. La Vie en Rose

"Bob and I are going to Paris on a tour put on by the UC Berkeley Alumni Association," George's mother, Isabella, said on the phone, as if making an important announcement. "We'd be happy to pay half your way if you'd like to come with us. I remember you spoke French very well in college."

Isabella lived to travel. Aside from the cruise of the Baltics she'd taken me on, and a disastrous trip to Mexico with Max, I'd never even been out of the country. When I was younger, I was too afraid my little world might disappear if I wasn't there to keep watch over it. Later, I hadn't wanted to go anywhere without George.

To an introvert, home is where your person is, but he told me he'd traveled so much with his parents when he was young he'd had his fill of it. I thought I could talk him into traveling after he retired, but after so many uneventful years together, I'd forgotten the law of impending disaster: if I stopped worrying about the worst, it would probably come to pass.

Isabella never said anything, but I knew she wished I'd been inspired to take some trips on my own after the Baltic cruise. But I feared my loss would increase from a dull roar to a full-on shriek without the aid of the familiar to dampen it. Timid to the end, I told her that I needed to think about it and that I hadn't spoken French in a very long time.

○ ○ ○ ○ ○

"I'll pay for the other half of your trip," my dad said when I told him about my in-laws' offer. I hadn't expected that. He usually told me what not to do.

"I don't want to impose on them," I said to Dad.

I thought of all the things that could go wrong while I was in Paris, from getting mugged in the Marais to having my house fall into a giant sinkhole when I wasn't there to keep an eye on it. See the world? No thanks, too fraught with imaginary peril.

"You're being a poor negotiator," he said. "I just said I'd con-tribute half. I can't believe I paid for you to go to law school."

Now that I was an adult, he was far better at assessing risk than when I was a teenager.

I'd always wanted to be one of those carefree women with piles of wavy hair and an armful of bangles, with their paisley duffel bags and little crystal talismans tucked into their bras, who hopped on a plane with absolutely no itinerary, open to anything. But I needed the travel plans of an overanxious bookworm with no sense of adventure.

Yet I had to admit a group tour put on by an alumni associ-ation came pretty close. "Kiss at least one guy who isn't Max," said Laura, probably worried I'd get back together with him even though I hadn't seen him in weeks and had been ignoring his pleas to make up.

To Do Before Vacation:

1. Have the gardener program the yard lights.
2. Get the burglar alarm checked.
3. Ask Caroline to house-sit while I'm gone.
4. Pray the house doesn't self-destruct.
5. Pray Dad doesn't die.

6. Buy more black T-shirts for the trip.
7. Buy more Chardonnay for when I return.

George's parents and I were part of a group of twenty-six travelers on a two-and-a-half-week tour of Paris and its surrounding areas. Our days were filled with lectures, guided walks, and museums. It was all lovely and well-organized, but at the welcome dinner I had to dig my fingernails into my palms to stop from breaking into sobs.

The group introductions had been awkward, with me explaining that Bob and Isabella weren't my parents but my in-laws. All three of us leaving out why my husband wasn't there, as if George were too busy at home coding Quicken to come with us.

"What's wrong?" my tour-mate Eliana whispered, putting her hand on my arm.

A scholar of Russian history, she was in her mid-sixties, petite, with a cap of perfectly coiffed gray hair and the minimalist black separates of a longtime New Yorker. Long divorced, she was traveling alone. I whispered to her that I was widowed.

She said quietly but with finality, "I thought so. You'll be fine." Then she patted my arm and nodded briskly.

I wished I had her certainty. During the next few days, as we made our way through the city, visiting the Arc de Triomphe, the Place de la Concorde, and the famous cafés, I saw only the empty space where George should have been by my side.

One day I skipped one of the lectures to go by myself to the Musée de L'Orangerie, entering the rooms with Monet's *Water Lilies* covering the walls. Suddenly I was wading into the ponds, feeling the petals, inhaling the indigos and mauves. There was nothing else, no George or guilt or missed opportunities. There were only petals. In the presence of art, I was outside myself.

Eliana was right. After that, I was fine. I started thinking of myself as a solo traveler instead of a widow and got used to seeing things without George by my side.

Since we'd never traveled together outside the United States, aside from a road trip to Canada in our early thirties, I had no memories of being with him at any of the places we were visiting. There ceased to be an empty space beside me because there had never been a George in those places. Nothing was missing. I was on a vacation from grief.

When Eliana and I went to the Musée Rodin, she had to stop me from walking through the garden of statues just one more time as I tried to decipher what each of the faces was trying to tell me. At the entrance to the Musée du Montmartre, Isabella charmed the entire tour group by spontaneously bursting into "La Vie en Rose."

Afterward, Eliana and I walked through the cobblestone streets in the rain, stopping beneath dripping leaves and red-and-white striped awnings, the shops lit up against the gray, the pastries in the windows looking like little gilded turtles.

"Look at that raincoat," Eliana said, pointing to a sleek orange slicker in the window of Petit Bateau. "That would look great on you. Go try it on." She politely said nothing about the shapeless parka, formerly George's, I was wearing, but she was so chic I could tell what she was thinking.

When I tried on the slicker, I stood up straighter, attempting to look like someone who sought out new experiences instead of running away from them. I pictured myself receiving a compliment on my new coat and saying, "Thank you, I got it in Paris"—instead of confessing I'd bought it online like most of my clothes.

I wore the slicker out of the store, hoping I looked like I might be French. I put my old parka in the shopping bag, later to be left behind at the hotel.

After shopping, Eliana and I went for a lunch of foie gras and blue cheese with Sauternes, sitting at a café with marble-topped tables and a long zinc bar. The rain was falling more gently now;

the sidewalks were bustling outside the thick glass windows.

"I wish I were more like you," I said, taking a bite of cheese on baguette, for once not thinking of Gene while eating blue cheese. The flavors were silky and biting, the Sauternes elixir-like, the tastes so much more intense than they were at home.

"In what way?" she said.

"Brave. You seem so good at traveling on your own." I wondered what it was like to be accustomed to navigating foreign airports, finding my way to an unknown hotel, and communicating in a new language using only a guidebook.

"I've done it for a long time. You just have to get used to it. These tour groups have been wonderful."

"But what if I hadn't found you on this trip?" I couldn't imagine eating dinner alone night after night in another country, looking sheepishly at all the couples and wondering what they thought, even though they probably wouldn't even notice me.

"Then you would have found other people," she said. "I do when I travel, and it's always been a lovely surprise."

She had a point. The group tour was going so smoothly there wasn't much to be anxious about. I would never jump on a random plane with crystal talismans in my bra jiggling merrily, but this trip had been quite doable.

After all the vacations he'd taken with his parents, George must have been an expert at international travel. They used to laugh together at family dinners over memories of canceled flights and misplaced hotel reservations that required them to rent a ridiculously tiny car or stay in a haunted *pensione*.

*Oh, George, why didn't you want to share any of the places you'd seen with me?* I guess he'd been content to stay home with his electronics, but it made me sad he never thought I should see those things too. With my fear of the unknown, I had never pushed him, but I hadn't known then what I was missing. Now I did.

# Available As Is

○ ○ ○ ○ ○

A few days later, the group went on a walking tour of Dijon, ending with lunch at the villa of an elderly French attorney who spoke no English.

Watching him silently pour the wine, elegant in his red sweater vest and navy-blue tie, I hesitated. *Be a little braver.* I'd tried out my French on a few outings, asking questions of shopkeepers and getting directions from museum guards—I'd even been asked if my accent was Canadian—but I hadn't yet attempted a full conversation.

Finally, I said, *"Je suis aussi un avocat mais je ne pratique pas pour beacoup d'annees."* Which means, "I am also a lawyer, but I haven't practiced for many years." I wasn't sure where that came from. I hadn't spoken French in more than twenty-five years. I couldn't even figure out how to program my garden lights, but maybe I wasn't that interested in my garden lights.

I was answered with a quick succession of French phrases. *"Je ne parle pas francais pour plus'que vigint années. Plus lentement, s'il vous plait."* ("I haven't spoken French in more than twenty years. Please speak more slowly.") In that moment, I realized my widow brain might yet reconstitute if only I could feed it more things that it wanted to eat.

Eventually the *avocat* and I managed to understand each other, more or less. Several people in the tour group had me act as their translator, having me tell him he had a beautiful home, finding out how long he'd lived there, asking what his favorite restaurant was and whether he could get them reservations there for dinner.

As I spoke for the group, Isabella looked on with pride as if I were her own daughter. I thought about the museum tour a few days earlier, where, upon seeing me, Isabella had given me a kiss hello and a gentle squeeze on the arm, prompting one of the women on the tour to say, "Your mother-in-law really loves you."

Every morning after our visit with the lawyer, I'd coil up my hair, clipping it in place; wrap my long navy scarf around my neck, the ends hanging down in front like the French women; and slip on my new slicker, ready to try out my French, to be just a little braver.

"I am Jean-Jacques . . . I mean, Jeff," said a gorgeous Jean-Paul Belmondo doppelganger with sculpted sideburns as he approached me in the cafeteria of the Louvre the next day when we were back in Paris. "I am lost. Could I borrow your map?"

When I handed it to him, he sat down, bringing his chair a little too close to mine. He told me he liked to haunt the Louvre on his days off. He said he owned his own business, not specifying what it was, but it might well have been gigolo to the tourist trade. Lost he was not.

"See how my heart beats for you," he said a few minutes later as we walked through the galleries together, putting my hand on his white T-shirt-clad chest under his black leather jacket.

"Are you a pickpocket?" I said, clutching my purse tightly, heedful of the repeated warnings over the museum intercom.

"*Non,* I just find you very attractive," he said, looking offended.

In response to his asking whether I was married, I told him I was *une veuve,* but aside from a quick *désolée* (sorry), it didn't seem to distract him from his pursuit. I rather liked him for his single-mindedness.

In Napoleon's apartments, we wound up alone in a dusty chamber dominated by an enormous bed with a fleur-de-lis bedspread. He gestured at it with one eyebrow raised.

"I like your hair, your outfit, the way that you move. You're sexy. I want you. Do you want me?"" he said as we sat down on the bench, his arm around me.

"Are you looking for a green card?" I hadn't known he was for sale in the museum gift shop.

"Non. Do you have your own room at your hotel?"

"Yes."

"I will make you an offer," he said. "Text me when you want me, and I will come to your room."

I let him kiss me so I could tell my yoga friend Laura I'd been kissed in the Louvre, but I had to tell him to get his tongue out of my ear, finally leaving to meet the rest of my group in the lobby.

"Do you want me?" he texted later that night.

"In theory" seemed a poor answer.

I thought of my failed hookup. Having Jean-Jacques come to my room offered possible theft, date rape, or worse, and I couldn't even google him. There was being brave, then there was causing my own personal Waterloo.

I offered to meet him for coffee, but wasn't surprised when I didn't hear back from him. He no doubt had already moved on to the next tourist. I did not throw caution to the wind, but clung to it proudly like a schoolgirl clutching her books to her chest. *Je ne regrette rien.*

On a rare night alone, I made pasta in my tiny kitchen at the hotel apartment, tossing it with salmon and asparagus left over from dinner the night before. I opened the marinated mussels and red wine I'd bought with Eliana at the nearby grocery store and ate at the minuscule table with its miserably spiny chair. My only view of Paris was of the rooms across the way. But it was the most complete I'd felt since George died.

For the first time, I had an inkling of a future. If I could be so moved by art, and if I could remember a language I'd loved but thought I'd lost years ago, I could try to live. Whatever I did, I would not be one of those women who was afraid to travel on their own because they'd always gone everywhere with their husbands. I would channel Eliana.

When we got home, I sent my in-laws a thank-you note for the trip. "I don't want to sound mushy, but I want you and Bob to know I love you," I typed at the end, then deleted, then retyped, finally leaving it in and putting the page in an envelope.

"Of course. It isn't mushy," Isabella emailed back two days later. "We love you too. We're family."

I wished I'd compromised more when George had still been alive. He and I could have gone to one of Isabella's dinners but then been excused from attending the next one. Or we could have gotten together with my in-laws on Christmas Day but spent Christmas Eve alone. We could have all taken a trip to Chile together, with all of us leading fuller lives.

My father once said the one thing he wished he'd done for my mother before she died was spend more time with her family, who he found difficult to get along with. I'd finally learned to consider mortality, but only after it was too late.

After sending the note, I booked my first international trip alone, nothing too risky, another alumni group tour, this time a ten-day trip to the Amalfi Coast. I'd be leaving in six months. I could only hope it would be my second vacation from grief.

Without Eliana or Paris to look forward to, dinner at home couldn't compare to a meal in my austere little room at the hotel apartment.

Working in my garden on a day too cold and misty for spring, I pruned excessively and took my aggressions out on the magnolia trees George had espaliered against the back fence. I sighed over the calla lily plants Max had brought me from his garden.

I moved on to power washing the concrete. The nozzle made thin lines of gray through the moss, the water mingling with a few stray raindrops.

"This sucks," I wrote in water cursive, shivering from the overspray.

I looked up, and there was Max in his black leather jacket, looking righteously indignant, his spiky hair silhouetted against the cloudy sky. I was wearing a bleach-stained sweatshirt, faded terry shorts, Wellingtons, and my dirt-stained canvas gardening hat with its dangling chin strap. I hadn't yet brushed my teeth that day.

"Just tell me what the hell is going on," he said. "You keep avoiding me."

He'd been trying to get together since I returned from Paris, but I'd been making excuses. I'd said I was sick, remembering the drive back from Tahoe and the feeling, no doubt exacerbated by my infection, that my entire life post-George had congealed in my stomach.

Yet I hadn't told him to go away forever. I had been keeping him in reserve just in case he turned out to be my last chance for companionship, even if I did have to pay for dinner so I could have someone to ask about my day.

"How many drinks have you had?" I asked, smelling the whiskey on his breath.

"Two. You picked that up right away. Are you okay? Why did you lie to me?"

"I'm fine. I just needed some time alone," I said.

"But I was so worried about you," he said, looking both angry and hangdog at the same time. "I don't know what I'll do without you. I love you and I've been so lonely. I thought you were out on more of your OkCupid dates."

"Yeah, I'm cheating on you with my garden," I joked unsuccessfully.

I was acting like I was thirteen years old: make me mad and I'll punish you by making you worry about me. I tried not to smirk, secretly pleased he'd been thinking I was out with other men. He must have thought my ability to organize my keys applied to my social life as well.

He helped me to spread a couple bags of bark over my azaleas. There was something endearing about a man working in the garden in a leather jacket, suddenly pressed into service.

Then he said, "Give me my stuff back."

"Now?" I said, incredulous, gesturing toward my muddy wellies. That was Max, offering a declaration of love, then encasing it in thorns.

I pried off the wellies, dashing into the house to gather up his ID bracelet, the Snoopy-print pajama bottoms he kept on my nightstand, the orange paisley jacket he'd given me because it matched my hair, and the whiskey bottle he kept in my bar. I gave them to him and went back to power washing. He stayed, watching me, looking as if he'd aged ten years in my absence, his tawny skin tinged with gray.

Finally I said, "I'm freezing. I need a shower."

"So go take one," he said, gently pushing me inside.

I expected him to leave, but when I emerged from the bathroom wrapped in a towel, he was lying on his stomach on the bed, and he still looked truly miserable. I should have told him to go, then locked the door behind me when I went inside. Instead, I'd left the choice up to him and let my loneliness make my decisions for me, even though the last time I had seen him had been horrible.

He offered to take me out for happy hour sushi. "Including drinks," he added with a wan smile. *Be brave. Say no.*

But hot sake and raw tuna are a lovely remedy for existential angst. So are tanned, well-muscled arms and green eyes framing high cheekbones. So was making him smile and finally wiping that sad look off his face even though he was an ass.

"Please take me back. I love you and I want this to work out," Max said over sushi, remembering for once to fill my cup too and not just his own. He sounded just like a little boy who hadn't realized something he loved could be lost.

His words "I love you" echoed in my head. Having never expected to feel love again, I couldn't let go of it, even for someone as flawed as Max.

I told myself he'd learned his lesson, that he would never behave like that again, that he valued me too much now that he'd had to live without me. I twisted his nervous breakdown into a course in self-improvement and fell back on the delusions of a middle-aged woman living alone in an empty house.

But I failed to value the peace that came with his absence. It was yet another thing I would have understood had I dated more when I was younger.

On the way home, I slipped Max's ID bracelet over my wrist like a good teenage girlfriend. Watching a movie in bed with him, I rested my cold feet on his legs over his yelps of protest. It was the first time in weeks I'd felt truly warm.

Max was not the love of my life, but he was a lover who made me feel alive. I told myself I was being a realist. He loved me in his own way. It was enough for now.

Now I know I was being an idiot. Not so brave after all.

# XIX. The Quiet Sundial

MORE THAN TWO YEARS AFTER GEORGE DIED, I was still seeking an epiphany about what to do with my life, so I finally went to see the sundial in his parents' backyard where his ashes were buried. It was a tall order for a patio ornament.

My in-laws' garden, with its huge, ornamental rocks, ancient bonsai trees, and hanging boxes of fuchsias, had often been featured on local garden club tours. They'd lived in the house for over fifty years, having bought it soon after George was born. He and his father had constructed much of it themselves.

Three feet tall, made of sand-colored stone, sitting between a Japanese maple and a tall columnar fountain, the sundial was shorter, squatter, and far less imposing than I'd imagined. Still, its inscription, *George Albert Hansen, July 29, 1959–April 10, 2013,* made my blood run cold.

Before seeing it, I could envision George floating in the ether, checking on his work group and murmuring solutions to frustrated coders. But the sundial made it plain he was now ash. I'd managed to avoid seeing it until now, coming over to my in-laws' only in the evenings when it was natural to stay inside.

This was where my husband wound up after I bailed out and Isabella took over. In retrospect, it was a good thing she had. I was so unhinged after his death I probably would have had his ashes interred at his cube at Intuit in a bitter tribute to his workaholism.

In the movies, the bereaved kneels down and chatters away at her beloved's gravestone, looking for a revelation. I never understood that. Either the deceased's soul is untethered from this earth so the bereaved could contact him anywhere, or else it's trapped at the gravesite and probably really pissed off about it. But I still had to try.

"George, we never had a chance to say goodbye," I whispered to the sundial. "Do you have anything you want to say to me?"

I'd always wondered, if George hadn't been in denial, whether there was anything he would have asked me to do when he was gone, like watch *Casablanca* and make Steak Dianne every year on our anniversary, or plant purple azaleas in our garden in his memory, or be there for his parents. I wondered whether he would have had any advice for me, like never sell the house, or buy a different surround sound processor, or no man will ever love you the way I did so get a cat.

Not surprisingly, the sundial did not reply. I waited a little longer just to be sure.

"You need to get out and meet more people," Isabella said, coming to sit beside me on her patio. "You should go to the Commonwealth Club or join that group, Table for Six, where they fix you up with people to have dinner with."

The Commonwealth Club had certainly worked for my dad and Jane when they met there all those many years ago. On the other hand, Nancy told me that when she went there after being widowed, the attendees were mostly women with very few men. This was in keeping with my view that most single middle-aged men did as little as possible while still managing to remain sexually active.

"Maybe I'll do that," I said vaguely. "But I do have a boyfriend. You've met Max."

"You mean the hippie?" she said with a frown. I guess he didn't qualify.

Before the Lake Tahoe incident, I'd brought him to dinner a few times with my in-laws, trying to avoid keeping him apart from them the way I had with Gene. I was trying to reassure them that I wasn't alone while simultaneously deluding myself into thinking that Max wasn't so bad since we could all have dinner together.

But when Isabella met people, she always questioned them about their educations and careers. Max was a junior college dropout with a blue-collar job. He was friendly and polite, and had offered my in-laws his condolences. He had even told them to call him if they needed any help around the house, but they didn't like to talk about George. Max's overtures had fallen flat.

Also, he had eaten not just his own dessert but the rest of ours when we didn't finish them, saying he hated to see good food go to waste. Isabella had looked away with a bemused, if faintly disgusted, smile.

"Yes, the hippie." It was easier not to argue.

In retrospect, I wished I hadn't introduced him to my in-laws. He was not a good man, and I saw him as temporary, yet I'd brought him to dinner with them because having someone to sit in the empty chair at the table for four seemed better than leaving it empty. I probably caused Isabella more worry than if I'd come alone.

It must have been hard for her to see someone who was not nearly the man that George had been sitting in his chair. I was embarrassed that with all my dating I hadn't managed to come up with someone more suitable. But she never said anything, and I assumed she'd vowed not to offer any judgment.

My dad had also suggested I try to meet more people by signing up for a UC Extension class on the wines of the Rhone Valley, as he had when he was single, or putting on an attractive yet modest outfit and taking in the latest exhibition at the de Young Museum where he'd had a lot of luck meeting women, and where he was probably one of the few men who came there by himself. All I'd managed to do was to meet a French gigolo at the Louvre.

I didn't want to go to a lecture on political paradigms at the Commonwealth Club, or Manichewitz and Mishegoss Night at the synagogue, or even half-priced Jell-O shots at Vinnie's Roadhouse. After spending all that time on my dating apps, and all those hours on bad meetups drinking too many nonfat chai lattes, I was tired of "Marketing Myself to Score Dates," the new kind of graduate degree for the middle-aged single. I didn't have the energy to go back online and try again.

"If I weren't married," Isabella said, smiling to herself, "I'd move to San Francisco. It has everything—symphonies, museums, opera."

"Mmmmm," I murmured. What did everybody have against Danville?

"You should live abroad for a while," she said. But I had my yoga girls and a writing group I loved. I had a boyfriend, albeit a deeply flawed one. I didn't want to run away from home without having something I was running to.

"Mmmmm."

"You live like an old lady," she added affectionately.

"Mmmmm." *Must not grind teeth.*

Isabella didn't want me to be alone, but more importantly, she wanted me to have a richly textured life, with or without a partner. She had made several efforts to introduce me to travel. It wasn't her fault if I couldn't arrange a better life for myself, and I was embarrassed I hadn't accomplished more since George's death, or before it, actually.

When my cosmopolitan nuclear physicist mother-in-law, who still worked every day, asked me what I was up to, I muttered abashedly about writing classes and yoga and redoing the garden lights (really grasping here), and no, I hadn't been thinking about doing anything with my law degree.

Whenever Isabella contacted me, she always started out by complaining she hadn't heard from me in a while. But she was really saying that she missed me.

She still didn't talk much about George, but she'd email me on his birthday and the anniversary of his death—a single crack in her veneer—saying how old he would have been or that he died exactly two years ago, as if she needed to acknowledge those dates with someone who missed him as much as she did. I'd learned to stop making excuses for not having contacted her sooner and just told her that I missed her too.

I glanced at the sundial on my way out. But wherever George was, he wasn't there.

That evening, as the light began to fade, I started to scatter the aqua-colored stones I'd bought at the nursery around the aloes George and I had planted in our backyard. It was the closest I could come to putting stones on his grave.

Each rock was a memory. Setting them down one by one, I thought about our first kiss, our first slow dance, the first time we spent the entire night together, and the first time he belted out "Born to Be Wild" at a karaoke night. I ran out of stones long before I ran out of memories.

It was twilight, when the outlines blurred and the air became gauzy. I stretched out under the pergola, on the white outdoor sofa with its turquoise striped cushions, the two redwood trees towering overhead, framed by the magnolia plants, the helix-shaped wind sculpture turning gently in the breeze. We'd thought about adding a pergola for years and had finally ordered one during George's last autumn, before he'd gotten really sick.

"Measure again, kitten," he'd said, directing me from his wheelchair. "You know what they say, measure twice, cut once." The pergola looked just as good as we'd imagined it would, but it had arrived the week after he died.

I was dozing off into half dreams when George appeared next to me on the sofa and said with the grin that I missed so terribly, "At least you didn't mess things up too much."

"Really? The bathroom remodel turned out okay?" I said, sitting up with a jolt. I tripped over my words and rubbed my eyes in disbelief.

"Yeah, it's great. I love the tile. Only you would pick a shade named Dorian Gray," he said. "And the pergola turned out exactly like I'd hoped. But I miss my old home theater system. When you had the stereo guys redo it, you went for looks over quality. I can't believe you got rid of my Bryston surround sound processor. Ease of use isn't everything. At least you kept my Aerial 10ts." Even from beyond, he was still trying to influence our audiovisual experience.

"I need things I can use on my own," I replied. "And those speakers weigh three hundred pounds each. I think I'm stuck with them for life." I decided to omit my lecture on how unprepared I was when he died. I'd complained enough while he was still alive.

"What's with Max? Why'd you have to go for someone like the Worm?" he said, grimacing, referring to his former friend Anthony by his nickname. Worm was an underachiever who, like Max, wanted to be a professional guitarist but, also like Max, spent way too much time getting high and watching TV.

"Max loves me," I muttered.

"If you say so. Sorry about Gene. I always liked him. But you need to stop hanging out with flatliners. Why did you ever date Denis? That guy couldn't say anything straight. And you should have just belted Lowell."

"It seemed like fun at the time." I felt myself blush, not realizing death had made him omniscient.

"But what really matters, the only thing that does, is that you're alive," he said, suddenly becoming serious.

"Why did you lie to me about dying? Couldn't you have told

me the truth?" I said, finally asking the question that had haunted me since he died.

"I always told you my truth, even though the doctors kept saying I was already dead. I refused to believe them, and I lasted way longer than they thought I would. We wouldn't have had any kind of life with you always thinking I was going to die at any second."

His eyes sparkled. He'd lasted four years after his diagnosis, which was far longer than his doctors had predicted. He'd beat the naysayers. Sort of.

"The last six months were hell," I said, raising my voice. "I didn't understand what was happening. I didn't know you anymore. Sometimes it seemed like you were already gone."

"I'm never gone. I'm in your memories. Not to mention my awesome, now much less awesome, home theater system. Drive the Consolation. By the way, I hate that name. I never would have gotten an automatic for me. I got it for you to remember how loved you are."

"Was. How loved I was."

"No. *Are.* You just have to believe it," he said. "We had true love for almost thirty-three years. I can't be with you anymore, but you still have that love."

Some people believed in angels. I believed in statistics about the rarity of male breast cancer, but I'd had George for the better part of a lifetime. It's just that the rest of that lifetime didn't seem so great without him.

"I'll always feel bad about how we ended."

"I know, but I'm not here to punish you," he said. Determination deepened each syllable. "I'm here to tell you to stop punishing yourself. You're going to have to find a way to be happy without me."

"I've tried. I can't."

"You haven't tried hard enough. You think my legacy is

Quicken. But it isn't. It's you. I have to believe I left you with enough love so that you can survive without me. If you give up trying, our life together was meaningless."

His image started to flicker a little, and a few silver sparks rose up from the edges.

"Don't go," I begged him. "I'm not doing this very well."

"Cook something good for once," he said, now only an outline as he faded away. "Just because I died the day after you made those scallops didn't make it the scallops' fault."

"I've hated scallops ever since."

"And aim higher. I never thought you were a bad writer. You just have to work at it instead of thinking everything should come easily," he said. "You know, the universe is random, but it isn't hostile."

Then he was gone, the air where he'd been gradually losing its charge. But he left me with free will.

I thought of George and me in our early twenties, when he had taken the lead and forged ahead with his engineering career. He had held my hand while I trailed behind him. I had never looked past his footsteps, choosing instead to let him decide our path.

He might have been a coder of almost infinite bandwidth, but he hadn't looked much past our front door, and I had rarely crossed the threshold. I had been too afraid of what I might find on the other side.

I finally realized that I hadn't been happy during the last years of our marriage. I'd gotten used to pushing those thoughts away like spoiled food, convincing myself that our limited, but well-tended, lives were how he had cared for me—I could finally have all the coddling and chocolates and sick days I wanted. But it kept me a child, happy to pull up the bars of my playpen and stay inside.

The weekend in 2009 when we had been waiting for George's test results, we had gone for lunch at the same Napa Valley bistro where we went the day that we got married. We'd sat down at "our" marble-topped table and had ordered the same rose-colored meal of pink champagne and lobster quenelles that we'd had all those many years ago.

"But what are you getting tested *for?*" I'd asked George yet again, uncertain since he'd referred only to unspecified tests.

"Everything," he had said with a laugh. "We'll find out on Tuesday."

The quenelles had been as nutty and buttery as they had been all those years ago, and the champagne had tasted just as yeasty, but I knew if I let my mind wander off those test results, they'd come back bad, my punishment for not having worried enough.

After lunch, George had said we should go for a walk, and he'd guided me over to our favorite jewelry store. He asked me yet again to try the necklace he'd had me try on during our last few trips, a chain of chunky, aquamarine cylinders like pale blue icicles, stunning but too expensive to buy. The necklace had lain just right, its heft substantial, the stones cool and smooth against my collarbones. The aqua had brought out my eyes.

*Now, I'll get to take it off,* I had thought with relief, not wanting a souvenir of Waiting for Test Results Day.

"We'll take it," George had said, and surprised me. The jeweler had put it in a blue-velvet box, dropping the box in a gold paper bag, putting matching foil on top, and tying a ribbon around the handles.

"Wonderful choice. I've seen you two in here looking at it before," he'd said. "Is it a special occasion?"

"Every day's a special occasion," George had answered, bowing and handing me the bag as if he'd just accomplished something really big, but I'd hated all the forced gaiety.

At dinner, I had told him we should return the necklace, that it was too expensive, and hoped that he would think I was just being practical.

"It might be the last thing I ever give you," he had said.

That's when I finally realized that he was scared too. He must have been worried since his two maternal uncles had already died of cancer. I had pretended to be thrilled about keeping the necklace. Even as he had been waiting for the hardest news of his life, he had tried to give me the most perfect day he could. It's just that he thought objects could fix feelings.

After he died, I had buried the necklace deep in my jewelry drawer, angry with it for not having healing properties, for not being what I needed. How much better it would have been had we been able to talk about being scared instead of hiding it under a froth of tissue paper, but like my father, George did not appear weak.

During the past year, I'd taken the necklace out of its box a few times and had looked for hidden meanings in the shimmering shades of aqua, but I had found only the realization that he had done the best he could for me. He had left me financially secure (no small feat in the overpriced Bay Area), with memories of the deepest love he had known how to give.

Caroline often said at the start of each class, "Approach your practice with a beginner's mind," meaning as if you were doing yoga for the very first time. It finally registered. We were all beginners, my dad after my mom's death, George with his cancer—when even a brilliant guy with almost infinite bandwidth couldn't withstand the lure of denial—me after his death when, despite having had lots of time to myself, I'd never really been alone before. None of us meant to do badly.

I could forgive George for narrowing our lives, especially since I never asked otherwise. But my forgiveness was bittersweet—we would never have the chance to talk now that I finally had a voice.

# XX. The Man Who Tried to Kill Me

IN THE MONTHS AFTER I RETURNED FROM PARIS, I decided to start having a future.

"I always feel like I'm hiding something when I meet someone new, like I'm lying about who I was when George was sick," I said to Will after writing group one day. Then I wondered why I'd said it.

He'd simply asked about my plans for the weekend. He would have thought I was crazy had I told him my house was haunted by my caregiver ghost, her bleach-stained sweatpants brushing by me in the hallway, still on her way to fetch George his morning Vicodin and Triscuits.

"Write about it," he said. "It's when we keep our secrets inside that they fester. When we tell other people about our guilt, it takes away the stigma." Kübler-Ross agrees, saying, "Telling the story helps to dissipate the pain. Grief must be witnessed to be healed."

Deciding that George was a friendly ghost, I finally kicked him out of our home office. I put my laptop where his computer used to be next to the window and cushioned the hard, Eames-style chairs he'd chosen with turquoise and red pillows.

I took the unfinished remote-controlled model Jeep he'd

been working on when he died off the shelf and planned to put it in the closet. Then, almost involuntarily, I threw it in the garbage, looking over my shoulder as if he might catch me, putting a ceramic Buddha head in its place.

*Sorry, George, but it's not like you're ever going to finish it. You're the one who said I should try to be happy.*

The next week my voice shook as I read aloud to my writing group, "More than two years after George died, I am still mired in shame. Memories of me yelling at him continue to haunt me. My burden following my husband's death: knowing I was a terrible caregiver and a bad person." I had to stop reading.

I remembered how hard George had tried to be helpful even as he faded away, sitting on the edge of the bed, his newly skinny arms trembling as he shimmied across the transfer board to his wheelchair, the sheets stained from the tears in his skin, his face twisted from effort. I had prayed he wouldn't fall in a heap by the bed and had wished that he understood he was dying. I was so very angry that this had become our lives.

My voice breaking, I handed my piece to Will to finish. He continued, "I need to stop reopening my wounds. But they cannot heal if they are buried in shame. George is at peace. And I need to be at peace now too."

*The Huffington Post* accepted my essay, but seeing it online was like sharing my reverse dating profile, the one that made me look irredeemable. But unable to change the past, all I could do was confess to it.

"You didn't do anything wrong," said the first comment to appear online. "It was the best you could do." A few hours later, I had more than eighty comments. Some caregivers shared their own stories, some admitted their guilt, and still others agonized over being unable to help their own loved ones. But they all said pretty much the same thing: "Stop blaming yourself. You're going to be fine."

I felt like I'd finally put on a pair of glasses with the right prescription. My caregiver ghost faded from the hallway with a tired smile.

She'd always wanted to leave; she just needed to be forgiven.

After that, I joined a pool of writers who submitted personal essays to national women's magazines. The writers had two days to submit their work, competing against each other to be published. I hated competition. It had been another one of my failings as a lawyer.

I read all the comments from my caregiver article again. *You deserve a future. These people think you should try.* Attempting to exile my brain with alcohol hadn't worked so well—maybe it was time to repatriate it.

Over the next six months, I had eight articles accepted by five different magazines, all of them about being widowed. Taken together, they formed one of those wood-framed puzzles with one piece missing, where if you slide the pieces together in just the right order, they formed a picture. But the puzzle pieces—remodeling rooms in one article, making women friends in another, rediscovering sex in a third (I didn't share that one with Dad)— had never formed a complete picture, only glimpses of something amorphous that might turn out to be less than terrible.

Almost all the photographs used to illustrate my articles showed a woman sitting alone next to an empty chair or lying on one side of a bed, her face averted from the camera, her emptiness palpable. Seeing what widowhood looked like to other people, I realized I'd been right to feel stigmatized. But perhaps those sad pictures related to the common perception of a woman of a certain age who was on her own regardless of whether she was widowed.

After my eighth article was published, the writers' pool that I had joined shut down. But by then I'd stopped carrying my work to writing group in a wrinkled manila folder and had replaced it with an orange leather portfolio like something an overzealous, slightly twee college student would have used.

I decided to take a five-week writing course in San Francisco on editing. My only regret was agreeing to have dinner with Max after my first class.

"Get in the car. Traffic's shit. I've been circling the block forever," Max said when he pulled up outside the building where my class was held. He was amped up and edgy, probably high on pot and pain pills with a drink or two under his belt, but he'd insisted he wanted to take me for dinner in the Mission District.

After we parked, he started walking quickly but aimlessly, fighting some inner restlessness, and circled the same blocks over and over, as if looking for something he'd misplaced. Unfortunately, it appeared to be his equilibrium.

Tired of following him through the Mission, I finally picked a sushi bar having happy hour. I thought we could hang out for a while and relax. My flabby brain was exhausted from being exercised in an intense three-hour class. But Max rushed through his meal like someone eating for the first time in weeks, then leapt up with a loud "Let's go," as if prodding a dawdling toddler.

He agreed to wait until I finished eating but perched nervously on the edge of his chair, eager to spring back up again. I got up reluctantly and refrained from suggesting we get another sake and stay awhile. I was still making excuses for not getting what I wanted, rationalizing that at least this time I wasn't deluding myself.

As we were walking back to the car, the light changed against us just as we reached the crosswalk of a busy intersection. I told him we needed to wait, but he grabbed my wrist and dragged me into the street with him.

A speeding car almost hit us. It missed us by inches and screeched to a halt with a loud squeal of brakes. I stopped to let it pass, but by then other cars were coming at us too. I stood in the intersection, frozen, watching the cars whiz by, terrified we'd be hit, my heart lurching into my throat.

"You don't trust me," he said after we'd finally reached the other side, running as fast as we could to the sound of more sickening squeals. "You don't even know how to cross a street. It would have been fine if you'd just come with me."

I slumped against the wall of a busy ice cream store, shaking with adrenaline, repeating over and over like a mantra, "We just almost died." People moved past us to line up for ice cream, ignoring us as he yelled at me, but I was too tired to move.

*You can't live like this anymore.*

"I should just leave you here. You can take the train home," he said, his eyes boring into me. I started walking toward the station, relieved to be rid of him, but he started walking alongside me, his voice rising as he worked himself into a frenzy. It was Tahoe all over again.

I willed him to leave. Just a few more steps and I'd reach the station, but he blocked my way just as I was about to head down the stairs, muttering, "Never mind, I'll give you a ride."

I wanted to take the train, but he wouldn't let me get by him. I pictured him running after me into the station, grabbing at me as I tried to buy my ticket and reach my train. Finally, I went with him to his car, still too stunned to think he might be suicidal, not wanting to attract any more attention.

"You almost killed me," I said, still finding it hard to believe. An hour ago I'd been elated over my new writing class. Now I was beaten down.

"You are such a bitch. I don't see how George ever put up with you," he said as he drove.

I would never forget those words. I'd still loved him a little before that day, a tired, vestigial kind of love, but those words killed what was left of it. A calmness wafted over me.

"You're abusive," I said slowly, to him but mostly to myself.

It was the first time I'd used that word to describe him, even to myself. *Abusive*, I mouthed silently, remembering the restaurant in Tahoe, to the other times he'd rushed me out of restaurants even though I'd barely finished eating, to his constant complaints about how selfish I was and how I owed him for staying with me.

Instead of valuing me more after I'd broken up with him, he'd gotten worse, thinking that I would take him back no matter what he did. He harbored a sick kind of contempt for me now that he knew how weak I was. Another piece of the puzzle slid into place. His language had become emotional abuse. I just hadn't acknowledged it. If I had, I also would have had to acknowledge that I'd been accepting it for a very long time.

At least, I thought, I hadn't accepted physical abuse. Then I remembered the time he threw a drink in my face when we'd been arguing and the way he'd laughed about it afterward. And the time we had been walking to the casino and he had run ahead inside, holding the door shut against me as I shivered outside in the snow, and had snickered inside with the people who were watching us. And today, when he had dragged me into traffic, against my will, yet I still agreed to go home with him. Oh yes, I'd accepted his physical abuse too.

For the rest of the ride, every time he started to say something, I'd interject the word "abusive," quietly at first, then growing louder each time he opened his mouth. I willed him to be silent until he finally stopped trying to talk and looked straight ahead as he drove, sweaty and distraught. I was scared he'd cause an accident, but in that moment, I could no longer bear the sound of his voice.

Half an hour later, we reached the train station where I'd left my car, a twenty-minute drive and I'd be home and this day would be over. I leapt out of his car and got into the Consolation. I exhaled with relief, but just as I was starting to back out, he pulled up behind me, blocking my car in with his. He'd trapped me. I got out of my car, uncertain what to do.

"You are being such a bitch," he said. He got out of his car and left it running in the aisle.

When I told him to move, he refused. My mouth went dry, and I needed a bathroom. *Think.* Best option: lock myself in my own car and call the police.

But just as I was about to get in, a deep voice suddenly asked, "Are you okay? What do you need?" As if he'd materialized out of nowhere, a man was standing next to me, middle-aged and heavily muscled with a short gray beard, wearing a blue striped button-down and pressed jeans as if he'd been going somewhere special.

In a voice so calm I didn't recognize it as my own, I said, "I need him to leave."

"Why are you being like this?" Max said. Then seeing the man standing next to me, he pleaded, lowering his voice, "It's Saturday night. Let's just go back to your place, baby."

The man turned to Max and said, placid but intimidating, sounding like he could wait all night, "I'm not leaving until you do. And I need you to leave now."

"She's my girlfriend. We were just having a little argument," Max said.

"I need you to leave," said the man.

"I told you, she's my girlfriend." But the man just stood there, implacable. Max hesitated, weighing his options, trying to think what to say next, but finally he got in his car and drove away.

The man's blonde companion walked over to join us now that Max was gone. "Do you know that person?" she asked. I knew I looked like a respectable lady, about their age, driving a nice car, and Max looked like a maniac.

"He's my, sort of, boyfriend," I said, "but he isn't usually like this." Not only did I know him; I'd been with him for over two years.

From articles I'd read, I knew that one of the signs of abuse was making excuses for the abuser's behavior. I just hadn't realized until half an hour ago that those articles applied to me.

"Are you going to be okay?" the man asked.

"Yes, we don't live together and he doesn't have a key," I answered wearily. I stopped myself from saying that I wasn't crazy enough to live with him. I must have already seemed crazy to have been with Max in the first place

I thanked the man and tried to hide my embarrassment, as if this was all a part of my plan. I nearly asked him whether he worked as a hostage negotiator or a SWAT team member, but I didn't. I didn't want to have to answer any questions about my own life.

"Sure. Take care," he said as he and his date walked away, but he still looked concerned. They were probably asking each other, "Why does she put up with a guy like that? This sort of thing has probably happened before, why does she keep taking it, I wonder if he's ever hit her, I hope she doesn't let him do it again."

It was George's birthday, July 29. I'd taken the date as a sign I should enroll in the writing class. I'd looked at it many times online but always talked myself out of actually going. *It's too far. They'll all be better than you. It takes too long to get to the city.*

I was embarrassed to admit that in my old life I would have been fearful of the fifteen-minute walk from the train station to the class and having to pass by the homeless folks and the closed-up storefronts. But now it was just another place. Max was far more dangerous.

Yet the date had become something more. George was looking out for me.

A few weeks earlier, I'd been in Sorrento for my tour of the Amalfi Coast. The trip had started out badly when my flight from San Francisco to Munich was late, leaving me forty-three minutes instead of the projected hour and a half to make my connection.

My seatmates on the way to Munich were a couple who snuggled and cooed at each other. When I looked over and smiled, eager to initiate the nervous conversation of the novice solo traveler, the man frowned and looked pointedly away as if I were rancid. At least he looked surprised when I got on the same tram as we made our ways through the bowels of the Munich airport. This time I glared at him, reaching my gate with nineteen minutes to spare.

At the welcome dinner, I wound up sitting with two couples who communicated in Couples Speak:

"We want to see as many of the ruins as possible."

"We'll meet you all back at the hotel since we want to take a walk together after dinner."

"We've heard the Amalfi Coast is so romantic."

I told them I was traveling alone, but didn't mention my widowhood. I didn't want to become the embodiment of their worst fears.

But when they asked me what I did, at least I could say I was a writer, instead of stammering the way I used to, "Not much, really, I used to be an attorney," as if needing to reassure them, as well as myself, that I had brain cells; they were just on hiatus.

The trip improved after I joined the few other women who were traveling alone, and my shyness dissipated over our first cocktail hour. Together we saw the pastel town of Positano, the blue waters of Capri, the temples of Paestum, and the ruins of Pompeii. We walked along the sun-drenched bay of Naples and tried the famous Neapolitan pizza, which was delicious if a little plain with its thin covering of tomato sauce and dots of mozzarella.

Like me, Kristin was an attorney, a yogi, and a shopper, with auburn curls and a curvy figure that made the Italian men shout "*Bella*" every time she passed by. We bonded over the merits of vinyasa yoga, cutting carbs, and finding the perfect Italian black leather jacket. During our evenings back in Sorrento, we'd window shop, then have dinner at one of the little waterfront restaurants, the seafood piled high on ice like an avant-garde sculpture.

Kristin said she was dying to go for drinks at the Hotel Vittoria, the *grand dame* of Sorrento with its manicured gardens, banks of bougainvillea, and a uniformed host who turned almost everyone away at the door. She was an Angeleno; it figured she'd want to go someplace gated.

The next night, dressed in our best clothes accessorized by our new Italian handbags, we held our breath and stood up a little taller when we reached the host stand. He let us pass, and we struggled to stay nonchalant as he seated us on the huge outdoor patio, all white marble with sweeping views of the sea, lights twinkling on the water, and patrons dressed like a layout in *Vogue*.

It must have been dinnertime for the locals, because almost everyone left soon after, leaving us alone on the patio. A man started playing the grand piano, singing lounge standards in a heavy French accent. Just as Kristin left for the restroom, he broke into the first few notes of "They Can't Take That Away from Me," George's and my song. It ended just as Kristin returned, as if the song were intended for me alone.

"Good, you're trying to be happy," I could hear George say. "Now dump the Worm."

Caroline house-sat for me while I was away. Upon my return, she told me that one night she'd had Nancy and Laura over for dinner, and the lights had started flickering on and off, remaining constant for a few minutes, then starting up again. By the third time, they were all saying in unison, "Hi, George! Good to see you too."

I liked to think that George was watching over the house,

keeping it safe from imaginary perils and welcoming my new friends. Perhaps he was starting to appear because I'd stopped being mad at him.

I thought I might be attributing too much to coincidence, but I knew the events of July 29 were his way of telling me I was in danger. He sent that man in the parking lot to help me. Max might have been suicidal when he ran into the street, in which case it was either grossly inconsiderate of him to try to take me with him or perversely helpful of him to leave me no choice but to break up with him.

"Let me make it up to you by taking you out for dinner. I'll let you decide when to cross the street," Max texted the next day.

"C'mon, baby, we've had some great times together," he texted the day after.

And we had. We'd hiked in Lake Tahoe, and seen all the headliners for free at the casino amphitheater, and lain together on secluded beaches in Marin, and made love on lazy afternoons. But he was going under, and I didn't want to go with him.

I stopped joking with my yoga girls that I'd settled for a hot guy with little brainpower. I'd settled for abuse, and on July 29, I could have died.

But getting rid of Max wasn't that easy.

"I don't think I can live without you. I'm going to kill myself," he texted the next week. A few minutes later, he added, "I'm so down. I'm really going to do it." Within an hour, he sent dozens more texts, all threatening suicide, ending with "I'm going to take all my pain pills. I've left a handwritten will at your house making you my executor."

When I got home, there was a roll of butcher paper by my front door, rolled up with a rubber band and a wilted rose from his garden, the will scrawled on it in jagged handwriting. Despite all his histrionics, he had never before said he was going to kill himself.

Thinking of his two siblings who committed suicide, I called the police and gave them his address. If he'd ever wanted to punish me, making me responsible for another death was the way to do it. But a few minutes later he texted that he was on his way over to my house. My stomach in knots, I called the police again.

"Let them come," he said from his car when I yelled to him that the police were on their way. "I want them to know how you treated me."

When he got to my house, he banged on my windows, screaming, "Open up. I still love you." His body was moving so jerkily he had to be on something.

I sat out of sight on my bathroom floor, recalling the dispatcher's final words, "Try not to engage with him." I realized this was not a man on the verge of suicide but a toddler expecting Mommy to pick him up if he screamed loudly enough. My sympathy for him evaporated like the steam rising off an overheated engine.

*Remember, abusive.*

There's a joke in Danville about how many police cars respond to every call, no matter how minor, because they have so little else to do. Four squad cars pulled up, their sirens blaring. The police asked Max to leave, but he wouldn't go.

He yelled, "That's my girlfriend. We just need to talk" and "I need to go inside to get my guitar."

I prayed the neighbors weren't home to witness the trashy widow fighting with her crazy ex-boyfriend. Finally, the cops arrested him, hauling him away in handcuffs as he shouted my name.

"Alcohol makes people do strange things," said one of the policemen as he was leaving. "If he comes back, call us. In domestic violence situations, you may need to get a restraining order."

I had become a domestic violence situation.

# 🍓 XXI. Widow's Peaks

"So, you are from Danville?" said a voice with an Indian accent one Sunday morning as thirty-four other hikers and I staggered up a steep incline that left me panting like an obscene phone caller.

The voice belonged to a thin man who looked to be about seventy with deep brown skin, high cheekbones, and huge piercing eyes under sleek gray hair. He had the mischievous smile of a ten-year-old boy.

"Yeah," I wheezed. When I'd arrived at the trailhead, the group leader, an affable, bald-headed fellow who looked like he climbed Mount Kilimanjaro as a warmup, had herded us into a circle where we'd given our first names and the towns we lived in before heading out.

"I am Arjun, also from Danville. Now speed up. You don't want to be in the back of the pack," my companion said.

I didn't see why not, but I tried to keep up as he grabbed my arm and propelled me forward.

I had joined a hiking group that met on weekend mornings to do "short" six- to ten-mile hikes after I kept waking up in the middle of the night thinking Max was trying to break in. Unable to fall back asleep, I'd lie there for hours, obsessing that I was going to die alone, desperately in need of a distraction other than men.

Max hadn't stopped texting me since the day after his arrest when he asked me to pick him up to retrieve his car from my house. He'd had to leave it when the police took him away. He talked about being arrested as if this was something we could already laugh about. The police had let him go after only a few hours despite my showing them the texts and the will, so I guess he'd managed to convince them that he wasn't suicidal, just really obnoxious.

He wasn't even ashamed of himself. He'd just been upping his bets the way he did at the blackjack table when he was losing, and expecting his luck to turn. Channeling the Hungover Widow, I told him to get counseling.

"We Danville people are fast," Arjun said as we started out. As we hiked, he chatted cheerfully, with no shortness of breath, about his meditation practice, his daily walks, and his spiritual beliefs, saying, "Wherever I go, I know that God is with me."

Perhaps God could give me a boost to get up the ridge.

"But you must forgive me, I am an old man grateful to have a beautiful woman to talk to," he said.

I wiped my sweat-drenched face, knowing I looked like a beet. Later I would learn that Arjun referred to all women as beautiful. It turned out we lived only a few blocks apart in the same housing development.

"Perhaps you would like to come with me on my morning walks sometime," he said when we stopped for our lunch break halfway through the hike.

"Uh, I'm not much of a morning person." He'd probably kill me.

"I have become one since my wife died four years ago," he said. "I need to keep to my daily routine."

"I'm widowed too."

"When my wife died, my chalice of happiness went from full to empty," he said. I had met a poet.

"I can relate," I said, telling him a little about George now that I could breathe again. His wife too had died of cancer.

"When our spouses die, they leave their bodies and jump into our hearts," he said.

Then he was off to take selfies with all the other beautiful ladies on the hike. He gave me a little shrug when he caught me looking at him, as if to say we must find what pleasure we can in this life.

As we were walking to our cars after the hike, he said, "Since we are neighbors, we could carpool to some of the future hikes if you'd like." I said I'd like that. It was a tiny ray of happiness piercing through my Max-induced fog.

"Great first effort today. Good to have you with us," our leader said as I was leaving. "We usually go for coffee after our hikes. Will you be joining us?"

I declined his invitation this time; I was so exhausted that I could barely make it back to the car to collapse on the sofa when I got home, finally able to sleep. But the next weekend I went for coffee after carpooling to the hike with Arjun and tried hard to keep up with him as he again took off ahead of the group.

I pushed myself up the hills as if to pound out my neediness, like crushing mint with a mortar and pestle. That evening Arjun texted me good night, adding the kiss-blowing emoji to his message—a welcome bit of charm among Max's twisted missives.

On our next hike, Arjun said, "That backpack you have is useful only for looking fashionable. Perhaps you would like to come with me to REI the next time I go shopping. They can help you select something more suitable."

The other hikers had much larger nylon contraptions, with loops for hanging hiking poles and extra gear, and holes for tubes to stay hydrated from the water bladders hooked inside. I had an extra-small fashion backpack with no hooks or loops, and I had to take it off every time I wanted a sip from my water bottle.

"I hope that's not all the water you brought," one of my fellow hikers said.

"Uh, no," I lied, looking down at my feet and realizing I was also wearing the wrong kind of shoes. That explained why I'd been slipping so much.

"So why have you started coming on all of our hikes?" Arjun asked me another time. By then I'd learned that under his flirty exterior, he was a retired mathematician with several degrees and a thorough knowledge of history.

"I just got out of a bad relationship," I said. "It lasted for more than two years. It was great at the beginning, but he went a little crazy toward the end." I trailed off, unable to continue.

"It's good you are out of that relationship," he said, suddenly taking my hand. "You know you can talk to me whenever you need to."

"I just might do that." But how could I explain that I'd settled for abuse?

"I'm usually around except for my yoga lessons and evening prayers and visits with my grandson," he said. "I lead a very tranquil life."

A few weeks later on one of the hikes, our leader said, "It's great to see you coming back. You didn't strike me as the outdoorsy type."

"I, um, just got out of a long relationship, so I have a lot more time than I used to," I said, once again panting on an uphill climb. I was apparently unable to walk and filter my words at the same time.

"A lot of people who hike with us are in transition," he said. "They're getting divorced or coming out of relationships. I can tell by how often they show up."

*But they weren't in abusive ones.*

With a pat on the shoulder he was gone, but turned up a few minutes later as if by magic to offer me one of his hiking poles when I started floundering on a steep downhill, since I lacked proper equipment of my own. That night, I texted Arjun to schedule our trip to REI.

I'd been putting it off, telling myself that I wasn't that into hiking, that the drives were too long, that sometimes I got lost trying to find the trailheads, that the hikes started too damn early. Yet I kept coming back. After Max, I felt more anxious staying at home than I did going to a new place, even if I did obsess whenever the hike announcement referred to limited parking or narrow roads.

Before the next hike, I carefully filled my new water bladder, sliding the plastic top into place with a satisfying little slursh, tucking it into my new green backpack, slipping my new poles through the loops at the back, and putting on thick olive-green socks emblazoned with the REI logo to match my new boots.

*You are too outdoorsy.*

I put a container of almonds and an apple in my backpack. I'd started getting a weekly produce delivery, so my fruit bowl wasn't always empty. I put the backpack in the passenger seat, where it bumped up satisfyingly against my Manduka yoga mat.

Most of the group were the cheeriest, most upbeat people I'd ever met, but I tried not to hold it against them. I looked forward to hearing their loud "hellos" across the parking lot, collecting a few hugs when I arrived.

Then we were off, walking single file on a ridge overlooking a leafy green valley. We caught a majestic view of the bay at the peak after a steep climb and used our poles (I finally learned to use mine with the help of a friendly fellow hiker) to steady ourselves on the way down.

As we wended our way through the trails, I thought of the circular path I'd walked with George, narrow and unchanging, and wished we had seen these vistas together. They might have informed our lives.

The group was yielding unexpected pleasures, from listening to people's life stories to dancing together at outdoor concerts to enjoying the equilibrium that came from a day spent in nature.

Many in the group were single, and when I heard them talking about the hiking vacations and evenings out that they were planning together, I could see more possibilities for an unpartnered life.

I was going on as many as four hikes a week, walking between thirty and forty miles, gradually wheezing less on the uphill climbs, and starring in *Mild*, my version of Wilderness Lite. There was a satisfying sense of order that came from following a set route, racking up the miles with nothing to impede our progress except mud and the occasional swelling stream, ending every trip right where we started. It was a relief after the chaos that was Max.

I needed to be someone other than his girlfriend, someone self-sufficient and unselfconscious, who didn't have a crazy guy texting her at all hours. My makeup sat untouched in the bathroom drawer, my skinny jeans stayed in the closet, and my hair faded from well-curated red to weird blonde from all my time outside. But despite a lack of visible symptoms, I was concealing a disease: my two longest relationships post-George had both been with emotionally abusive men. That pretty much ruled out self-sufficient.

Even OkCupid's inane compatibility questions wouldn't have dared to ask, *Would you date somebody abusive?*

Never again.

*Then why did you?*

Why I Stayed with Max:

1. I thought I should stop being such a princess (his words).
2. He said he loved me.
3. Sex.
4. He was a cheap date.
5. I thought if I gave more, he would too.
6. Bad food is good for portion control.

7. We had some good times, at least at the start.
8. Sex.
9. The alternative was sleeping alone.
10. I could help him to change.
11. I could stop at any time (as if).
12. Inertia is not a food group.

With slightly different wording, many of the items on my list were the standard reasons people gave for staying with emotional abusers. I certainly hadn't meant to sample abuse the same way I'd tried the Rotary Club or the synagogue book group, but I hadn't been able to recognize it for what it was.

My research showed that with intermittent emotional abuse, people often perceived their relationships as good enough or even loving. They saw each episode as a onetime slip. Verbal abusers behaved illogically, and people used to healthy relationships kept failing to guess how their abusers would act because their own experience allowed them to predict only rational behavior. Expecting sanity from their abusers, they stayed with them, hoping each episode would be the last.

I'd thought I could help Max, or at least keep him in check, but I'd failed to understand that he was beyond my control. In retrospect, I needed to believe I could save somebody after losing George.

I spelled out the facts of my case as if I were writing a legal brief—lonely, inexperienced widow, initially love-struck man who was always available—then shared my story in an online women's magazine, once again offering advice by negative example. With every word, I realized I could have put a stop to Max at any time.

With every outburst, he chipped away at me, and each time I took him back, I lost a bit of myself. I could still hear him ranting, his voice becoming more ragged with every word.

"You made me drive like that because I was upset" and "You're so selfish you owe me just for putting up with you."

After Gene, I thought I would never again fall into abuse. Clearly, I was far weaker than I'd thought, and telling myself I wouldn't let it happen again provided little comfort. I'd picked men who seemed crazy about me, at least at first, and so long as I needed that infusion of approval, I would always be vulnerable. God, how I hated that word.

I had to be willing to be lonely. Maybe even for the rest of my life, but the alternative was far worse. My final dating lesson: do not settle.

I lost over two years making excuses for Max, and by the end, I could have died. The only thing I could take away was that you never know what you'll put up with until it happens. The knowledge that my loneliness had caused me to tolerate abuse was truly humbling.

The next Saturday morning as I was getting ready for my hike, I heard shuffling outside my window. "Open up. We need to talk," said a raspy voice. Max. My stomach lurched.

"Go away," I yelled.

"I still love you. How can you hate me after all we've been through?"

*After all you've put me through.* But I'd made my own share of late-night phone calls, asking him why he didn't treat me better, why he was hurting me, then telling him a few minutes later that I'd missed him and asking him to come over and spend the night. I had been afraid that the raven might alight on my shoulder after too many nights alone.

We had reached our crescendo together, Max and I. I had just backed off while he had toppled over the edge. The last time we'd gone to Tahoe, he had lost $20,000 gambling. He had blamed his luck on the whim of the cards, but I knew it was because I'd managed to channel my anger onto the blackjack table where he was playing.

Now I saw his words for what they were—the demands of an abuser. He couldn't acknowledge his brutality, calling it something we'd been through together to make me complicit. He demanded I let him into my home as if it were his right.

I had spoken my last words to him when I had him arrested. I only hoped I didn't have to do it again. But I was far angrier at myself for not having ended it sooner.

"Are you going somewhere?" he said, seeing me standing in the window in my hiking shorts and T-shirt. "I could go with you."

He looked great, well-rested with a new haircut and brand-new tennis shoes. As if attempting to kill us both had been good for him.

"Fuck off, motherfucker," I heard a deep voice growl, then realized it was me sounding like Linda Blair in *The Exorcist*.

Max flinched, staring at me through the window, his eyes wide with disbelief. Why wouldn't they be, when I'd always relented in the past? He stood frozen for a moment, then slunk away, taking his new haircut with him.

Even though he stopped coming over, he kept plaguing me with texts. "You'll die alone" and "You'll never get laid again," he wrote. Apparently the two were equated. He apologized the next day after sleeping it off.

"I went to counseling like you told me to and I found out I have borderline personality disorder," he texted a few days later, as if expecting to be praised. A few days after that, he wrote, "I really think you should pay at least half the fine for my arrest. It's partly your fault." This suggested that whatever counseling he was getting wasn't working too well in the personal responsibility department.

I turned on my burglar alarm during the day, since I was unable to ignore his texts in case he said he was on his way over. Nancy offered to let me stay over in her spare room. Finally, Caroline asked why I kept inviting his energy into my life. She quoted some wise Sanskrit saying I didn't really understand. But I'd finally come to see the value of peace.

I blocked him, still afraid he might come over again, but his fear of incurring more fees if I had him arrested again would have to be enough. Money had always been his deepest love, whether it was saving a few bucks on drinks or betting thousands on blackjack. He threw his money away, then begged it to come back, just like he had with me.

I last heard about him a few months later when a woman contacted me through Facebook telling me she'd run into Max at a bar. He was falling down drunk, stumbling over to her table, saying he'd been ruined by love, and showing her my picture. She thought I should know.

After we chatted a bit, she said that after hearing him talk about me, she was surprised to discover I was actually nice.

# XXII. Just Another Single Woman on the 680 Corridor

"ARE WE STILL MEETING TOMORROW? Is 7:30 a good time to pick you up?" Arjun texted a few weeks after our shopping trip. He was referring to our Sunday morning hike with the group, a nine-mile trek through the hills of Marin down to the beaches of the Tennessee Valley.

"Let's make it 7:10 to be sure there's still parking," I answered, always pushing up the time. When he arrived, I discovered I'd forgotten my sunglasses and had to run back to the house to get them, eating up some of the extra minutes I'd demanded.

"Now I know why you always say you want to leave earlier," he said when I returned. "By the way, you should be very selective in who you choose to date. You have a lot to offer a man."

I blushed, not realizing he'd been watching me run into the house from his rearview mirror. After we'd carpooled to a few hikes together, people started asking if Arjun and I were a couple. It was probably because we teased each other like one, but we were just friends, drawn together by our losses and our getting of each other's jokes.

He reminded me of my writing pal Will, with his vegetarian diet and dedication to service. I admired his spirituality, the grace with which he accepted his loss, and the way he kicked all of our younger butts on the uphill climbs.

"I'll be spending less time hiking in the fall," I said once we were on our way.

"Why is that?"

"I'll be starting a master's degree in writing, so I'll be in class sometimes. And I'll have assignments to turn in."

At fifty-three, I'd returned to my senior year of college, this time making a better choice of studies than majoring in compulsive dating. I was following my own blog post on overcoming loneliness: find something you like to do, then figure out how to do it with others.

I couldn't think much past the start of the program, and I had no plans after graduation. But it was like opening the windows in a stifling room. I'd collected letters of recommendation from my writing group pals Will and Lee, as well as my writing teacher, not recognizing myself in their words yet finally seeing progress from the wraith who sought only to obliterate her brain.

My ghost was such a chameleon—sometimes she was a chic translator living in France, or an English professor adored by her students, or a yoga teacher who specialized in klutzes, but whoever she was, she knew what she wanted. Attending graduate school might be enough for her to stop being so superior and share a little of her adventurousness with me, helping me to see more possibilities.

Ironically, the graduate program used a pass/fail system. There would be no grades. I just hoped getting admitted didn't mean that my dad would get sick.

When I'd told him about the program, he smiled as if I'd just given him a gift. One of his favorite expressions was "use it or lose it," meaning your intellect will deteriorate if you don't exercise it. He said he wished he could take the program with me. He was no doubt relieved my brain had returned (though he probably wondered where it went in the first place).

He was such a lifelong learner, interested in almost every class listed in the online Coursera catalog. Even in a program with no grades, he'd be the only student to get an A++.

When I told him that I was nervous about going back to school after so many years, he said, "Deb-or-ah, you've had so much loss. You have survived so much more stress than most people your age. You're a success."

I never thought so. But recovering from grief was moving the puzzle pieces infinitesimal amounts, feeling you weren't accomplishing much, yet hoping something would finally come into focus.

"That sounds like a good idea," Arjun said as we pulled into the parking lot. "Although I'll miss you on our hikes."

"I'll miss you too."

"So, last night I went to a meetup where we all went dancing at this bar," I overheard our leader telling Arjun once we started out on the trail. "I was with my buddy, and there must have been ten women to every man. They all seemed so desperate. We danced with as many as we could, but it was like we were their prey."

"That doesn't sound too painful," said Arjun with a wink.

"No, it was just really sad. I'd heard there were a lot of middle-aged single women on the Danville-San Ramon 680 corridor," our leader said. "Now I know for sure."

George used to call me his rose after the character in Antoine de Saint-Exupéry's *The Little Prince* because loving someone made both of them special. I'd gone from being George's rose to just another single woman on the 680 corridor, all of us competing for a small pool of available dick.

When I'd mentioned dating to several women in the group, to a one, they'd told me they hated the process so much they decided to stop and were happier for it. Listening to those comments from our hiking leader, I could see why. Who wants someone who sees women as raptors and men as field mice?

A relationship might be something for these women to think about in the future—perhaps as a last priority, after they'd finally finished reorganizing their sock drawers—but it was probably still too much trouble. Better to avoid the whole mess. They'd already raised their kids, they told me, equating the men they dated with children.

Perhaps my dad had been the last single adult male in the Bay Area. In which case, there hadn't been another since 1979, when he had gotten together with Jane.

I still wanted to fall in love, but Max had thrown me. Even now I sometimes heard his voice, spewing poison at me to dispel his pain, begrudging me my right to a good life. Dating left me wary, and I missed the softness I'd had when I was married, when I was truly loved.

My heart had grown an outer shell of disillusionment. Allowing myself to love again would mean letting that shell crack and fall away, and I wouldn't be able to do that for a while. I was looking for a needle in a haystack, and so far, I'd had a lot of pricks.

But I'd still gone back online—if I wanted to find love, I had to seek it out. Taking Laura's advice, I'd made a list describing my ideal guy so that I wouldn't waste what was left of my dwindling love energy.

Debbie's Guy:

1. Can be a grown-up if necessary
2. Gets my sense of humor
3. Is good with time apart, but not too much
4. Wants to travel
5. Socially appropriate (the opposite of Max)
6. Non-workaholic (sorry, George)
7. Emotionally available and affectionate

8. Quiet and not vengeful about former partners
9. Financially secure and stable
10. ~~Likes~~ Loves Danville

Perhaps George and I could have changed to be less like the two redwood trees in our backyard that grew so close together no sunlight passed between them, and more like the cattail plants that blew away from each other, then came back again. We would have spoken our own languages when we were apart. He would have coded a new program in HTML, and I would have discussed museums with a tour group.

But George and I would have understood each other when we were back together. I liked to think of him as being as agile as the code he had written, as capable of evolving as befitted an engineer of almost infinite bandwidth.

But in reality, while we never would have divorced, we probably wouldn't have changed much either. I pictured myself at seventy, still scolding him to finish the home theater project, returning the clothes I bought online that he didn't like, and never making any of my own plans. He would have been hurt had I gone away traveling for weeks, and I doubt he would have wanted to come with me.

My next relationship would not be the all-encompassing union my marriage had been. Falling in love with George had been like falling into a river, learning to swim, clinging together through dangerous waters, each of us the other's only life raft.

I wanted an anachronism to my oxymoron, a well-mannered gentleman who equated sex with love, a solid man who'd be there for the rest of my life. Where would I be now had I just acknowledged that from the start? I could have skipped trying to relive my college years and wanting to have fun and being down for almost anything, heh heh.

But I hadn't been sure of what I wanted, and I'd craved new

experiences, like dating a man who was terrifically attractive (great for about an hour), and having my first fling (like eating junk food), and seeing what was out there (a giant discount store full of damaged merchandise).

I still had the relationship box checked off on my profile, but I'd added at the end, *I am looking for a long-term partnership. If you are looking for something temporary or kinky, I applaud your self-knowledge, but please do not waste your time contacting me.*

Dating was like a 1950s high school movie where so many men were only trying to make conquests, seeing women as either good girls or bad. I didn't like it that way, but I was keeping my poodle skirt on and one saddle-shoed foot firmly on the floor.

My prospective partner might even offer to read one of the books assigned in my graduate classes so that we could discuss it over chocolate croissants and decaf espressos.

The thirty of us climbed slowly down the steep path to the beach. The uneven rocks that cluttered the walkway shifted under our feet, and loose dirt puffed up around us. I skidded a few times, crouching and holding on to the boulders lining the trail. My palms dug into rock, and I hoped I didn't fall and take out anyone below.

When we reached the beach, the scene reminded me of my walks with George. The pearly sky met silvered water, and wisps of fog hovered overhead. I went to stand alone by the water's edge.

I imagined myself walking in, enveloped by iciness, the chill shocking what was left of my heart—a moment of regret, maybe a few of panic, then a blissful feeling of floating, the way I used to fall asleep before George got sick. When the loneliness hit, I was like the little mermaid when she walked on land with her new legs, inching along on the edge of a knife, every step painful.

"What are you thinking about?" asked Arjun, coming to stand beside me.

"I miss George. I don't like it here. I want to be home having brunch." I was never very good at Sundays.

Were my dad there to ask me how old I was, I would have told him I was ten, the age when I needed to feel safe after my mom died instead of being forced to play dodgeball, a truly diabolical game for a child who already believed she'd been singled out for special punishment.

That steep trail down to the beach had become my dodgeball, leaving me on my own trying not to get hit, or in this case, not to skid down the loose dirt. Tears were dripping past my sunglasses, bathing me in self-pity.

"It is good to feel these things," Arjun said. "It's cathartic. There would be something wrong if you didn't feel sad sometimes."

"I should be happy to be in this beautiful place," I said, rubbing my eyes. I felt the absence by my side, like one of those sad widow photos in the women's magazines.

"Looking into the waves is spiritual," Arjun said. "They remind me to be grateful for the many wonderful years I did have with my wife, even though they ended much too soon."

I too usually found the ocean to be comforting, but today it signified only mortality. The waves died as they broke on the shore. I had gone from walking together to walking alone, from sheltered by love to exposed to the elements, until, like the little mermaid, I too became sea-foam.

"But even though my love for my wife will never end, I want to find someone to share meals with, to travel with, and to hold hands with," he continued, the sound of the crashing waves lending gravitas to his words. "Someone who is as happy to see me as I am to see her. And that feeling will continue for the rest of our lives."

"I want that too," I said.

"As an older man, the physical is of far less importance to me," he said, but the glint in his eye told me otherwise. Having both known long-lasting love, we sought it again, but I might never find it.

Then I thought about an essay I'd had accepted in a publication I'd only dreamed about. In yet another appearance by Georgie the Friendly Ghost, it was scheduled to come out the day of my wedding anniversary.

I'd spent the evening with Laura at Danville's trendiest restaurant, all halogen lighting and well-coiffed women in high heels, a far cry from the dreary widow photos that illustrated my articles. I'd worn the aquamarine necklace George had given me, finally forgiving it for not being able to save him. I saw it as a reminder of our love and tried to find hope in the shades of aqua.

Coming home after dinner, I'd expected to feel sad, but the unfinished stereo cabinet had morphed into sleek new shelving, the gray leather sofa was almost completely covered in girly pillows, and my orange coffee table had a scarlet orchid on it.

When I opened the front door, the first thing I saw was the leather wall hanging I'd bought in Italy of a woman looking out from what appeared to be swirls of fabric, as if deciding whether to push them aside to see what was out there. She smiled a little as if expecting to like what she found.

She encouraged me as I prepared for an upcoming group tour of Barcelona, and Nancy and I were talking about taking a trip to Rome on our own later in the year. That night I managed to quiet the rodent on my own, and it slept softly against my rib cage.

My current assignment: reimagining being on my own as part of a good life, not an incomplete one. I pictured better widow photos, a woman hiking with a group, sitting in a lively class, alone in bed with a great book, at peace instead of looking over nervously at the man lying next to her. I was already getting notices of upcoming author talks and orientation sessions as part of the MFA program.

Another one of Caroline's sayings in yoga class was "You are enough, you have enough, just as you are." I envisioned a life of promise.

"Time to head back. We're leaving in a few minutes," said our leader with his usual pat on the shoulder as he came by to round everyone up.

As Arjun and I climbed back up the path, he offered me his hand in the steep places so that I didn't freeze up like I had on the way down. I stayed for the after-hike ice cream and the photos we took of one another to commemorate the day. My eyes looked a little puffy, but they were clear.

Arjun bought us each a vanilla ice cream cup, vanilla being our favorite flavor—and we ate them outside. The creamy white droplets ran down our fingers like the passage of time.

A few nights later, I got a text from Arjun telling me to let him know if I wanted to go for brunch sometime. I texted back that I'd signed up both of us for next week's hike. Outside, I heard the flap of the raven's wings as it took off in flight.

# About the Author

Debbie Weiss is a former attorney who earned her MFA in creative nonfiction from Saint Mary's College of California in 2020. A native of the Bay Area, she turned to writing after George, her husband and partner of more than three decades, died of cancer in April 2013, and she found herself single and living alone for the first time in her life. Weiss's essays have been published in *The New York Times*'s "Modern Love" column, *HuffPost*, *Woman's Day*, *Good Housekeeping*, *Elle Décor*, and *Reader's Digest*, among other publications. She lives in Benicia, CA.

## SELECTED TITLES FROM SHE WRITES PRESS

She Writes Press is an independent publishing company founded to serve women writers everywhere. Visit us at www.shewritespress.com.

*Daring to Date Again: A Memoir* by Ann Anderson Evans. $16.95, 978-1-63152-909-2. A hilarious, no-holds-barred memoir about a legal secretary turned professor who dives back into the dating pool headfirst after twelve years of celibacy.

*First Date Stories: Women's Romantic to Ridiculous Midlife Adventures* by Jodi Klein. $16.95, 978-1-64742-185-4. A collection of hopeful, hilarious, and horrific tales—plus dating tips and inspirational quotes—designed to remind women in their mid-thirties and beyond that not all first dates are created equal, and sometimes they can be the beginning of something wonderful.

*Not a Perfect Fit: Stories from Jane's World* by Jane A. Schmidt. $16.95, 978-1-63152-206-2. Jane Schmidt documents her challenges living off grid, moving from the city to the country, living with a variety of animals as her only companions, dating, family trips, outdoor adventures, and midlife in essays full of honesty and humor.

*Finding My Badass Self: A Year of Truths and Dares* by Sherry Stanfa-Stanley. $16.95, 978-1-63152-290-1. Fighting midlife inertia, Sherry Stanfa-Stanley decides to stare down fear through The 52/52 Project—a year of weekly new experiences designed to push her far outside her comfort zone and into a better understanding of herself.

*Miracle at Midlife: A Transatlantic Romance* by Roni Beth Tower. $16.95, 978-1-63152-123-2. An inspiring memoir chronicling the sudden, unexpected, and life-changing two-year courtship between a divorced American lawyer living on a houseboat in the center of Paris and an empty-nested clinical psychologist living in Connecticut.

*The Joy of Uber Driving: A Wild Ride to Self-Love* by Yamini Redewill. $16.95, 978-1-63152-567-4. In this wild, unabridged journey through the rearview mirror of an actress/singer/costumer/photographer/single woman turned Uber driver in San Francisco, Yamini Redewill reveals how she went from Hollywood depravity to East Indian spirituality—and from lifelong victimhood to self-love—through loving and serving her passengers.